Before the
WORLD
SERIES

Before the

WORLD SERIES

Pride, Profits, and Baseball's First Championships

Larry G. Bowman

NORTHERN ILLINOIS

UNIVERSITY

PRESS

DeKalb

Published by the Northern Illinois University Press, DeKalb, Illinois 60115

Manufactured in the United States using acid-free paper

All Rights Reserved

Design by Julia Fauci

Library of Congress Cataloging-in-Publication Data

Bowman, Larry G.

Before the World Series : pride, profits, and baseball's first championships /

Larry G. Bowman.

p. cm.

Includes bibliographical references and index.

ISBN 0-87580-307-5 (alk. paper)

1. Baseball—United States—History—19th century. I. Title.

GV863.A1 B695 2003

796.357'0973'09034—dc21

2002032606

To Sarah Margaret Merten Bowman

Contents

Acknowledgments

I owe debts of gratitude to several people who aided me during the months that I labored on this book. Two first-rate researchers and writers, the late Jerry Malloy and Bryan Di Salvatore, generously shared information with me and always provided good ideas for further research. My neighbors, Steve and Marian Kester, proved quite helpful. Steve, a retired professor of microbiology, read the manuscript with the scientist's eye and frame of mind, and he always offered useful opinions on the chapters he examined. Marian is my daily walking partner, and while she read the entire manuscript with a keen eye, she also patiently endured my endless conversations concerning baseball in the 1880s. I owe Marian special thanks for her assistance and her forbearance.

I thank my son, Curtis Bowman, for the time he devoted to reading and criticizing the various phases of the manuscript. In addition to the numerous hours he spent reading rough drafts, Curtis, who is a busy scholar, also took a good deal of his valuable time to teach me the intricacies of a new computer and how to cope with the peculiar ways of alien software. As he is a better than average baseball fan himself, Curtis always offered useful criticisms and regularly suggested means to clarify turgid sentences. Laura Eaton ably assisted Curtis with the final preparation of the manuscript. Kevin Butterfield, my editor at Northern Illinois University Press, offered many useful suggestions along the way. Thanks to everyone.

I wish to dedicate this book to my late wife, Sarah Margaret Merten Bowman, who died on October 30, 2001, after a valiant, forty-two year battle with multiple sclerosis.

—Larry G. Bowman
June 2002

MY FATHER died on July 28, 2002, only two months after he had been diagnosed with cancer. When he went into the hospital, his manuscript still stood in need of some minor changes before it could advance into page proofs. We discussed what needed to be done, and I completed the revisions for him. Since none of my corrections was substantive, the book is as he intended it to be.

We had hoped that he would live to witness the publication of his book, but it quickly became clear to us that his cancer would swiftly kill him. Seeing his book through the press was thus left to me. The task entrusted to me has been a bittersweet one. Many of my memories of my father are associated with baseball, such as his stories of his youthful playing days in Kansas, his years of coaching several of my teams as I was growing up, and the work on baseball history that occupied the second half of his academic career. My joy in these memories has been tempered by the sad knowledge that my father will never see the culmination of a lifetime's devotion to baseball. I can only hope that this book finds readers who share my father's delight in the game.

Laura Eaton, who helped me to edit the manuscript, also assisted me with the page proofs. Sandra Cannon compiled the index, and Laura helped me to revise Sandra's work to accord with my father's wishes as I understood them. Sandra did most of the work on the index, but I alone am responsible for its finished form. I would like to thank Laura and Sandra for their assistance.

Donna Bowman, my father's sister, and Patricia Goley helped to take care of my father during his terminal illness, allowing me to complete my work on the manuscript in a timely fashion. Words cannot convey my gratitude to them. I am also grateful to Sid and Wynell Cockrill, Steve and Marian Kester, Ron Marcello, and Joyce Snay. They have helped me to deal with the practical consequences of my father's death. The peace of mind that they have given me has made my task that much easier.

—Curtis Bowman
January 2003

Before the
WORLD
SERIES

Introduction

Modern baseball fans consider the season-ending World Series to be as predictable as the autumn display of deciduous trees signaling the conclusion of summer. October conjures memories of Babe Ruth's heroic home run in the 1932 World Series, Don Larsen's perfect game, the Brooklyn Dodgers' heroics and anguish, Willie Mays's catching of Vic Wertz's long drive into center field, Carlton Fisk's home run in the sixth game of the 1975 World Series, and other unforgettable moments of championship play. The World Series is a peculiarly American institution that held the sports-minded public in its thrall throughout the twentieth century. The lore of the contemporary series, now international in character, is woven throughout the societal fabric of America and Canada.

If, however, one were to quiz contemporary fans about Old Hoss Radbourn's pitching feats in the 1884 World's Championship playoff, or the heroic effort of Detroit's Dan Brouthers to play on a badly sprained ankle in the Detroit Wolverines and St. Louis Browns championship series in 1887, or the roles of superstars such as Cap Anson, John Montgomery Ward, Charles Comiskey, Arlie Latham, and Tim Keefe in the playoffs of the 1880s, it is likely one would draw a blank face from the nominal fan, perhaps an amused or tolerant stare from the fanatical baseball fan with a sketchy sense of the history of the game. Sportscasters, sportswriters, and other sports-minded professional folk may have a vague knowledge of the games in the 1880s, but overall, the seven playoffs between the National League of Professional Base Ball Clubs and the American Association of Base Ball Clubs, beginning in 1884 and concluding in 1890, are shrouded in the mists of obscurity.

Baseball's origins are keenly debated by scholars, but it is evident that the game's forebears first appeared in England and emigrated to North America with the earliest settlers. By the time of President Andrew Jackson, Americans were playing a hybrid game, a mixture of One Old Cat, stool ball, cricket, and other pastimes employing a stick and a ball. By the 1830s and 1840s, the term *base ball* had become a fairly commonplace name for the emerging sport. Regional versions of "base ball" (most notably the "New York game" and the "Massachusetts game") were played in the years immediately preceding the Civil War. A group of men in New York City had a particularly heavy impact on the game's evolution. In 1845 Alexander Joy Cartwright, a bank clerk and later a partner in a stationery shop, convinced a group of his friends to form the New York Knickerbocker Base Ball Club. The Knickerbockers, though not the first club in the United States, proved unique. The organization was driven by a collection of enthusiastic men who popularized the game in America's largest city and simultaneously began the complicated task of defining not only the rules but also appropriate dress, playing fields, and etiquette. Other clubs in the New York City area soon emulated the Knickerbockers, and the New York interpretation of baseball steadily gained footing in the northeastern, urban sector of the United States. In an effort to promote the sport and to standardize playing rules, representatives of several baseball clubs met in New York City in 1857 and formed the National Association of Base Ball Players, which proved moderately successful in its quest to organize and standardize the game. Its appearance clearly signaled that baseball had become more than just a fad.

Baseball flourished in spite of the Civil War. Soldiers took the game to war with them and taught it to others. After the war, veterans took it home, and the baseball craze burgeoned across the nation. Several developments documented the game's rising popularity, such as the Cincinnati Red Stockings' famous U.S. tour in 1869. The Cincinnati club, originally designed to boost civic pride and yield profits to the team's financial backers, traveled to the East Coast and recorded fifty-seven victories against one tie. The tied game, a contest with the Haymakers of Troy, New York, ended suspiciously when the Troy club quit the field after the sixth inning. Allegations that gamblers had influenced the Haymakers' decision abounded but were never verified. After completing the eastern tour, which included an official reception by President Ulysses S. Grant after the team thrashed the Washington Nationals, the Red Stockings returned to Cincinnati for a grand reception. Shortly thereafter, the club departed for several exhibition games in California, traveling on the newly completed transcontinental railroad. The Red Stockings' accomplishments thrilled observers everywhere. Astute baseball fans knew that all the team's players were paid professionals, and that other municipalities were certain to spawn similar clubs.

The emergence of a professional dimension to baseball led to the creation of the National Association of Professional Base Ball Players in 1871, and the new organization subsequently gave birth to a player-controlled league, usually called the National Association (NA), whose members formed teams in several cities of the Northeast. Within a decade of the Civil War, baseball had become ubiquitous. Baseball reached into nearly every nook and cranny of society. Boys played baseball in vacant lots and pastures, men and boys played baseball in the parks and village streets, church members played on church grounds after service on Sundays, college students played baseball on their campuses and club grounds, even girls and young women played baseball, though to a lesser extent.

The game's rising popularity was evident in the U.S. Army, for example. Men in the armed forces played ball wherever they were stationed. Men from all sections of the nation came together in the game, transcending normal social mixing of nineteenth-century America, and off-duty soldiers sought entertainment and amusement in ways common to their civilian environments. During the Civil War, soldiers in the Union Army often used baseball to while away hours between assignments. Some historians, George B. Kirsch among them, advance the thesis that the melting pot influence of service in the war helped to turn baseball into a national pastime.[1]

The popularity of baseball with soldiers posted far from home provides a barometer of the growing craze for the game. David L. Spotts, who served with the Nineteenth Kansas Volunteer Cavalry in 1868 and 1869, recorded how baseball occupied the minds of soldiers in the field. The Nineteenth Kansas volunteers were recruited in eastern Kansas to augment the U.S. Seventh Cavalry launched against the Cheyennes and Kiowas wintering in southwestern Indian Territory in 1868–1869. The force led by George Armstrong Custer was delegated to punish the Indians who raided settlements in western Kansas during the summer of 1868. The government's objective was to coerce the Cheyennes to move onto reservations rather than allow them to roam their traditional hunting grounds between the Red River and the Platte River. Custer's campaign, which preceded his more famous Little Big Horn campaign of 1876, was relatively successful, but the Nineteenth Kansas did not directly clash with the Indians; the volunteers played a supporting, noncombatant role to the Seventh Cavalry. Spotts and the nearly twelve hundred Kansas volunteers mostly marched, enduring hard weather and short rations and suffering boredom and homesickness. Once the Nineteenth reached the vicinity of modern-day Fort Sill, Oklahoma, in mid-January 1869, they spent the remainder of the month in camp.

To alleviate their boredom, men in the Nineteenth organized baseball teams and promoted intercompany play. Spotts recorded in his diary on January 20, 1869, that the restless troopers "are getting up an interest in baseball and may soon form a league, and in that way the companies will get to know each other."[2] A few days later men from Spotts's company, Company L, hosted a team of players from Company A and defeated them (7–2). The losing players protested the game, claiming that the umpire, a trooper from Company H, had favored his friends in L Company.[3] In the midst of a campaign among hostile Indians on a far-flung corner of the frontier, men played baseball and complained about the umpiring—a most impressive statement of the game's growing popularity and its tightening grip on American culture. According to Spotts's account, the soldiers built a diamond, practiced vigorously, and played several games, but the efforts to create a league ultimately failed. Bad weather and a lack of equipment hindered the soldiers' efforts to engage in wholesale competition. The ball was "made of yarn with something inside to give it weight covered with leather from an old boot." Games were often called because the crude baseballs simply tore apart when struck with bats. Describing Company L's second game, Spotts declared, "The game was almost a fizzle as the baseballs were soon knocked to pieces, and they had only two."[4]

Baseball rose in popularity in post–Civil War America, and professional baseball was born when the National Association of Professional Base Ball Players (NA) formed in 1871. This loosely governed the activities of organized teams and signaled the transition of the highest level of the game from a fraternal sport to a commercial enterprise, but it failed to create a stable environment for its players and clubs. Its administrative affairs were often in chaos, teams failed to complete season schedules, players jumped from team to team, ballparks were often rowdy sites, and gamblers flocked to the games. In a period of only five years, the NA had acquired an unsavory reputation.

Professional sports of all denominations struggled to raise their level of respectability in the 1880s. Prizefighting had an especially noxious reputation, for example. Reporting a prize fight in 1883, the *New York World* observed that the crowd attending the match was "made up of sporting men, athletes, gamblers, roughs, thieves, arabs, and that great brute element that underlies all civilization and only comes together when there is a hanging, a mob or a fight."[5] Although no one would have equated a baseball crowd with the throngs attending prize fights, there nevertheless was an association between the two in Victorian Americans' perceptions of the NA's shortcomings as a regulatory agency.

Keen-eyed businessmen such as William Ambrose Hulbert of Chicago, however, sensed that baseball was to become a major sport. He suspected that the game offered potential profits to those who could organize and control its marketing, and to this end he and a group of like-minded associates met in New York City in 1876, seeking to revolutionize professional baseball. Hulbert's plan was simple. He and his peers created the National League of Professional Base Ball Clubs (NL) and placed control of their new league in the hands of the team owners rather than the loosely confederated players. In the era of the robber barons who had begun carving their empires in oil, steel, banking, railroads, and other vital economic sectors, Hulbert sought to replicate the goals of Andrew Carnegie, John D. Rockefeller, and their powerful contemporaries. His main goal was profit, but the founders of the National League cloaked their movements with rhetoric, freighted with high motives. Baseball, they contended, was in a slough of despair and disrepute; only a new league, carefully regulated and with the power to enforce its pronouncements, could redeem the game from its current state of disorder and lack of respectability.[6]

Ballparks were not considered suitable sites for the more genteel Americans, and realizing their reservations about attending National Association games, Hulbert set out to alter this perception. Article 2 of the National League Constitution set forth the new league's goals:

> *The objectives of the League are:*
>
> 1st. To encourage, foster, and elevate the game of base ball
>
> 2nd. To enact and enforce proper rules for the exhibition and conduct of the game
>
> 3rd. To make base ball playing respectable and honorable
>
> 4th. To protect and promote the mutual interests of the professional base ball clubs and professional base ball players; and
>
> 5th. To establish and regulate the base ball championship of the United States.[7]

The aim to increase decorum and professionalism was apparent, underlaid with measures designed to limit competition and maximize profit. Publicly, the founders of the NL appeared locked in a quixotic crusade to cleanse baseball of all the hurtful influences facing it.[8] This, in part, was true. Several of the NL's operational rules clearly expressed the league's intention to appeal to a better class of patrons. To achieve the goal of attracting desirable spectators (the popular term for fans in the 1880s was *cranks*) to their ballparks, the National League founders took several steps to set themselves apart from the National Association; the NL clearly forbade Sunday games, banned alcohol on ballpark premises, established fifty cent admission to attract respectable patrons to its ballparks, and promised league-enforced regulation of players' conduct. All of the high-minded provisions of the new League's constitution supposedly struck at the more heinous evils fostered by NA contests. Hulbert and his associates sought diligently to create a sanitized, stable environment in which to reap profits from the purses of middle-class Americans.[9]

One facet of the revolution wrought by the National League's founders, one they perhaps did not anticipate, was that article 2, section 5, inadvertently established a foundation for the World's Championship Series destined to appear in the 1880s. With the appearance of the NL, the NA quickly collapsed, and it was not hubris for the National League rightfully to claim its victor the champion of the United States. For the six seasons from 1876 through 1881, NL teams held franchises in many of the major cities in the eastern and midwestern regions of the United States, and none of the other professional leagues, destined eventually to be termed "minor leagues," successfully challenged the NL.

All this changed, however, when the American Association of Base Ball Clubs (AA) was formed in 1881 and began playing its own brand of baseball in 1882.[10] Inevitably, as the AA succeeded in several cities, a debate emerged as to whether the upstart league or the NL played the better baseball. In only a year or so, conventional wisdom decided that a championship series between the rival leagues was the only means to resolve the question of supremacy. The possibility of some sort of playoff system between the two leagues appealed to nearly everyone associated with major league baseball; owners, of course, anticipated financial gains, players saw extra income, the press saw good sporting news, and the American sports fans saw an opportunity to witness a spectacle unlike any previously known in the United States.

In early 1883 the National League, the American Association, and the Northwestern League (a flourishing professional league in the Midwest) entered into an agreement in which they pledged to respect each other's player reserve lists and territorial rights. The so-called tripartite agreement also conferred major league status on the NL and the AA, and the notion of a postseason series between their pennant winners gained momentum.[11] Even so, it took the NL and the AA another two seasons to establish the first championship series between them. James D. Hardy Jr. refers to the 1880s postseason series as "Paleozoic and rather haphazard" in many ways, an apt description.[12] The championship games were certainly haphazard, and to modern-day fans they seem ancient and quaint. Nevertheless, the championship games of the 1880s laid the groundwork for the twentieth century's most famous sporting event, the World Series.

CHAPTER ONE

The 1880s

The Times and the Game

The 1880s were among the most turbulent decades in the history of major league baseball. Three new major leagues—the American Association, the Union Association, and the Players' League—were established to challenge the dominant National League, and all three had died before the 1890s were fairly begun. The major league players established an ill-fated Brotherhood of Professional Base Ball Players to protect themselves from the excesses of rapacious management, and baseball's rules and play steadily evolved toward an outward appearance that modern fans would readily recognize. In its turbulence and constant refashioning, baseball was a microcosm of everyday American life, as the nation entered into the glories and the horrors of the American industrial revolution with all its promises and threats.

The Times

Abetted by a burgeoning urban population with income to spend for entertainment, professional baseball flourished in the late nineteenth century. Population growth and a trend toward urban concentration highlighted the post–Civil War years. In 1860 slightly more than five million people (16 percent of the population) lived in cities of eight thousand residents or more; by 1890 more than eighteen million (nearly 30 percent of all Americans) lived in cities of that size.[1] On the eve of the Civil War in 1860, only ten American cities had populations of seventy-five thousand or more. By 1870 twenty-four cities exceeded that population, and by 1890 thirty-nine cities (including New York City, Philadelphia, and Chicago, which each boasted more than one million residents) registered seventy-five thousand or more inhabitants.[2] Propelled by the heavy immigration of foreigners seeking to build new lives in America and the high birthrate after the Civil War, America's population doubled in the thirty years between 1860 and 1890, rising from 31,443,321 to 62,622,250.[3]

As the 1880s dawned, American society faced massive changes in nearly all areas of national life. At the outset of the decade, the nation's population numbered slightly more than fifty million. By the 1890 census it had reached more than sixty-two, a growth of twelve million, which represented an increase of slightly more than 24 percent for the decade. The North Atlantic Region and North Central Region, as the Census of 1890 labeled the geographical areas from Boston to New York City and westward to Chicago, accounted for 81 percent of the total growth.[4] The locales in which major league baseball first flourished experienced explosive growth and provided men such as Hulbert, Albert Goodwill Spalding, and Christian Von der Ahe with unprecedented opportunities to build their baseball empires.

The principal factor fueling the rapid expansion of the population in the 1880s was immigration. Between 1840 and 1880 the average influx hovered around 2.4 million per decade, but the 1880s brought a flood of immigrants.[5] Between January 1881 and December 1890, a total of 5,036,633 people, mostly from Europe, entered the United States and settled primarily in the industrializing parts of the nation where employment was readily available.[6] This meant in 1890 that at least one of every twelve Americans had arrived in the country within the past ten years. Cities teemed with populations that were foreign to the Americans produced by earlier waves of immigrants. The new immigrants tended to replicate much of their Old World culture once they arrived in New York City, Boston, Philadelphia, Chicago, and other urban centers, which often created the impression they were aloof to American traditions.[7] The new Americans eventually adopted American customs and fads, however, their offspring usually preceding them, as they accepted American ways and customs and sought to assimilate into the melting pot.

Some historians argue that the new European immigration also changed the dominant Victorian American attitude toward recreation. Dale A. Somers postulates that the way foreign-born city dwellers "brought their own native amusements[,] and above all a European dedication to the active pursuit of pleasure, also stimulated urban interest in recreation."[8] Recent immigrants' intense interest in popular forms of leisure activities helped the success of major league baseball in America's urban centers. An immigrant's acceptance of baseball as a part of his new culture advanced his quest for recreation and at the same time indicated partial assimilation into American society.[9] Baseball unquestionably benefited from the sudden rush of immigration, as the new Americans accepted the game as a part of their adopted world, and professional teams found dedicated patrons among America's newest arrivals.

While immigration abetted municipal growth in the 1880s, other factors also contributed to the rise of an urban population ready to adopt baseball for entertainment. Prior to 1880 the majority of Americans were tied to agricultural occupations, but with the rapid industrialization of post–Civil War America, this also changed. Beginning with the 1870s Americans started to leave their rural environments and move to cities in search of better employment. The 1880 census recorded for the first time in the nation's history that more Americans (8,807,000) held nonfarming jobs than those (8,585,000) who labored in agriculture. Americans steadily found employment in industries promoting urban growth. By 1890 the shift from farm to city was apparent in employment statistics; nonfarm workers in American outnumbered farm workers 13,380,000 to 9,938,000. Between 1880 and 1890, the mostly urban, nonfarm workers' wages rose from $386.00 to $475.00 annually.[10]

Stated another way, by the end of the decade, the rapidly growing urban classes had approximately three billion dollars more to spend than in 1880. Naturally, this did not mean that baseball automatically had patrons ready to spend three billion dollars to enjoy professional ball, but it did mean that the professional leagues had a prospering consumer base from which they could benefit. It is not surprising that the 1880s was the only decade in history that four different "major leagues" courted the baseball enthusiasts. The growth and proliferation of leagues (though only one was to survive beyond the early 1890s) were fostered by the astonishing demographic shifts in the structure of American society, the extraordinary economic growth, and the free-booting entrepreneurial spirit that typified the 1880s.

Not only did American cities grow in numbers, but they changed in physical appearance as well. Until the 1850s, American cities were compact in structure and could be termed "walking cities." Howard Chudacoff and Judith Smith described American cities as "characterized by their compactness. Located near harbors or river junctions, they focused their activities on the waterfront. Here wharves, warehouses, mercantile offices, and small manufacturing establishments were built, because access to water transportation was of principal importance."[11] The heaviest users of the city streets were pedestrians. Streets were jammed with wagons, carriages, and animals, but the feature that would most intrigue a modern onlooker was the heavy pedestrian traffic on the avenues of pre-1880s American cities.

By the 1880s the walking city began to die out, a victim of the industrial revolution and the unprecedented growth from internal migration and U.S. immigration. It was replaced by what social reformer Jane Addams and others of her turn-of-the-century generation termed the "modern city."[12] Once-compact cities began to sprawl outward. Where people once easily walked to work or recreation, now the distances became too large, and in some instances too dangerous, for pedestrians to stroll. Cities in the late nineteenth century were paradoxes (as indeed are the great urban areas of more modern times). Parts of the cities were fashionable, obviously prosperous, inhabited by elements of society who had found success in the frequently unplanned, unbridled urban and industrial growth so common to the late nineteenth century. Other facets of city life presented a depressing picture. Life for too many of America's urban dwellers was harsh, on the streets, in the tenements, in the factories and shops:

> Disease spread rapidly and death rates increased alarmingly in urban centers. Disasters were commonplace and widespread in their destructiveness. Problems of crime, fire, noise, odor, and sanitation were everywhere apparent. Street-cleaning, garbage collection, and traffic management were complicated by the inefficiencies of municipal governments, whose responsibility in those areas was ill-defined. The last half of the century saw the introduction of water-purification systems, street-lighting, garbage-disposal procedures, and new fire-fighting equipment, but improvements seldom kept pace with the growth in population and in the enormity of urban problems.[13]

The modern industrial city offered fresh hope and unparalleled opportunity to many Americans, but it was not without peril and horror for the poor, the illiterate, and the lower classes who were victimized and discriminated against in their struggle to survive the impersonal milieu and emerging urban societies of industrializing America. But the emerging industrial city's sheer size posed considerable difficulties to its inhabitants. In the 1880s the market, the workplace, or the ballpark often were too far distant from urbanites' homes for them to stroll there. The streets separating residents from their destinations were often plagued with street thugs as well.

Mass transportation, designed to cope with the demographic and physical growth of American cities, emerged as the solution to these problems, and the rise of public transportation systems certainly enhanced the viability of major league baseball. New baseball parks appeared everywhere, especially in cities where new National League teams were installed or where American Association clubs attempted to establish themselves; and as new and bigger ballparks were built in the rapidly swelling cities, they were often moved farther to the cities' outer limits, since real estate in the older, more developed areas became too valuable for limited, seasonal use by major league franchises. At the beginning of the 1880s, American cities of populations of fifty thousand or more boasted 1,584 miles of street railways powered by animals, electricity, steam, or cable; by 1890 this total had risen to 3,200 miles, an increase of 102.35 percent for the decade.[14] Transporting large numbers of fans to ballparks became a fairly simple process as the network of city railways grew in the 1880s.

Historian Harold Seymour observes that owners of transportation companies also recognized "that ball games were well patronized, and found it profitable to co-operate with the ball clubs," thus becoming some of the sport's first promoters.[15] Frank Robison and his brother, Stanley, in Cleveland were among the group of baseball executives and owners who were tied also to the traction company businesses, and as Seymour asserts, they and many of their colleagues viewed baseball as a way to stimulate their own interests.[16] Car lines sold tickets to games as a part of the service they rendered their patrons, and the rapidly growing traction companies in major league towns obviously profited by the presence of ballparks along the rail networks.

As urban transportation improved in the 1880s, the sophistication of the U.S. railway infrastructure facilitated movement of teams from one site to another. Between 1880 and 1890, the miles of track in the United States nearly doubled from 86,762 to 166,558 miles.[17] Much of the new mileage was constructed in the West as the nation fulfilled part of its "manifest destiny" by linking the Atlantic and the Pacific Oceans with an efficient transportation system, but a portion of the newly installed tracks significantly improved the intercity network of the Midwest and the Atlantic seaboard, which directly benefited major league baseball. In 1886, for example, all the National League franchises (Boston, Chicago, New York, Washington, Kansas City, Detroit, St. Louis, Philadelphia) were connected by the Michigan Central Railroad, which enjoyed a virtual monopoly on the teams' travel arrangements.[18] Telegraph companies grew in scope and permitted easier transmission of newspapers' accounts of teams' out-of-town games to anxious fans following their team's progress against league rivals. Telephones, another innovation allowing quick transmission of news of players and games, became more a part of daily life as telephone wires increased from 34,000 miles in 1880 to an astonishing 240,000 by 1890.[19]

The noticeable rise in comprehensive metropolitan newspapers also aided the growing popularity of major league baseball. During the 1870s and 1880s, major cities in the United States became homes to a new breed of newspaper, wanting to inform readers on a broad spectrum of topics. Local news remained the primary staple no matter how large or sophisticated the city, and crime, corruption, society events, sports, and civic affairs still dominated the newspapers of the 1880s.

Baseball was well reported in metropolitan newspapers in the 1880s. Sportswriters for major newspapers, an emerging professional fraternity, traveled with their hometown teams and filed daily reports, telegraphed to their editors, so that fans could follow their heroes' progress. The 1880s saw the maturation of newspapers' coverage of baseball because readers relished the sports news. Frank Queen's newspaper, the *New York Clipper*, served as the prototype for the new sports-oriented journal. By the 1880s baseball coverage consumed a good portion of its space, especially after the paper employed Henry Chadwick, who proved one of baseball's foremost popularizers during the post–Civil War era. Others soon realized sports journalism offered profits, and the 1880s witnessed the birth of two specialized journals, *Sporting Life,* headquartered in Philadelphia, and

Sporting News, situated in St. Louis, each of which emulated Queen's successes and focused on reporting baseball, college football, the stage, billiards, prizefighting, horse racing, and other topics of interest to America's growing sports fans. Amateur and professional baseball were America's most popular team sports in late nineteenth century, and neither wanted for coverage in the press.[20]

Sports-minded city dwellers quickly identified with their local teams as intercity rivalries developed. The press, eager to boost circulation by exploiting hometown interest in game outcomes, carefully reported the emerging scene to a public captivated by the spectacle of professional athletes doing battle for civic honor. As the sporting public identified with their clubs, NL and AA owners and players took their places as minor icons of American popular culture, gaining instant celebrity for that handful of people who carried the local standard in the baseball wars. Identifying with the gifted few made fans feel they belonged to a special group, bound together by a common interest. Big-time baseball became synonymous with metropolitan America. If one lived in St. Louis, one loved the Browns or the Maroons. If one lived in New York, one loved the Giants or the Metropolitans. Supporting the local team became a civic duty. Baseball became an integral part of city life.

The Game

A superficial glance at baseball in the 1880s would suggest that it was the same as during any other decade of the game's existence: A team of nine men took the field to prevent another team of nine men from scoring runs while at bat. Modern baseball fans and 1880s cranks, were they allowed to converse about their favorite game, would have an immediate rapport. Unlike basketball or football enthusiasts from two different eras, they would not need to define their terms before they could meaningfully discuss their favorite game. A first baseman is still a first baseman, whereas in football the concept of a strong safety might puzzle someone who had followed Walter Camp's great Yale teams. Football teams with a defensive unit, an offensive unit, and a special team unit, a kicking team, and cheerleaders on the sidelines probably would seem more circus than sport to a football fan resurrected from the turn of the century. A basketball fan from 1900 might suffer considerable confusion were he to attend one the "March Madness" playoffs games. He would see elaborate timing devices, several referees frequently blowing whistles for incomprehensible reasons, and a host of other differences. All team sports, baseball included, have undeniably evolved since the nineteenth century, but the charm of baseball is that its outward appearance remains nearly the same from one generation to another. Dean Naismith probably would be a bit puzzled by a

The 1889 Chicago White Stockings pose for a team picture as interested cranks look on.

(Courtesy of Jay Sanford, Arvada, Colo.)

term such as a *box and one,* and Walter Camp would have no idea what a *nickel package* was, but Hoss Radbourn or King Kelly would instantly comprehend discussions of the "hit and run" or "suicide squeeze" even though their generation of ballplayers did not use such terms. Bruce Catton, the eminent historian of the American Civil War, writing in the 1950s, observed, "A gaffer from the era of William McKinley, abruptly brought back to the second half of the twentieth century would find little in modern life that did not seem new, strange, and bewildering, but put in a good grandstand seat back of first base he would see nothing that is not completely familiar."[21] If one took the time to explain the designated hitter, the artificial turf, and the floodlights illuminating the field to the McKinley-era gentleman (who may have heard of some early efforts to light playing fields in his own time), Catton's argument still bears scrutiny.[22]

While the basics of playing major league baseball remain essentially the same a century and a quarter later, the environment has changed dramatically. First of all, ballparks in the early part of the 1880s were small and of wooden construction, often suffering calamitous fires and sometimes collapsing, injuring fans. In the early twentieth century, the small and sometimes flimsy ballparks were replaced by concrete-and-steel constructions, both larger and more durable. In the late nineteenth century, nearly all the clubs played in parks that accommodated less than ten thousand spectators. The Chicago White Stockings, for example, played home games in two parks during the 1880s. Both were small stadiums. Lake Front Park served as Chicago's home field in 1883 and 1884, and its capacity seating was only five thousand; moreover, its dimensions were only 186 feet down the left field foul line and 196 feet to right field. When the White Stockings moved to West Side Park in 1885, they played in an upgraded environment, but it was not much larger. The foul lines were only 216 feet to the fences.[23] Boston's South End Grounds seated sixty-eight hundred, St. Louis's Sportsman's Park by 1886 had been renovated to accommodate twelve thousand fans, and Brooklyn's Washington Park, after several improvements, seated only three thousand spectators.[24] Three ballparks, by 1880s standards, were huge. Pittsburgh's Recreation Park seated seventeen thousand; Philadelphia's NL franchise played on Philadelphia Baseball Grounds, which had room for fifteen thousand patrons; and the Polo Grounds in New York City, after the AA New York Metropolitans moved to Metropolitan Park and the Giants and the Mets no longer shared fields separated by a canvas fence, became the site of the first major league crowd to exceed twenty thousand when, on Memorial Day, May 31, 1886, the Giants hosted the Detroit Wolverines in a morning/afternoon doubleheader that attracted 20,709 to the second game.[25]

Attendance statistics for major league games in the 1880s are sparse and notoriously unreliable. Most figures were supplied by newspaper men reporting the games, who provided their readers rounded off estimates. Statements such as "about 4,000 sweltering fans" or "2,000 dissatisfied aficionados of baseball" decorated their accounts. What is apparent, however, is that attendance at major league games varied greatly. Some towns were better baseball towns than others. In 1884, for example, Boston and Providence engaged in a titanic struggle for the National League crown. In the nine games played in Boston, the average attendance was 4,948, but when the Beaneaters and the Providence Grays played nine dates in Providence, they averaged only 2,200 paid admissions.[26] Boston was a larger city than Providence, but the main reason the Grays did not draw well at home was because Providence fans never really took the Grays to their hearts. By 1886 Providence no longer had a major league franchise.[27] Boston, New York, Chicago, and St. Louis were noted for their rabid fans. In good years and in bad, these franchises drew substantial numbers to their parks. Cincinnati was a good baseball town. So, briefly, was Detroit in the mid-1880s. The Philadelphia fans were noted, then as now, for their support of their local heroes and for the abuse they heaped on their opponents. One obvious fact remains, however: the business of baseball was played on a smaller scale in the 1880s. In 1885 the Chicago White Stockings played fifty-six home dates, and had they filled the ballpark for every game (which they did not), total attendance would not have exceeded 280,000. Modern teams draw that many fans to a single home stand of six or seven games.

In the 1880s the rules governing the game were in a dramatically evolutionary state. Rules governing pitchers and hitters changed noticeably during the decade. At first, the pitcher delivered his pitches from within a pitcher's box that was six feet square. At the beginning of his throwing motion, the pitcher was obligated to have his back foot on the rear line of the box, located fifty-five feet five inches from the hitter. Whereas the distance between the pitcher and the hitter remained the same throughout the 1880s (it was not set at sixty feet six inches until 1893), the size of the pitcher's box steadily shrank. By the end of the decade, the box was a square four feet by five feet six inches.[28]

In the early 1880s, baseball's rules forbade a pitcher to elevate his hand above hip level while delivering a ball to a hitter. It steadily became common practice for pitchers who faced a crisis situation in a game to ignore the rule and raise their throwing motions above hip level, in an attempt to generate more velocity on a pitch. Both major leagues tried to halt the trend toward overhanded pitching, but finally, in its annual conference held in Washington, D.C., on November 21 and 22, 1883, the National League removed the ban on overhanded deliveries by pitchers.[29] The American Association initially opposed the change, and specifically addressed the question in its meeting three weeks later. The delegates to the convention unanimously voted to maintain the rule forbidding the altered style of pitching.[30] Two years later, AA owners relented and sanctioned overhanded pitching. By 1885 pitchers who preferred to do so routinely used overhanded motions to deliver pitches in both major leagues. Some, who had developed a style to accommodate the old rules, stayed with the side-arm motion.

A hitter was not retired on three strikes until 1888. In 1882 it required seven balls to walk a hitter; this figure was lowered to five in 1887, and finally to the more familiar four balls for a base on balls in 1889.[31] Until 1887 a hitter could call for a high or a low pitch, which allowed him to concentrate on a zone in which the pitch was to arrive. He was also allowed, if he chose, to use a bat that was flat on one side. Hitters normally employed the flat side of the bat for bunting. In 1893 official baseball rules required that the bat be perfectly round. Pinch-hitting was unknown in the 1880s, and teams were not allowed to substitute players unless a debilitating injury occurred. Even then, such substitutions required the consent of the opposing team. By 1889, however, teams were allowed to designate one player as an extra player, and he could enter the game after a completed inning. In 1891 the substitution rule was further liberalized so that any player on the field could be replaced at any time.[32]

Pitchers had a distinct advantage in the 1880s. Pitchers with thirty or forty wins per season seem, at first glance, evidence of vanished titans in the game. Hoss Radbourn of the Providence Grays, for example, won more than 160 games between 1881 and 1884; Tim Keefe of the New York Metropolitans and later the New York Giants averaged 35 wins per season between 1883 and 1889; Silver King of the St. Louis Browns averaged 37 wins a season from 1887 to 1889.[33] Radbourn won nearly as many games in four years (167) as Sandy Koufax won in his entire twelve-year career (169, counting World Series competition).

Major league pitchers were talented men in the 1880s, but they labored in a different game. It should be noted first that Radbourn and his contemporaries stood approximately five feet closer to the hitter than after the distance was set at sixty feet six inches in 1893. Since they threw with mostly a side-arm to underhanded motion, pitchers in the 1880s greatly reduced the stress on their throwing arms. They also used a ball that was often battered, soft, dirty, and practically unhittable long before the game ended. Major league rules in the 1880s required the home team to present the umpire with two new baseballs prior to the game—and he was more or less expected to make do with those.[34] He could be supplied with new baseballs if those in play became too battered for further use, or if they were lost. Spectators politely returned balls fouled into the stands, but by the end of a contest a baseball was often in shabby condition. Hitters in the 1880s often hit something resembling a dingy sponge rather than a modern game-quality ball. All of these factors only served to make life easier for a pitcher.

Teams' appearances became standardized in the 1880s. Prior to that time, professional baseball teams donned whatever uniform style and color that pleased the ownership. But in the 1880s this haphazard policy slowly disappeared. By the mid-1880s there emerged the practice of the home team wearing white uniforms and the visitors wearing gray or some other dark-colored uniforms, and finally, in 1911, major league baseball codified the policy of home team in white and visitors in darker colors.[35] Although the style of uniforms altered over the years, players' attire, today and then, is not radically different in appearance, especially when compared to the evolutionary development of football players' garb from that era to today's gridiron warriors. Baseball's appearance changed, but this change was comparatively slight compared to other sports.

One noticeable difference between the modern game and major league baseball in the 1880s was the size of the teams' rosters. Today's major league teams compete for the bulk of the season with a twenty-five-man roster, but in the 1880s it was common for teams to play the entire season with rosters of fewer than fifteen men. Even though the major league teams of the 1880s played schedules of about thirty to forty fewer games than the modern norm for a season, rosters at first glance seem fragile. In the style of baseball in the 1880s, pinch-hitters and relief pitchers were unknown so no one worried about right- and left-handed percentages, and defensive specialists on a roster were phenomena for the future. The usual practice was for a team to have eight position players who played the bulk of the season at their respective posts. In addition to the regulars, a roster routinely carried two more players. These players were jacks-of-all-trades, filling in wherever needed on the field. Pitching staffs were usually composed of three or four stalwart pitchers who resolutely pitched most of the innings played. Since substitutions could occur only after a player was injured, a faltering pitcher was sent to an outfield position, and one of his teammates already in the lineup took his place in the pitcher's box. During the 1880s, rosters of the championship NL and AA teams that played in the postseason championship series never exceeded sixteen players and usually hovered at twelve men.[36]

A few teams in the 1880s used players to double as field captain and as "manager." Adrian Constantine "Cap" Anson of the Chicago White Stockings, Charles Comiskey of the St. Louis Browns, John Morill of the NL Boston team, and Tim Murnane also of the Boston team, all played and managed simultaneously. But most teams adopted the practice of placing a non-roster member of the team in the manager's post, and a new profession was born. Men such as Jim Mutrie, Frank Bancroft, Jim Hart, and Harry Wright found places in baseball as successful managers. In the 1880s, managers were a good deal more powerful than today's counterparts. They not only made the lineups, chose the pitchers, and performed the usual duties of a manager, they also had more control over the players' daily lives, often administering fines and punishment on a scale that would astonish modern managers. Players were rebellious in the 1880s, but ownership and management exercised enormous influence on the major leaguers.

On-the-field control of baseball teams has changed in another way. As professional, nonplaying managers became commonplace in the 1880s, they took more decisive control of their teams' strategies. Most managers began to use base coaches to help direct offensive action against an opponent. Nowadays teams carry men whose principal function is to serve as first- or third-base coaches, to relay the managers' decisions to hitters and base-runners. Coaches, or "coachers" as they were termed in the 1880s, were members of the teams waiting for their turn at bat who doubled as interim base coaches. By the mid-1880s, "coachers" became a common sight in major league play, and soon minor league and amateur baseball teams were using base coaches as well. In the 1880s, however, many of the coaches saw their function as not only to assist the offensive conduct of a team's attack on an opponent but also to heap verbal abuse upon rival pitchers in order to annoy or unnerve them. Vile and ugly verbal abuse became commonplace in the 1880s. Two teams in particular excelled in the use of abusive "coachers." The Chicago White Stockings (NL), led by the redoubtable Cap Anson, and the highly volatile St. Louis Browns (AA) were baseball's acknowledged leaders in "kicking" (the contemporary slang term for challenging umpires' rulings) and in vociferous, sometimes vulgar, and always colorful coaching from the first- and third-base corners.[37] Walter Arlington "Arlie" Latham of the St. Louis Browns had no equal as a "coacher." He prowled up and down the third-base line howling insults at the opponent's pitcher, trying to steal signs, and attempting to distract the opposition. Hometown fans loved him. Cranks on the road hated him. Partly because of Latham's antics and those who emulated him, coaching boxes were defined in the rules issued in 1887, and although the guidelines for base coaches today are not identical to those of the 1880s, the concept was inaugurated then.[38]

The 1880s saw accelerated experimentation with new equipment to improve players' performances. A casual glance at the advertisements featured in sports journals demonstrates this changing aspect of baseball. Fielders' gloves, improved bats, protective gear for catchers, and other paraphernalia found their way into baseball. Some old-timers tried to play the game the way it was played in previous decades, but items such as catcher's masks, chest protectors, and shin guards made far too much sense to be long ignored by the players; furthermore, such equipment made it safer for catchers to play closer to the hitter, a defensive innovation that obviously improved the game. As late as 1884, for example, many catchers used only a pair of gloves with the fingers trimmed short to receive their pitchers. These hardy gentlemen positioned themselves well behind the hitter to field the ball on the first bounce and struggled to hold runners to their bases. It is not surprising that many catchers found their task nearly impossible, whereas the hitters and runners enjoyed an extra few feet of advantage. In spite of setting up well behind hitters, catchers were frequently injured. Moses Fleetwood Walker, the first African American to play in the major leagues, was a good case in point. Walker joined the Toledo team in 1884 as a catcher and played most of the season, but he was released in late summer owing to an injury he received from a foul tip.[39] Walker, as most of his brethren behind the plate, could not avoid serious injury in the mid-1880s since protective gear was in its infant stages. By the next decade catchers, still vulnerable to injury as are their modern counterparts, at least enjoyed improved gear to protect their hands and bodies.

OLD JUDGE CIGARETTES   Goodwin & Co.,
                        New York.

Doc Bushong posing for Old Judge Cigarettes in 1888. Note the gloves on Doc's hands.

(Courtesy of Jay Sanford, Arvada, Colo.)

Umpires are a constant in the game of baseball. Their knowledge of the rules, their judgments of rapidly unfolding game situations, and their unquestioned integrity are vital to a well-ordered, efficiently played contest. Umpires also create the perception of an impartial environment in which teams succeed or fail by virtue of skills or shortcomings. From the very beginning of organized baseball, umpires were targets for abuse from players and fans alike, but no credible authority ever argued that the game of baseball could proceed without them. Players kicked over umpires' decisions, and fans frequently verbally abused them and, on rare occasions, physically attacked them.[40] Finley Peter Dunne, the Chicago journalist who covered the White Stockings in the mid-1880s quoted the attitude of his mythical "Mr. Dooley" toward umpires:

> Whin I was a young fellow nawthin' pleased me betther thin to go out to th' ball grounds, get a good cosy seat in th' sun, take off me collar an' coat an' buy a bottle of pop, not so much for the pop mind ye, f'r th' refreshment, because I niver was much on pop, as to have something handy to reprove th' empire with whin he give an eeronyous decision.[41]

Mr. Dooley's observations about the niceties of the game probably classified the bulk of the abuse fans heaped on "empires" other than verbal attacks from the stands. Modern fans, were they treated to a faithful recreation of ballpark environments in the 1880s, most likely would be startled by the fans' behavior.

Baseball umpiring in the 1880s was often the center of controversy, largely because games were officiated by only one umpire. Umpires could not possibly see everything at once. An umpire intently watching a play at first base understandably failed to notice the third baseman grab a passing runner by the belt to impede his progress to home plate. Or an overworked umpire could not see a runner fail to tag up at third base as his eyes followed a long fly ball to the outfield. Calling balls and strikes, following the line of flight of a baseball, monitoring the activities of baserunners who chose to cut corners as they ran the base paths, or punishing opportunistic infielders who tripped runners or blocked the base paths were umpires' responsibilities; but one umpire could not be expected to perform so many crucial functions simultaneously. Even though they missed plays, failed to see infractions of rules, and often riled players and spectators by failing to punish obvious transgressions, the beleaguered umpires managed to conduct the games. In an effort to improve the quality of umpiring and to add some incentive for better officiating, the American Association held an emergency meeting in Cincinnati on July 2, 1882, and decided to hire a staff of paid umpires; the National League followed suit and also hired League-paid, League-approved umpires at its annual meeting later in the year.[42] While experiments employing more than one umpire in a contest occurred in the 1880s, the usual practice was for one man to try to call all aspects of a contest. Today's fans, accustomed to seeing four umpires on the field during a game and six during championship play, would not be at all surprised for a game to be cancelled if only one umpire was available at game time. One man, they would surely argue, could not perform all the umpiring tasks. Nevertheless, the umpires of the 1880s took a nearly impossible task and did the best they could.

Another prominent aspect of major league baseball in the 1880s was the role of superstition in the minds of players, owners, and fans. Players in the twentieth century had their quirks about how to prepare for a game, and how to conduct themselves on the field. Whether it is dining on chicken prior to each game, blousing the pants at the knee rather than the ankle, or whatever idiosyncrasies players may demonstrate, modern baseball superstitions are fairly innocuous when compared to those of the late nineteenth century. Nineteenth-century players had the usual range of superstitions one finds with athletes from time immemorial. But players in the 1880s took superstition a bit more seriously than their modern counterparts.[43]

A popular view in the late nineteenth century was that the bulk of professional ballplayers were largely drawn from the lower end of the socioeconomic scale of American society, and as a result, they were less well educated and more prone to superstitious practices. An article in the *Chicago Tribune* dated April 6, 1890, asserted this and then proceeded to proclaim that the nature of major league baseball was changing, that new, more refined, more polished players were appearing on major league rosters and that the more egregious superstitious practices were slowly leaving the game.[44] Although it became conventional wisdom that baseball superstitions were largely the product of uneducated and uncouth minds among the professional players of the 1880s, many scholars dispute this theory. The great philosopher Benedict de Spinoza, for example, observed that men would never be superstitious, "if they could govern all their circumstances set by rules, or if they were always favored by fortune: but being driven into straits where the rules are useless, and being often kept fluctuating pitiably between hope and fear by the uncertainty of fortune's greedily coveted favors, they are prone to credulity."[45] Other scholars agree with Spinoza on the matter of the universality of superstition among men. Gustav Jahoda points out that C. G. Jung and Sigmund Freud agree that "superstitious beliefs and practices are deeply rooted in man's unconscious mental processes; both held that superstition is not a thing of the past or confined to the less educated—in fact it is regarded as a part of everybody's mental makeup liable to come to the surface under certain circumstances."[46]

So, it is likely that the *Chicago Tribune*'s assertion that superstition in baseball was largely the product of lower-class thinking was incorrect. What is apparent, however, is that players, management, and spectators in the 1880s were prone to make more of a display of their superstitious concerns than participants in later decades in baseball. Players might be alarmed if they saw a cross-eyed spectator, or anxious to see a wagon full of barrels on the way to the ballpark, or determined to follow certain pre-game rituals to ensure good fortune; these personal habits were fairly innocuous and harmless, sometimes amusing. But the *Tribune* roundly censured the use of mascots by baseball teams, declaring them "generally chosen for some hideous peculiarity, such as a dwarfed hump-back, or crossed eyes. If a little negro, black as the ace of spades, dwarfed in every limb, and with crossed eyes could have been secured the ideal mascot would have been presented to the gaze of the baseball world."[47] Modern baseball fans and historians have been prone to view the use of misshapen or dwarfed African Americans as mascots as a product of the undeniable racism that infected the 1880s and to some extent probably promoted the practice. But there may have been other, more complicated reasons underlying the practice as well.

Folklorists assert that nearly all races and societies from earliest times have accepted the notion that hunchbacks, dwarfs, and deformed people with squinting or different colored eyes possessed powers to protect people from misfortune.[48] Perhaps the earliest historical example of this phenomenon occurred in ancient Egypt. The household god known as Bes or Bishu has been described as a dwarfed embryo-like god with a tail, a broad flat nose, the ears of a cat, long arms, and crooked legs. He was a talisman against sorcery, and he was placed on or near bedrests to keep evil spirits away from sleepers.[49] Evidence indicates that Bes was imported into Egypt from Nubia, and modern archaeologists have excavated scores of clay figurines of Bes from Egyptian sites, which indicates he was pervasive in early Egyptian society. After Alexander the Great conquered Egypt, the Phoenicians, a seagoing, commerce-minded people of the Mediterranean, developed extensive relations with Hellenic civilization and adopted Bes into their pantheon of deities. Being the peripatetic people they were, the Phoenicians quickly introduced him to other parts of the Mediterranean world.[50] This probably led to the introduction of Bes into the emerging western European societies' lores of superstitions where the concept eventually rooted itself. According to Maria Leach, the term *mascot* derives from the Provencal word *masco* meaning "little magician."[51] As a result, a Nubian god adopted by the Egyptians eventually penetrated western European culture and then came to America as part of our forefathers' cultural baggage. Bes may have been lost in the mists of centuries of travel, but he or his descendant emerged in ballparks in America late in the nineteenth century. Whatever route he took to enter popular culture, Bes mutated into a somewhat grotesque practice of keeping mascots, a standard feature of major league baseball in the 1880s. That this was also a time of rampant racism certainly made the adoption of mascots (not necessarily African Americans) more acceptable to the Victorian Americans who patronized baseball.

The principal duty of the nineteenth-century mascot was to fend off the "hoodoo" (bad luck) placed upon their teams by opposing mascots or cranks, to serve as lightning rods against misfortune.[52] When a team was on the road, for example, the players dressed in their hotel and made their way to the ballpark by carriage or public conveyance. The trip to the ballpark was a public event in which the team advertised its presence in town and simultaneously baited spectators to attend the afternoon's contest while heaping scorn on the cranks' local heroes. During the parade to the park, the mascot was prominently displayed to discourage pedestrians from placing a hoodoo on the team as it journeyed to the game site. Once in the park, the mascot usually glared at the opposing team and mascot (if it featured one), extended his arms, and shook his fingers and hands at them. This served the double purpose of fending off a hoodoo and casting one at the opposition in return. Then during the game the mascot served as the bat boy, chattered to his team on the field, entertained the cranks by dancing, singing, and prowling about the bench area, and kept a vigilant watch for evil spirits that could have an untoward effect on the game's outcome.[53] Mascots were entertainment for the fans, but they served a more important function: They served as talismans against misfortune. Many players and fans, most likely, did not take the diminutive charm-makers too seriously, but the mascots were common sights in professional baseball into the early twentieth century.

Racism in baseball definitely reared its ugly head in the 1880s. At the outset of the 1884 season, major league baseball underwent its single experience with African American players prior to Jackie Robinson in 1947. The Toledo team opened the 1884 season with Moses Fleetwood Walker on its roster. Walker, who played amateur and minor league baseball, got his opportunity when the need for players became acute in 1884. Three major leagues (the National League, the American Association, and the newly formed Union Association) competed vigorously for personnel, which temporarily opened the door, however slightly, to black players. Only two black men—Moses and his brother, Welday Wilberforce Walker—played in the major leagues that summer. Both men played for Toledo. Moses was the regular catcher, and Welday played a handful of games as an outfielder. Welday was quickly released, and Moses lasted most of the summer until an injury brought his season to an end.[54] After the 1884 season, none of the major league teams featured African Americans on their rosters until after World War II. A few rugged individuals, Moses Walker among them, remained in minor league baseball a few years more and pursued their dreams, but by the end of the 1890s even the minor leagues were completely white.[55] Jim Crow reigned supreme in America in the 1880s and 1890s, and baseball reflected that tragic chapter in the nation's history. Although many sportswriters, fans, and others had begun to view baseball as America's national game, it was also an enterprise that capitulated to the racist views of the majority of Americans who actively or passively condoned an era of intolerance.

Major league baseball in the 1880s was a time of massive growth in the numbers of leagues, teams, and players who manned the rosters. The lords of baseball attempted to create what amounted to a horizontal trust to control the game, just as the captains of industry sought to control profits and to limit competition in their fields. Most major league franchises exhibited the prejudices of Victorian America and ingratiated themselves with a respectable, ticket-buying public by espousing the popular views on race, labor, and morality. The 1880s were a decade of players' unrest, seeing the eventual organization of most of the major league players into a brotherhood that fought the more odious practices foisted on them by the ownership and management. The decade was marked by phenomenal economic growth and significant transition in American society, and the sport and business of baseball mirrored those changes.

Interleague Play

The Years 1882–1883

Between 1876 and the start of the 1882 season, the National League enjoyed six years of dominance in eastern and midwestern cities as professional baseball built its audience. Originally instituted as an eight-team league, the NL diligently struggled to maintain that format. During its maiden season in 1876 the League, whose constitution called for teams to be placed in cities with populations of seventy thousand or more, started teams in Boston, New York, Philadelphia, Hartford, Cincinnati, Louisville, Chicago, and St. Louis. Six of the eight original sites for League franchises were among the ten largest cities; the Hartford and Louisville teams were outside the top ten urban areas in the nation. Only Hartford was below the population requirement and its membership required a special exemption by a vote of the NL owners.[1]

Although the National League survived its inaugural season, it was not without controversy. As the season came to an end, the New York and Philadelphia teams (twenty-six and thirty-four games out of first place, respectively) refused to make their final western road trips to play their rivals, and each was in consequence expelled.[2] Both teams had endured financial tribulations during the season, and they sought to limit their expenses by avoiding costly travel to play what appeared to be meaningless games. Hulbert and his associates determined that these teams' conduct left the League no alternative but to expel them, even though this left it without franchises in the two largest cities. One of the evils that the emerging NL had roundly condemned in the National Association had been the frequent failure of NA teams to complete scheduled play. If the new league was to differentiate itself from the older, more inept association, NL officials reasoned, then its constitution and playing schedule must be enforced and New York and Philadelphia must be chastised. Maintaining its image as a vigilant and if necessary vengeful organization suited the NL's quest for credibility among fans, even though such action placed approximately two million potential patrons beyond its immediate ticket sales. Such action also planted the seeds of opportunism among those outside the National League who were interested in capitalizing on professional baseball. After the expulsion of New York and Philadelphia, the NL functioned with fewer than eight teams. In 1877 and 1878 it operated with only six teams; in 1879 it returned to the full eight-team format, which was maintained until 1892 when it expanded to twelve teams following the war with the Players' League and the subsequent collapse of the American Association.

Between 1876 and the beginning of the 1882 season when the American Association arose as a challenger to the dominance of the National League, the NL underwent frequent changes in its membership. Only Boston and Chicago stayed the course during the first six years, proving bulwarks to its existence. Cincinnati maintained its membership through the League's first five years of operation, but eventually the Queen City's team was also expelled. Cincinnati, which claimed special status owing to its large German immigrant fan base, openly flouted NL rules and sold beer to fans and permitted semiprofessional teams to play Sunday games at its Bank Street grounds. German Americans celebrated what many term the "Continental Sabbath." Hardworking German American fans, consistent with their cultural norms, evidenced no prejudice against recreational beer consumption at games and readily patronized the semiprofessional games on Sundays. Purists saw this as being in open defiance of NL authority, as a perversion of two of its hallowed principles.[3] After repeated warnings, after the 1880 season concluded, the Cincinnati franchise was expelled for multiple infractions of the NL constitution.[4] While this action remained consistent with the League's stated objectives, the expulsion of Cincinnati constituted a major setback. Although the Red Stockings performed poorly and only once finished in the upper half of the League's final standings, Cincinnati was the cradle of professional baseball and, if the breach could not be closed, was a prime location for a rival to appear. Hulbert, NL president at the time, entertained the idea that the Cincinnati ownership might be persuaded to recant and rejoin the League, but his hopes for such a rapprochement proved fruitless.[5]

The remaining openings in the National League witnessed many occupants. In addition to the Boston, Chicago, and Cincinnati franchises, each of which functioned as NL anchors for five of the six first years of its existence, fourteen different cities served as members to keep the membership balanced at either six teams (as circumstances mandated in 1877 and 1878) or the desired eight teams. For varying lengths of time St. Louis, Hartford, Louisville, New York, Philadelphia, Providence, Milwaukee, Indianapolis, Buffalo, Cleveland, Syracuse, Troy, New York, Detroit, and Worcester, Massachusetts, each functioned as an NL team from 1876 through the 1881 season.[6] Frequent restructuring of NL membership naturally confused the fans and perhaps gave the impression that the League was unlikely to survive another season. Nevertheless, it persevered, changed, and confounded those predicting its imminent doom.

Considering that the National League owners viewed themselves as saviors of professional baseball and that they endured major difficulties in organizing and maintaining the League, it surprised no one that they both ridiculed and feared the upstart American Association when it came into existence in 1882. Several factors automatically promoted chilly relations between the two leagues. First of all, the Association posed a threat to the League's six-year hegemony as America's "major league." When the AA opened its season in 1882, it featured franchises in Cincinnati, Philadelphia, Louisville, St. Louis, Baltimore, and Pittsburgh. None of the AA teams directly challenged an existing NL franchise for fans' loyalties and dollars, but NL leadership knew other challenges were inevitable.[7] Direct confrontation occurred the following year. In 1883 the Association placed teams in New York City and Philadelphia, as did the League, and this presented two groups of baseball fans with opportunities to compare the different styles of play and fueled the emerging controversy as to which league played the better baseball.

National League owners certainly were alarmed by the emerging American Association's underlying marketing philosophy. The AA adopted an admission price of twenty-five cents per game, undercutting the standard fifty cents NL admission. The AA quickly demonstrated it had no prejudice against Sunday games or the sale of alcoholic beverages. In the eyes of men such as A. G. Spalding and his allies in the NL leadership, these attitudes toward some of the League's most cherished principles were harbingers of disaster for all. Spalding later described his initial concerns:

> The American Association made its appeal to public sympathy and support by proposing an admission fee of twenty-five cents to all games, instead of fifty cents, as charged by League clubs. It was claimed by promoters of the new association that League magnates were coining wealth through an unreasonable charge at the gates; that the exorbitant fee was prohibitive so far as the working man was concerned; that the League was making Base Ball a rich man's game; that none but nabobs could see games anymore. The effect of this competition was serious to the interests of the game in some ways. Unrestricted Sunday games in violation of law and wide-open liquor traffic could not but be prejudicial.[8]

Spalding later revised his opinions and admitted that the competition between the two leagues proved beneficial, but in 1882 he and most of his cohorts looked upon the AA with both dismay and alarm.[9] After having successfully neutralized the old NA, after struggling with the problems of organizing a new league, creating a reserve rule that bound players to their clubs, controlling expenses and players' salaries, and attracting fans to sanitized ballparks, the NL owners naturally viewed the AA with pardonable hostility.

Both the National League and the American Association experienced difficulties in the 1882 season. For much of the summer, NL owners feared that the Troy and Worcester franchises (the two teams compiled totals of 53 wins against 114 losses) would fail to complete the season, which would upset the NL schedule.[10] If the stricken teams faltered and left the League before completing the season, Chicago would be most sorely affected since the White Stockings' final three games were with the Worcester Ruby Legs.[11] Anticipating the worst, and expecting Troy and Worcester to default, Providence and Chicago, locked in a tight pennant race, agreed to play a nine-game series to decide the NL championship once the regular season schedule was completed.

As events turned out, Troy and Worcester did not collapse, and the White Stockings finished in first place. Since his White Stockings won the pennant outright, Spalding tried to back out of the agreement for a postseason championship series. Providence, seeing a chance to claim a League championship via the previously arranged series of games, insisted on meeting the White Stockings. According to the *New York Times,* before the season was finished, the nine games were arranged in order to decide the championship should the Troy and Worcester clubs withdraw from the race. Both clubs stayed in to the end, and it was generally understood that if the Providence club won the most games it would claim championship honors.[12]

In actuality Spalding found himself in an ideal situation. No matter the outcome of the playoffs with Providence, he could always claim his team the champion since it unquestionably won the pennant during regular season play. Honoring his commitment set a good example of gentlemanly conduct for others to emulate, and there was the potential for welcome postseason profits. Providence hosted Chicago for the series' opening games and promptly took a commanding lead by winning all three in Rhode Island. The fourth game was played in the Polo Grounds before a crowd of four thousand spectators, and the White Stockings reversed the Grays' momentum, recording their first win in the playoffs. After moving the playoffs to Chicago, Spalding's team continued to play well and won three of the next four games with Providence.[13] The series finally concluded in Fort Wayne, Indiana, in late October where Chicago won the final game and prevailed five games to four.[14] Spalding's White Stockings undeniably validated their claim as the NL champion both by winning the most regular season games and by taking the series from Providence. Meanwhile, Spalding certainly polished his image as a statesman and, since the special nine-game series was well attended, reaped unexpected profits. Providence got its chance to contend for a championship by unorthodox means, and although the Grays were frustrated, everyone prof-ited from the experience.

In the midst of all this confusion over who was rightfully the NL cham-pion, Cincinnati's Justus Thorner decided to enter his Reds (AA) into the spirit of postseason playoffs among champions and near champions. The Reds won the AA pennant in 1882, and Thorner and his associate Oliver Perry Caylor, who was in many ways the primary force driving the Reds, hit upon an idea to earn both money and prestige in the postseason by scheduling games with the Cleveland, Providence, and Chicago NL clubs.[15] Games with Chicago carried many implications both for the Cincinnati club and for the American Association in general.

Caylor and Thorner's Cincinnati Reds (AA) first challenged the Cleve-land Blues (NL) to a three-game series for what amounted to the champi-onship of Ohio. The Blues' record in 1882 was fairly unimpressive. Cleve-land ranked fifth in the final NL standings with a modest record of forty-two wins and forty losses, finished next to last in runs scored and next to last in hits, but seventh in slugging percentage. Better than average pitching kept the Blues mildly competitive in 1882. The Blues' pitching staff—which consisted mainly of James McCormick, who started sixty-five of Cleveland's eighty-four NL games and won thirty-six while losing thirty—compiled an earned run average of 2.75, third best in the NL. Mc-Cormick and his colleagues gave up only 743 hits in 751 innings.[16] Even though the Cleveland Blues were an NL team, their record was not one to inspire fear in any opponent.

The Cincinnati Reds fared far better. They compiled a record of fifty-five wins and twenty-five losses for a sparkling winning percentage of .688, fin-ished first in hits, runs scored, and slugging percentage, and finished the season eleven and one-half games ahead of second-place Philadelphia.[17] Cincinnati also featured strong pitching. William Henry White, who car-ried the distinction of being the first major leaguer to wear eyeglasses while on the field, pitched fifty-four of Cincinnati's eighty games in 1882, winning forty and losing only twelve. He led the AA in innings pitched with 480 and gave up only 411 hits to opponents.[18] The Reds' pitching staff gave up only 609 hits in 721 innings and registered a stingy earned run average of 1.65 while issuing only 125 bases on balls.[19] In their respec-tive leagues the Reds' and the Blues' pitchers recorded some impressive feats, but in the areas of hitting and runs scored the Reds held a slight ad-vantage. A cross-state rivalry intrigued baseball fans in Ohio, and Cincin-nati did not appear to be overmatching itself with its NL counterpart. Thorner and Caylor and the leadership of the Blues anticipated a fairly profitable encounter when their teams met, and each group saw the pres-tige of their respective leagues at stake.

When the American Association president, Dennis McKnight, learned of the upcoming match between the Reds and the Blues, he made no attempt to conceal his annoyance with the prospect of the AA champion striking out on an independent course. McKnight felt that such action, especially if the Reds did poorly against the Blues, might well jeopardize the AA's status in the eyes of baseball fans across the nation. McKnight's viewpoint was not unique to him; most of the AA leadership adamantly opposed scheduling postseason games with the NL while so many outstanding issues between the two leagues remained unresolved. Consequently, McKnight issued a statement that banned games with NL opponents at the end of the 1882 season.[20] Undaunted, Caylor and Thorner resorted to subterfuge. They released their players from their contracts and invented a "wealthy admirer" who volunteered to pay the players' salaries for the series. After the owners had devised what they thought a workable scheme to circumvent McKnight's edict, the Cleveland-Cincinnati series came to fruition on October 3. Even though Cincinnati's victory in the second game was the AA's first win against the NL, Caylor and Thorner watched sadly as their Reds lost two of the three games and Cleveland claimed the championship of Ohio.[21]

Once the games with Cleveland concluded, the Reds' leadership then surprised the baseball world with the announcement that, in spite of McKnight's stern warnings, a two-game series with the Chicago White Stockings, the NL champions, would also take place. The White Stockings, currently involved in their nine-game series with Providence, were the premier team in major league baseball, and the Reds seemed to be both overmatching themselves and risking McKnight's wrath at the same time. Led by Cap Anson and Michael "King" Kelly and a pair of formidable pitchers (Larry Corcoran and Fred Goldsmith, who combined to win most of Chicago's regular season victories), the White Stockings clearly were a step up from the Cleveland Blues. The *Cincinnati Commercial* declared:

> The Chicagos are the veteran team of the choice ball-players of this country, who have won the League championship for three years, and it would be folly for any one to expect their defeat at the hands of the Cincinnati team of lighter material. Still the good playing which the home champions have done at times during this summer leads many of their friends to hope to see them play the champions a close and exciting game, and have the possibility of beating them.[22]

Regardless of Cincinnati's underdog status in comparison with the White Stockings, the city's baseball fans were in a state of intense agitation when the Chicago team arrived on the morning of October 6, 1882. The White Stockings arrived on the Erie Railroad, checked in to the Grand Hotel, dressed for the game, and proceeded to the ballpark for the locally momentous contest. According to the *Cincinnati Commercial,* about three thousand people turned out for the contest, and to their delirious joy and astonishment, the Reds won the game 4–0.[23] The next day, however, an estimated thirty-five hundred fans saw their Reds fall 2–0 to the White Stockings. Nevertheless, the Reds obviously acquitted themselves well before the largest crowd of the 1882 season in Cincinnati and won their rabid fans' affection. After the game, the White Stockings departed for the East Coast to prepare for their upcoming games with Providence, and the Reds entrained to St. Louis for a final game with the Browns prior to being dismissed for the season.

By the time the Chicago series was underway, the Reds were under intense pressure from McKnight, who now threatened to expel them from the American Association if they did not end their illegal postseason adventures. Thorner and Caylor finally succumbed to McKnight's blandishments and cancelled Cincinnati's upcoming games with Providence. Even so, the Reds attained a certain amount of glory and prestige by playing a good three-game series with Cleveland and splitting two games with Chicago. Sharp-eyed owners in both the National League and the American Association noticed that the Cincinnati-Chicago set of games drew about sixty-five hundred spectators. Such fan enthusiasm for interleague championship play offered potential profits, if the two rivals could settle the divisive issues that plagued their relationship.

Cold weather finally arrived in the early autumn of 1882, and teams in both leagues ended their postseason play and disbanded for the winter. Both NL and AA owners now found time to assess their seasons, lay plans for next year, and ponder their relationships with their rivals both within their leagues and without. On December 6, 1882, the National League convened its annual meeting in the Dorrance Hotel in Providence, Rhode Island, and transacted the usual season-ending business. Such matters as formally declaring Chicago the NL champion, reinstating blacklisted players, and forging minor changes in playing rules constituted most of the actions taken by the owners.[24] For the AA owners, the most significant part of the NL meeting was that the League appointed a committee to meet with AA representatives to discuss outstanding differences concerning the reserve rule, schedules, and other matters of common interest. So when the American Association leaders held their annual conference in the Grand Central Hotel in New York City only a few days later, the matter of a potential peace treaty with the NL appeared imminent. Even so, the Association prepared for another season of tension with the League. In the event that the "peace conference" did not materialize or proved futile, the AA forbade any of its teams to meet with opponents from the rival league.[25] The ban on play outside the AA carried a proviso, however, declaring that if the conference committee concluded satisfactory arrangements with the NL, then interleague play would be condoned. For the moment, games with the NL were forbidden.[26]

Obstacles to interleague play—and eventually to championship series—vanished in early 1883 when NL and AA representatives assembled for a "harmony conference." The historic meeting took place in the Fifth Avenue Hotel in New York City on February 17, 1883, and led to what was termed the National Agreement, which some have styled the Tripartite Agreement. Three men representing the National League (Arthur Soden, John Day, and Abraham G. Mills) met with three leaders of the American Association (Lew Simmons, O. P. Caylor, and Billie Barney) and the president of the Northwestern League (Elias Mather) to seek accommodations among the principal professional baseball leagues in the United States. The conference resolved several issues that had been troubling the relationship between the NL and the AA, which if left untended threatened to ignite open and bloody warfare. The Northwestern League was the junior partner in the deliberations and mainly played the role of spectator. Mather fully realized that peace between the NL and the AA served his league's interests, and he gracefully acquiesced to the role of observer rather than full-scale participant. Three divisive issues were addressed and resolved. All three leagues agreed to recognize each other's contracts with players; conference participants pledged that their leagues would avoid raiding rival leagues for players; and they agreed that interleague play was an acceptable concept.[27]

The National Agreement also set other standards. It established minimum salaries of $1,000 for ballplayers in the NL and AA, and a minimum of $750 for the Northwestern League, in effect, establishing that league's status as a "minor league."[28] The agreement created an Arbitration Committee composed of three members from each of the signatories' respective leagues, whose function was to resolve future disputes arising among or between members of the National Agreement.[29] It carefully set standards of conduct regarding the business end of the game, but the National Agreement skirted the issue of formalizing playing rules for its members. Each league was permitted to maintain its own playing rules. As a consequence (much as in modern baseball), where the two major leagues adopted different policies on the designated hitter, the NL and AA functioned with slightly different rules throughout much of the 1880s. While the first National Agreement held profound ramifications for the relationships between players and owners, for rival leagues such as the Union Association (UA), which arose in 1884 to challenge the NL and the AA, and the Players' League (PL), which appeared at the end of the decade, the National Agreement removed the final obstacle to interleague play. Now it was just a matter of time before the reality of a postseason championship series formally emerged.

Only seven weeks after the National Agreement was drafted, interleague play began. Championship games did not occur in 1883, but the NL and the AA first tested the waters with preseason contests in April as they prepared for their regular seasons. On April 7, 1883, Baltimore hosted the Philadelphia Athletics (NL) at Newington Park in the first interleague exhibition game. Philadelphia took command of the game in the first three innings and finally won the contest 6–3; although the score was respectable, the playing was ragged, and a total of thirteen errors marred the contest.[30] Cold and rain plagued the East Coast in early April 1883, and several games on April 8 were cancelled. When weather conditions improved on April 9, several more teams got their interleague play under way. The first game between the newly created New York Metropolitans (AA) and the fledgling New York Gothams (NL), soon to be the Giants, drew a good deal of attention. The teams later shared the Polo Grounds in 1884 as a home park, and the rivalry between the two captivated the imaginations of baseball fans throughout the New York City area and beyond. Tim Keefe, destined later to become the stalwart of the Giants' pitching staff, started the game for the Metropolitans, and as it turned out, the game proved something of a disaster for AA hopes. The Mets committed nine errors and lost the game 8–1, even though Keefe allowed only one earned run.[31] From that point until the opening of the regular season, several of the NL and AA teams clashed in interleague games. Some of the teams in both leagues, such as the Providence Grays (NL) and the St. Louis Browns (AA), shunned interleague play and contented themselves with intra-squad games, contests with college teams, or workouts against local amateur, semiprofessional, or minor league contingents. As far as interleague play was concerned, New York, Cleveland, Boston, and Philadelphia NL teams played heavy schedules with the New York, Philadelphia, and Baltimore AA franchises. The rival teams in New York and Philadelphia played multiple game series against each other, and these contests actually constituted a good portion of the preseason interleague experience. The New York Metropolitans (AA) were especially involved in the testing of the NL brand of baseball and fared poorly in the bargain. Between April 9 and April 28, 1883, the Mets played thirteen contests with NL teams and lost the first twelve. Finally, on April 28, the Mets reversed their misfortunes and defeated the Gothams in the Polo Grounds.[32] All told, the Association performed poorly against its rival. According to the *New York Clipper,* the NL and AA teams sandwiched at least twenty-four games into their schedules while often facing cold, damp weather. The NL won twenty of the contests.[33]

Fears of some of the American Association owners were realized in the preseason games; the National League appeared to establish its supremacy over the Association. Nevertheless, timid AA owners could not ignore the fact that the games drew healthy crowds when the weather was even only slightly cooperative. Fans seemed willing to endure cold and wet to see the leagues demonstrate their prowess, and on good days the attendance was impressive. On April 30 in Philadelphia, for example, a throng of ten thousand turned out to see a contest between the two Philadelphia teams.[34] Games between the two leagues often drew crowds ranging from two to four thousand. Finally, in early May, the two leagues opened their regular seasons, and fans and players alike now focused their energies on the pennant races. While defeating rivals occupied the attention of teams in both leagues, there was now the postseason potential of an October renewal of the preseason rivalry between the AA and the NL, which baseball fans awaited with some anticipation. Their first concerns, though, were the fortunes of their local heroes in the pennant races underway.

Baseball fever was at an unusually high level in the spring of 1883. Both the major leagues and the Northwestern League, the Interstate Association, and college teams attracted attention and ample press coverage as they opened their seasons. Countless amateur and semiprofessional teams also occupied local interest. Americans everywhere seemed consumed by a passion for the game. Not only did fans find college men, amateurs, and semiprofessionals competing with the professional teams for attention, but other types of teams began to appear in 1883. In Philadelphia, for example, unusual teams announced their formation and sought to attract fans to their games. According to the *Clipper:*

> Baseball fever is raging uncommonly high this season. The thirst for players is so great that in Philadelphia they are ransacking hospitals in order to make nines. One set of cripples is called the Snorkey Baseball Club, in honor of the hero of the famous drama "Under the Gaslight." Like him the players of this team have but one arm apiece. The team chosen to antagonize the Snorkeys are called the "Hoppers," from the fact that they are one-legged men, or at least supposed to be.[35]

The Snorkeys and the Hoppers were not destined to carve a niche for themselves in baseball's list of immortals. One-armed and one-legged players might draw curious spectators and provide the players with some fun and perhaps a little pocket money, but their game was a novelty that soon vanished. Nevertheless, the newspaper account of the Snorkeys' formation demonstrates that baseball was king of the summer in America. Some historians have asserted that baseball and its popularity helped to calm cities such as New York in the 1880s. Adrian Cook, for example, observes that, even though the 1880s were times of low unemployment and comparatively good wages, they were also years of overcrowding and social dislocation; yet there were no riots (relatively common in earlier decades), and Cook argues that the "rise of professional baseball and football provided an alternative to rioting as a form of communal weekend entertainment."[36] Whatever the merits of this theory, no one who reads the newspapers of the 1880s can reasonably deny the widespread support for baseball in all levels of America's rapidly diversifying urban populations.

Once the National League and American Association concluded their regular season's play in early October 1883, several teams entered into interleague exhibition play. No one suggested that any of the games constituted a championship series between the leagues; fans, players, and owners alike viewed the exhibition games for what they were. The games had no official effect on anything. Unofficially, however, games between the two major leagues were keenly observed since the prestige of each was indirectly involved in each contest.

Postseason play in 1883 proved extensive despite the cooler weather and earlier sunsets that reduced opportunities to play and made ballpark environments less attractive to customers who felt the chill of approaching autumn. In the 1880s games began in mid-afternoon. Steven Riess, writing about starting times for major league games, points out that games in Chicago, for example, usually began around half past two since the Chicago Board of Trade closed early. New York City games usually started at half past three. This gave the Wall Street crowd time to make the long trip north to the Polo Grounds. Washington, D.C., games usually awaited the arrival of the government clerks, who finished their workday at four o'clock.[37]

Weekend contests always drew larger numbers of fans when working men turned out to enjoy a game and perhaps a beer or two. As autumn arrived and the amount of daylight for ball games declined, the exhibition games often were six innings in length. Fans historically turned out in numbers sufficient to make postseason play prior to 1883 a worthwhile financial enterprise, and when the added luster of interleague play arose, the monetary advantages compounded.[38]

The prospect of interleague competition in the autumn was measurably enhanced when both major leagues experienced exciting seasons in 1883. The National League's Boston Beaneaters unseated the powerful Chicago White Stockings as league champions after a stirring season in which the White Stockings, led by the surly and talented Cap Anson, finished a close second. The Beaneaters had got off to a slow start in 1883. At the end of May, they were in sixth place, lagging behind the defending White Stockings by six games. By August 27, the Beaneaters were in fourth place trailing Cleveland, Providence, and Chicago, with a record of forty-four wins and thirty-two losses. In early September, however, the Beaneaters began an impressive winning streak and won nineteen of their final twenty-two games. This was good enough to propel them to the pennant four games ahead of the Chicago White Stockings.[39]

The Philadelphia Athletics and the St. Louis Browns energized the American Association's season as they fought for the pennant. Philadelphia nearly lost it in Louisville, Kentucky, when they played a season-ending four-game series with the Eclipse. Louisville was in fifth place as the season drew to a close and did not figure to be much of a challenge to the Philadelphia juggernaut. The Eclipse proceeded to win the first two games in the series and reduced Philadelphia's lead over the St. Louis Browns to one game. Finally, on September 28, 1883, the next-to-last day of the season, the Athletics won an eleven-inning game against Louisville, giving Philadelphia a two-game lead over St. Louis.[40] The next day the Eclipse again defeated the Athletics; the St. Louis Browns won their final game; and Philadelphia won the pennant by a single game.

As events established in 1883, the two major leagues functioned in comparative harmony. The Arbitration Committee set up by the National Agreement of February 1883 held its first meeting at the Fifth Avenue Hotel in New York City on October 27–28, 1883. The *New York Clipper* reported that the committee found "its full and creditable endorsement in the result of the season which has just closed with a record of unexpected financial prosperity, of thorough harmony and without a single instance of individual dishonesty in the club-ranks of either association calling for punishment at the hands of the judicial tribunal."[41] Owners in both major leagues could not have asked for more: Prosperity, harmony, and honesty, so the Arbitration Committee declared, reigned supreme.

Profits, pride, and prestige, reinforced by the license granted by the National Agreement, compelled the major leagues to reexplore the potential bonanza of interleague competition. The first postseason contest of 1883 between the two major leagues occurred on October 1, when the ex-champions of the NL and AA, Chicago and Cincinnati, in something of a continuation of the previous year's games, opened a three-game series in Cincinnati. All three games were well played, and to the delight of the Reds' fans, Cincinnati won the opening and closing games of the set with the White Stockings.[42] For the next three weeks NL and AA clubs played each other an additional forty-seven games.[43] Finally, the interleague season's play came to an end in St. Louis on October 27, 1883, when the Browns took the final game of a four-game series from the Cleveland Blues. Once the interleague play was concluded, the NL again emerged triumphant over the AA. The NL finished with twenty-nine wins compared to the AA's eighteen. Three games were declared draws owing to inclement weather or darkness. Once again, the NL, posting a winning percentage of .617 in postseason play, appeared to establish its hegemony over the AA. One significant event did not occur. The Boston Beaneaters (NL) and the Philadelphia Athletics (AA) did not meet each other in postseason play. Nothing resembling a championship series between the two leagues occurred in the autumn of 1883. Nevertheless, interleague competition flourished in 1883 facing no insurmountable obstacles on or off the playing fields, profits were recorded, and the cranks heartily approved the concept of League and Association teams clashing on the diamond. As 1883 came to its conclusion, most knowledgeable baseball insiders assumed that next year a championship between the major leagues' pennant winners was a certainty.

The Beginning

Providence versus New York, 1884

Interleague play in 1883 proved profitable to both the National League and the American Association. It also signified a ratification of an uneasy peace treaty between the two major leagues, but the sense of tranquillity in major league baseball was short-lived. As teams prepared for the new season in 1884, the leadership in major league baseball understood that the upcoming year offered a fresh, potentially costly challenge. A third major league, the Union Association of Base Ball Clubs (UA), now emerged as a rival to the NL and the AA. Once again, the major leagues were stalked by the prospect of players perhaps defecting to another league, by the specters of new teams competing in NL and AA towns, and by the potential warfare between ruthless owners and opportunistic players.

St. Louis resident Henry V. Lucas, railroad heir and baseball fanatic, spearheaded the effort to organize the new major league.[1] The *New York Clipper* reported the UA's upcoming organizational meeting in the autumn of 1883:

> The organization of a new association will no doubt result in some advantages to baseball in one form or another, but it surely will bring disadvantages. It will enable players, for a short time at least, to demand better wages than they are getting now; but contemporaneously it will enable these players to be independent rather than the association that professes to start out as independent. It will render the task of disciplining professionals much more difficult than it is now, and no one will pretend that ball-players are less in need of disciplining than the rest of mankind.[2]

Keeping discipline among the players may have been a concern among the owners of the NL and AA franchises, but it was the prospect of another battle for fans' loyalties and dollars that made them anxious.

Lucas and his associates assembled in Pittsburgh on September 12, 1883, and elected Henry B. Bennett president of the new league, proceeding to lay the foundation for a third major league. The Union Association's intent was unmistakable: to challenge the National League and the American Association in some vital baseball markets. In addition to admitting charter franchises, UA leaders reviewed the playing rules of both the NL and the AA and in the main adopted them. Perhaps the most significant action taken at its formative meeting, other than creating a rival to the NL and the AA, was the UA's declaration that it would recognize all existing contracts binding ballplayers through their current terms. In effect this meant that, once the 1884 season was concluded, the UA's founders felt no obligation to resist signing players from other leagues since the great majority of players were bound by one-year contracts set to expire in the autumn.[3] Disgruntled AA and NL owners now facing unwanted competition, delighted players sensing new outlets for their services, and fascinated fans, all realized that the upcoming season promised to be unique. The prospect of warfare among the rival leagues added spice to a baseball world already in ferment.

In 1884 baseball fans were treated to an unprecedented spectacle. The National League opened the season with its usual complement of eight teams, all of which were holdovers from the previous year. The American Association, however, partly encouraged by NL owners, staked out new territory by adding teams in Indianapolis, Brooklyn, Washington, D.C., and Toledo.[4] As a consequence, the established major leagues increased their franchises by one-quarter, expanding into areas they had heretofore ignored. With the new UA franchises, the number of major league teams doubled overnight. Many Americans, heretofore outside ready access to major league baseball, prepared to enjoy a season of top-quality play. At the same time the sudden growth in major league franchises, brought on by the birth of the UA and the AA's expansion plan, created a pressing demand for players to fill the new teams' rosters. Teams sought players everywhere, whereupon baseball executives soon realized that the nation did not have enough major-league-quality players to meet their needs.

Clear examples of the paucity of major league talent appeared quickly in the AA's expansion program. Early in 1884 one of the AA's new entries proved a good choice for a club. Brooklyn, the third-largest city in the United States in 1880 with a population of 566,663, grew rapidly during the decade and nearly doubled in size.[5] Even though the Brooklyn Trolley Dodgers fared poorly in 1884, posting a record of forty wins and sixty-four losses, the size of the city's population and the local thirst for baseball sustained the team until it won the AA pennant in 1889.[6] Other franchises in smaller cities did not match Brooklyn's success at the ticket window. The other three newly added AA franchises—Indianapolis, Toledo, and Washington, D.C.—were ill-fated choices and disappeared from the AA team roster in 1885. The club in Richmond, Virginia, that replaced the Washington team during the 1884 season also failed to survive the winter and passed into obscurity. Nevertheless, the AA's expansion program appeared to make sense in early 1884.

Following the Union Association's odyssey in 1884 was a challenge for even the most dedicated fan's attention and patience. At the outset of the season, the UA established an eight-team league. From the very beginning of the association's existence, however, teams failed to form, faltered once they entered competition, and disappeared with the elusive speed of summer lightning. By the time the UA's sole season was completed, twelve different teams carried its banner. Only the St. Louis Maroons (who ran away with the UA pennant), and the Cincinnati Outlaw Reds, the Baltimore Monumentals, the Boston Reds, and the Washington Nationals played more than one hundred games. Four franchises (the Milwaukee Cream Citys, the St. Paul White Caps, the Wilmington Quicksteps, and the Altoona Mountain Citys) played twenty-five or fewer games.[7] Some of the teams (such as the Maroons) were well stocked with competent players, and others (such as the Altoona franchise) were not. Altoona tried to compete with a roster of amateurs and local players. It collapsed late in May and was replaced by a team from Kansas City. On August 7, 1884, the Keystone club in Philadelphia collapsed. Shortly thereafter, the Wilmington team of the Eastern League joined the Union Association, played eighteen games, and on September 12 suspended play. The Chicago Browns fared poorly at the ticket window, transferred to Pittsburgh on August 25, renamed themselves the Stogies, and died eighteen games later.[8] The UA's performance in 1884 proved bewildering for baseball cranks, but it certainly provided variety. Fans who relished the game as a sort of secular religion always had new events to ponder and digest. Teams were born and perished, marginal ballplayers briefly appeared on "major league" rosters, owners scrambled for means to survive the baseball war of 1884, and fans ultimately witnessed something new, the death of a major league. The Union Association vanished during the winter of 1884–1885.

For the most part, the National League and the American Association had basically ignored the upstart. Other than in St. Louis, where the Maroons enjoyed a good deal of success on the diamond and competed for attention with the St. Louis Browns (AA), most UA teams did poorly in ticket sales. Although the Maroons distressed Christian Von der Ahe, the Browns' owner, neither the AA nor the NL truly felt threatened. According to the *New York Clipper,* nearly all interest in the Union Association season was lost because the contending teams were unevenly matched.[9] Within the first weeks of the 1884 season it became apparent that the new league was unable to recruit competent players in sufficient numbers to man teams claiming major league status.

Several events in the National League and the American Association marked the 1884 season as an unusual one. The Chicago White Stockings

(NL) produced home runs with unprecedented fury in their home ball-park. Minuscule Lake Front Park's dimensions were only 180 feet to the left field fence, 300 to center field, and 196 to the right field fence. Through the 1883 season, balls hit out of the park were considered two base hits, but in 1884 the ground rule was changed and any ball hit over the fence was a home run. Capitalizing on the new rule, four of the White Stockings hit twenty-one or more home runs in 1884. Ned Williamson led the barrage with 27 homers (only two were hit on the road) as the team posted an amazing total of 142 for the season.[10] Williamson's record endured until Babe Ruth broke it in 1919. The entire National League hit only 322 home runs in 1884, which meant that the White Stockings produced nearly half the league's output. Four teams (the Providence Grays, the New York Gothams, the Philadelphia Quakers, and the Cleveland Blues) each hit fewer home runs than Williamson, and all but three teams in the AA hit fewer than twenty-seven home runs. The following year the White Stockings moved to the slightly larger West Side Park, and home run production returned to "normal" levels when they hit only fifty-four. Even though the ballpark was small and home runs were relatively cheap, Chicago's Ned Williamson added an interesting sidelight to the 1884 NL campaign.

Although the White Stockings startled the baseball world with their fire-power at the plate, Chicago finished fifth in the season's standings. The NL pennant went to the Providence Grays, who featured a phenomenon of their own. Pitcher Charles G. "Hoss" Radbourn won fifty-nine games for the Grays in 1884. Prior to that year Hoss's pitching feats were substantial. He joined the Grays in 1881. Beginning with his initial year with Providence until his historic season of 1884, Radbourn won 106 games in three years while pitching 1,431 innings.[11] As awesome as these annual performances appear, they were only the prelude to Radbourn's amazing feat in 1884. He and Charles Sweeney were the mainstays of the Grays' pitching staff, and in July 1884, after Sweeney quarreled with his manager and left the team to later join the St. Louis Maroons (UA), Radbourn, who earlier had been briefly suspended, assumed the bulk of the pitching chores. Once the season finally concluded, Radbourn had compiled some monumental statistics: He led the league with 59 wins, pitched a Herculean 679 innings, gave up only 528 hits, struck out 441 hitters, and posted an earned run average of 1.38.[12]

Radbourn's stamina was remarkable. Commenting on Hoss's successes, *Sporting Life* declared that "Radbourne is certainly the boss pitcher for staying power, and much wonder is expressed how he can stand the strain of pitching game after game. One secret of his success is that he does not pitch for record, but when he has a game well in hand he saves himself by easing up on his delivery."[13] Hoss may well have been ahead of his time in the way

The 1884 Providence Grays posing before the grandstand in their home park.
(National Baseball Hall of Fame Library, Cooperstown, N.Y.)

he learned to pace himself. No major league pitcher ever approached his single-season record for games won. Other NL players had banner seasons in 1884, but Radbourn's tenacity and successes eclipsed everyone's.

The American Association also had an unusual season, partly from the fact that the league expanded to twelve teams. With the UA competing for players and the AA's need for players to man the rosters of an expanded league, many players, who had been minor leaguers in 1883, found themselves on major league teams. Inadvertently, the AA opened the door to the only experiment of employing African American players in the major leagues prior to the end of Jim Crow's reign in 1947. One of the teams added to the AA in 1884 was the Toledo Blue Stockings. The Blue Stockings were composed mostly of the men who had played for the Toledo team in the Northwestern League in 1883. Moses Fleetwood Walker was among the Blue Stockings who found themselves elevated to major league status, and he rather unexpectedly earned the distinction of becoming the first African American major leaguer. A native of Ohio and formerly a student at Oberlin College and the University of Michigan, where he played baseball while failing to take degrees, Walker joined the Toledo team in 1883 and established himself as a competent catcher and a modestly talented hitter.[14] Walker's tenure with the Blue Stockings in 1884 was cut short by injuries, and he was released before the season ended. "Fleet's" accomplishments were modest. He caught forty-one games, played one game in the outfield, went to bat only 152 times, and made 40 base hits for an average of .263.[15] Certainly a combination of injuries common to catchers in his era and the undeniable stress of the racial baiting and hostilities directed at him by opponents and fans affected his play. Nevertheless, he was a legend-making addition to the saga of the American Association's 1884 expansion program. Commenting on the peculiar nature of the season and the diversity of players called to major league rosters in a year of unprecedented expansion, one newspaper observed, "Columbus has a deaf mute and Cleveland a one-armed pitcher, Toledo a colored catcher and Providence a deaf centre-fielder; and yet these men can earn about $2,000 per annum apiece."[16] Marginal players enjoyed a summer in the sunshine of major league baseball, and then most of them returned to minor league teams in 1885 or drifted out of baseball. Walker recovered from his injuries and continued playing minor league baseball for several years before returning to his native Ohio where he operated an opera house in Cadiz. After retiring, he moved to Cleveland and died in 1924.[17]

The 1884 season proved an interesting one. In the National League the Providence Grays, behind the steady and awesome pitching of Sweeney and Radbourn, battled the defending champions, the Boston Beaneaters, for the NL pennant. Boston had its own pitching phenomenon in the person of Charles Buffinton who won forty-eight games, but overall, the Grays had the better team and won the pennant by a margin of ten and one-half games. Pitching proved the strength of Providence. The Grays were, comparatively speaking, a light-hitting team, finishing fifth with a team batting average of .241, fifth in runs scored, and sixth in home runs, but first in earned run average with a sparkling 1.61.[18] The Grays and the Beaneaters faced each other a total of sixteen times during the season and drew 59,393 patrons to their games; the games in Boston averaged 4,948 in paid attendance (for 66 percent of the total), whereas those in Providence averaged about 2,200.[19] Part of the disparity in the home attendance figures was because Boston was the larger city, but another part was because the Grays, for all their success on the diamond, never really enthused their hometown fans. Providence was in its fifth season as a member of the National League, and the Grays never drew well at home. For home games in 1884, other than those with the Beaneaters, the Grays averaged about one thousand paid admissions.[20] After the 1885 season the Providence club vanished. Nevertheless, by mid-August of 1884, the Grays appeared likely to win the League pennant, and dedicated fans in Providence anticipated a championship playoff with the AA's standard-bearer once the season concluded.

In 1884 the American Association experienced a bit more tumultuous a season. Forced to cope with the difficulties of its expansion program, it also was dealing with the usual problems brought on by a season of keen competition. New York's Metropolitans, playing only their second AA season, handily won the pennant when they outdistanced the second-place Columbus Buckeyes by six and one-half games with a record of seventy-five wins and thirty-two losses.[21] The Mets, much as the Grays, featured strong pitching and modest hitting. Two pitchers, Tim Keefe and Jack Lynch, each won thirty-seven games for the Mets that season and posted an earned run average of 2.46, second best in the AA. The team collectively hit .262, which only Philadelphia topped with a .267 average for the season. The Mets were in most ways a better-balanced club than the Grays. Many baseball fans, both astute and otherwise, argued that the AA was home to several teams of low quality; and NL partisans steadily maintained that some of those clubs fell far below major league standards. Cranks everywhere anticipated a series between the two leagues' champions, which would, many reasoned, offer some resolution to these arguments about the rivals' relative strengths.

Near the end of August, prospects materialized for a championship playoff between the National League and the American Association. Although there was a month remaining in the season, it appeared that the Providence Grays were likely to win the NL. The *New York Clipper* reported at the end of August that "the first time this season Providence now holds a winning lead in the pennant race, the record to date showing the Providence team to lead Boston by a percentage of .75 to .69."[22] The paper went on to speculate that, since Providence and Boston had finished their games with each other, the Grays appeared to be in good condition. The Grays enjoyed a four and one-half game lead over the Beaneaters and faced only second division competition for the remainder of the season. Meanwhile, in the AA, the New York Mets were locked in an exciting race with the Columbus Buckeyes and led Columbus by two and one-half games. Neither the Grays nor the Mets were certain to win the respective leagues' pennants as the final month of the regular season began, but they were the favorites in the races.

Frank Bancroft, the NL Grays' manager, certainly viewed his team as the favorite. In mid-August he addressed a letter to Jim Mutrie, the AA Mets' manager, suggesting a three-game, postseason championship series between their clubs.[23] Arrangements for postseason championship play in the 1880s were unique to major league baseball, and the task fell to the teams. It was not until 1905 that major league leadership took control of championship play and directed the National Commission to devise rules and guidelines for the emerging world series. So Bancroft's challenge was not viewed as an independent or self-aggrandizing act.[24] He and the Grays' ownership were free agents and could do as they pleased. Bancroft's letter to Mutrie was simple and to the point: He suggested a three-game series in New York City, that each team raise one thousand dollars and place it in escrow, and that the winning players take the two thousand dollars once the championship games were finished and divide it among themselves as they saw fit.[25]

Bancroft's strategy intrigued the baseball fans. He obviously felt his team was superior to the Mets and hungered for a playoff between his Grays and the Mets. He offered to play all three games in New York City. Bancroft understood the Providence fans' ambivalence toward his team and recognized that New York City fans were rabid about their teams. He also knew that a playoff there offered better hope of national attention and monetary rewards. In addition, somewhere in the back of his mind, Bancroft must also have relished the opportunity to beat a New York team in New York. During his years in baseball, he witnessed the growth of New York baseball fans' attitudes concerning their beloved clubs. New York fans made it abundantly clear that they considered a team such as the Providence Grays representatives of a community beyond the pale of urban civilization.

Bancroft vainly awaited a reply to his letter to Mutrie. About a month after he issued his written challenge, Bancroft arranged a face-to-face meeting with the Mets manager in Detroit, Michigan. There, on September 19, 1884, in a tense meeting, Bancroft again challenged the Mets to a three-game playoff and suggested that the teams split the gross receipts rather than put up one thousand dollars each for a winner's purse.[26] According to the *Clipper*, Bancroft, a little to his surprise, received some criticism over his suggestion that the players ante money for a prize. In an effort to justify his original idea, he wrote:

> I regret very much that anyone would misinterpret our intentions, and not understand the drift of our challenge, which is as follows: We disband about the middle of October, and many of our best players have arranged to go hunting, fishing, etc.; but if the Mets make it an object they will remain intact as a co-operative nine, and play the three games, and, after consulting with them, we thought a prize of $2,000 made up by each team would prove sufficient inducement to all concerned to bring about the test between the teams. As the players subscribe the funds themselves to make up the prize, we think it a pretty sure guaranty that they intend playing the games in a manner to elevate the game instead of degrading it.[27]

To avoid further criticism, Bancroft withdrew the suggestion that the players create a purse and replaced it with one in which the teams split the gross receipts. Mutrie countered with an offer rejecting all of Bancroft's proposals save that teams split the gate receipts.[28] Splitting the gate receipts reserved to the Mets all profits from concessions and any other income generated by the proposed series; Bancroft summarily dismissed the offer, and the meeting proved fruitless.

Mutrie, annoyed by Bancroft's aggressive conduct, managed to put Bancroft on the defensive after the Detroit meeting. His strategy was clever: If a playoff failed to materialize, he could always claim the Grays proved unwilling to meet his Mets. If a playoff developed on Mutrie's terms, the Mets retained the potential to reap additional profits by reserving to themselves any income from auxiliary ballpark enterprises. Over the next six weeks rumors abounded both that the Mets and the Grays would meet and that they would not. Finally, Mutrie publicly announced he intended to "claim the championship of the world for the Metropolitans if Bancroft did not accept his challenge."[29] Events took an odd turn; Bancroft had issued the original challenge and suddenly he appeared to be avoiding the mighty Mets. Mutrie cleverly employed the New York City press to bolster his position. Meanwhile, Bancroft seethed with resentment over how his small-town team was being manipulated by big city newspapers and an unscrupulous scalawag like Mutrie. If and when a series occurred, Bancroft had an account to settle with Mutrie and the Mets.

Finally, early in October, Bancroft and the Grays succumbed to Mutrie's pressure tactics and consented to a three-game series in New York City.[30] The games were scheduled for Thursday, Friday, and Saturday, October 23–25, in the Polo Grounds.[31] *Sporting Life* reported:

> The details were arranged at New York last week. The clubs will divide the receipts and expenses alike, and no restrictions will be placed on the pitchers, the winning club to be entitled to the championship of America. These will probably be the greatest games ever played, and will be the first time in history of the game that the championship teams of the two associations have met in a formal series to decide supremacy.[32]

After a good deal of posturing, Mutrie and Bancroft finally reached a compromise that suited each. A split of gate receipts met Mutrie's original proposal, and Bancroft now had the opportunity to showcase his team in the nation's largest city against the rival pennant winner before some of the most rabid fans found anywhere in America. The elements for an epoch-making series seemed at hand.

Prior to the 1884 season the Mets had played home dates in the New York Gothams' Polo Grounds. In 1884, however, the Mets occupied a new and hastily constructed park, Metropolitan Park, on 108th Street near the East River. Players, none too fondly, called it "the Dump" as it was located on the site of an old city dump. It was small and located across the river from a factory that often contributed noxious fumes to home games, which further detracted from the park's ambience. Jack Lynch of the Mets, a thirty-seven-game winner in 1884 and known for his sense of humor, observed that the Dump was a place where a player could stoop to field a ground ball and "come up with six months of malaria."[33] Because of the Dump's deplorable conditions, the Mets returned to the Polo Grounds on July 17, 1884, where they played the remainder of their home schedule.[34] So, even though the Polo Grounds ballpark was officially a National League park, the Mets did not surrender the home field advantage when they agreed to play the Grays at the Polo Grounds. The Grays were familiar with the Polo Grounds, which somewhat softened the apprehensions of Bancroft and his club who were playing the entire series on the road.

Preparatory to the upcoming series, fans in Providence and New York City made plans to celebrate their clubs' successes. In Providence, even though the town remained somewhat cool to its team, the public demonstrated its approval of the Grays' accomplishments in the NL. When the Grays returned to Providence from their last road series after clinching the League pennant, the players were met at the railroad depot with a twenty-one-gun salute and were escorted to the City Hotel where they were each presented with a new suit of clothes and a gold badge commemorating the championship season.[35] Providence baseball fans seemed unaffected by the fact that their team was scheduled to play a championship series away from home, and the festivities, though lightly attended, were joyous nonetheless.

In New York City, local authorities planned an evening parade for October 22 to compliment the Mets on their successful season and to inspire them for the series set to commence the next day. Unfortunately for the Mets and their fans a cold front arrived that afternoon, and the parade was cancelled owing to rain and a raw wind that swept through the city.[36] The vigorous, blustery weather proved something of an omen for the Mets. Playing conditions were far less than ideal, and the prospect of facing Hoss Radbourn on a damp field in chilly weather certainly did little to improve the Mets' hopes against the Grays. Nevertheless, the Mets, the Grays, and baseball fans everywhere anxiously awaited the long-sought showdown between the National League and the American Association.

As New Yorkers prepared to witness the first world's championship of baseball, they viewed the games as just one aspect of an already eventful year. Their city continued to change on a daily basis. Earlier in the year, they had been shocked by the failure of the brokerage firm Grant and Ward. Former president Ulysses S. Grant's partner had mismanaged the firm, leaving the Civil War hero embarrassed and nearly penniless. The Grant and Ward failure created a small financial panic in New York City, but the effects were neither permanent nor catastrophic, except that the ailing General Grant found himself financially ruined. While the Grant tragedy was playing itself out, another tycoon of the age, John D. Rockefeller, commissioned the construction of a nine-story building at 24–26

Broadway to house his recently formed Standard Oil Trust. Rockefeller's building joined a growing array of skyscrapers that altered the city's appearance and made Manhattan Island one of the urban wonders of the world. Taller buildings arose as real estate became increasingly expensive, and water tanks atop the taller structures became hallmarks of the city's rising skyline. Architecture rapidly outstripped fire-fighting technologies, and the tanks were reservoirs to feed water into sprinkling systems designed to control fires on levels above the reach of firemen's hoses and ladders. The Metropolitan Opera House, the product of William H. Vanderbilt's social ambitions, concluded its first season in 1884, and all about the city there were signs of commercial progress and cultural developments. Electric lights now twinkled along the city's more fashionable sectors and business district; Edward S. Clark's famous apartment house, Dakota Apartments, opened to tenants; and pedestrians struggled to deal with the growing traffic and confusion manifest on the streets.[37]

New York was a city known for its advances in commerce and culture, and also for its complexity. New York City, as well as Brooklyn and adjacent municipalities, sheltered not only the wealthy and the illustrious but a thriving middle class, masses of immigrant communities, and an underclass of desperately poor workers. The entire urban area was nationally renowned for its diversity. Coney Island symbolized the newly emerging urban environments, for example. One of Coney Island's landmarks was a wood-framed, tin-skinned hotel in the shape of an elephant, and it became common for visitors to the amusement center to declare they intended to "see the elephant." One could ride the newly introduced roller coaster, dine in modestly priced restaurants, wade in the surf, or satisfy carnal appetites in a visit to "the Gut" adjacent to the amusement park area.[38] In a small area ordinary visitors could proceed from acceptable middle-class pursuits to others of much more dubious nature. New Yorkers visiting Coney Island understood these differences and either passed them by or indulged themselves as their appetites dictated. Few seemed excessively worried by the contiguous nature of virtue and sin; after all, New York and Brooklyn were teeming cities where everyone pursued their own interests without judging others too harshly. For all its glory and shame, New York City was the nation's premier metropolis.

As the day of the playoffs arrived, New York fans recalled that, earlier in the year, the Mets and the Grays had played three preseason games, and that the Grays had won all three, scoring a total of thirty-four runs to ten for the Mets.[39] Now the Mets' partisans hoped to witness their team's redemption. As the world's championship approached, Mets' fans speculated on how their team would fare against Radbourn in cold weather. Radbourn was virtually unhittable in good weather. How could the Mets hope to punish him in damp, cold weather when he would be throwing a soggy ball? New York City had enjoyed balmy autumn weather the first three days of the week, but on Wednesday evening the first hint of approaching winter struck the city, and for the remainder of the week, an overcast sky accompanied rain and a piercing wind assailing the city and the fans in Polo Grounds.[40] Weather conditions certainly favored a strong pitcher such as Radbourn.

In spite of the daunting weather conditions, about twenty-five hundred fans filed into the Polo Grounds to witness the first game. As the excited spectators entered the park, they were presented with a "souvenir in the form of a handsome steel engraving of all the prominent players," courtesy of Mr. Pierre Lorillard who, in addition to his interests in tobacco, was a well-known baseball fanatic.[41] As the fans took their seats and braced themselves against the wind, they eagerly watched the players exercise lightly in preparation for the game. Unlike modern championship sporting events, the pre-game scene was not cluttered with celebrity introductions, marine color guards, soloists, or player introductions. There was little fanfare accompanying the opening of what amounted to the first World Series in baseball's history.

Providence won the coin toss and elected to take the field first and reserve the last at bat. The Mets failed to score in the first inning. In the bottom of the first inning, Tim Keefe, the ace of the Mets pitching staff, strode to the pitcher's box before a chilled but excited crowd. Keefe, in the beginning of an illustrious career in which he won 342 games, proved edgy. He hit the first two batters he faced; then during a series of wild pitches, a passed ball, and a sacrifice, the Grays scored two runs without making a hit.[42] The Mets, faltering in the first inning of the first game, never recovered from their inauspicious opening. After the first inning Keefe settled down and pitched well, but Radbourn proved masterful throughout the contest. Two runs proved enough for Hoss. He allowed the Mets only two hits (Keefe got one of them) and shut them out 6–0.

Reports of the first game focused nearly as much on the weather as on the game itself:

> A cold, raw wind, almost a gale force, swept over the grounds, and soon painted the noses and fingers of the lookers-on a pretty but uncomfortable blue. Many ladies braved the weather, but they probably mentally resolved never to do it again—at least until the weather was warmer. The wind whirled the ball in so many directions when it was sent into the air that it is remarkable that only two errors were made.[43]

Both errors were charged against Providence, but Radbourn's steady pitching easily offset them. The Mets were soundly defeated, and their fans found little comfort in the knowledge that Radbourn was scheduled to pitch the second game. Considering Hoss's mastery that summer, the prospect of facing him again was none too inviting. His record of winning games on consecutive days in 1884 was awesome, and the Mets' partisans apprehensively awaited his second appearance in the series.

The second game proved equally disappointing to New York. The weather remained disagreeable, and Radbourn, who again faced Keefe, proved unhittable. He allowed the Mets only three hits and held them to just one run.[44] Radbourn defeated Keefe on consecutive days, and by modern standards each man recorded phenomenal pitching feats. The first game lasted nine innings in spite of the cold and growing gloom toward the end of the contest; the second game lasted seven innings before being called on account of dismal playing conditions and failing light. In slightly over twenty-four hours Radbourn and Keefe each pitched sixteen innings in less than ideal conditions, and each day they pitched complete games. Keefe surrendered a total of ten hits and nine runs in two games, and Radbourn gave up only five hits and one run. Keefe pitched well enough in the second game to win the contest, but the Mets simply could not hit Radbourn's curve ball and change-of-pace pitch.

The weather again proved daunting for the fans. Only one thousand spectators, considerably less boisterous than the previous day, turned out to see the contest, and at game's end there was little doubt as to which of the teams legitimately claimed the title of world champion. Although the Grays easily won the first two games, the series was not, in the estimation of the Mets' management, completed; the teams had agreed to a three-game series, not a best of three.

On October 25, as only three hundred fans arrived at the Polo Grounds to witness the third game, the Grays balked at taking the field in cold weather and before so few fans. The weather had gotten nastier overnight, and the Grays argued that so few fans scarcely justified enduring the cold to play another, essentially meaningless game. According to the *New York Times*, when the Grays gazed into the stands and saw so few spectators, they

> turned up their noses and said they would not play. This displeased the officers of the Metropolitan club and Mr. Arthur Bell, the Treasurer, reminded them of the small attendance at the games in Providence, and said he would not disappoint his patrons if there were only ten present in the inclosure. This brought Bancroft's pets to their senses, and they willingly entered the field. They tried to stop the game by refusing to accept any umpire the Mets would name, and in order not to allow them any loophole by which to postpone the contest with the Mets they said they would accept any person Joe Start [the Grays' team captain] would name, even if they selected their own manager.[45]

Stung by Bell's well-placed remarks and in a gesture of both resignation and resentment, the Grays chose Tim Keefe as umpire. Keefe who performed so creditably in the first two games was not scheduled to pitch in the final game. Known as "Sir Timothy" for his courtly manners and sense of fair play, he was a man of impeccable integrity.

The last game of the playoff finally got under way. The weather was exceptionally cold, the players were uninspired, and the fans were puzzled by all the pre-game wrangling between the Mets and the Grays. The game proved a dismal experience. Mutrie sent rookie pitcher Jim Becannon to the pitcher's box for the Mets, and the Grays, who had argued the game was a meaningless one, again chose Radbourn to start the game.[46] Hoss took the field for the third time in three days and proceeded to defeat the Mets 12–2 in a six-inning game called because of growing darkness and bone-chilling cold.

The Metropolitans played poorly in the final game. Their regular second baseman, Dasher Troy, was unavailable for the game, and they inserted Tom Forster as his replacement.[47] Forster had spent most of the 1884 season playing for the Pittsburgh Allegheny team in the AA, and he was enlisted at the last moment to fill out the lineup. As the *Times* described it, the Mets "played recklessly in the field and failed to give young Becannon any kind of support. Reipschlager [the catcher] distinguished himself behind the plate by making a half dozen errors. He was very kind to the visitors and presented them with three-quarters of their runs."[48] Providence, or perhaps Hoss Radbourn, demonstrated an unmistakable superiority over the AA's standard-bearer in the first world championship. Radbourn's pitching feat in championship play was not surpassed until Christy Mathewson pitched three shutouts against the Philadelphia Athletics in the 1905 World Series, and even then, Mathewson's brilliant performance has to be qualified by the fact that Radbourn had no rest days while compiling his astonishing record. Except for the second game, when the Grays defeated the Mets 3–1, none of the contests was really ever in doubt. The Grays dominated the Mets.

Financially, the series was not especially successful. Less than four thousand people attended the games. At fifty cents per ticket, gate receipts could not have much exceeded two thousand dollars. Contemporary accounts failed to report the total income from the games, the amount deducted for expenses, and how much money, if any, the teams divided. At best, each team earned a pittance.

The 1884 series was unsettling for the American Association. The Mets won the pennant fairly easily in 1884, and they were demolished by the Grays and Radbourn in postseason play. Since its inception, the AA steadily claimed parity with the NL, but interleague play and the championship series rendered this assertion suspect in late 1884. Nevertheless, the

AA eagerly wanted to continue the series in 1885 as it sought to establish a claim of parity with the NL, and the NL readily accommodated its rival in order to maintain its self-declared hegemony in professional baseball.

Several lessons emerged from the first championship. Autumn weather often is balmy and beautiful, but the 1884 games faced the beginning of winter's wrath, which, along with the Grays' dominance of the Mets, negatively affected gate receipts. Mindful of the harsh weather experience of 1884 and in an effort to avoid early autumn cold spells, the playoffs began a full nine days earlier in 1885. Stealing a week on winter certainly provided no guarantee against uncomfortable weather during championship games, but it was the only means available to address the problem. No one seriously mentioned changing the start times for games. Series games in 1884 began at the usual time for major league games, three o'clock. Baseball authorities everywhere accepted the notion that later starting times were essential in attracting fans to major league games. Consequently, games in the championship series stretched the later innings of a contest into the cooling part of the afternoon as sunset rapidly approached. By starting two hours earlier, games shortened by twilight could have been avoided, and midday sunshine might have warmed fans late in the autumn. But conventional wisdom continued to prevail. Except for on weekends, baseball executives continued the practice of late afternoon starting times for games. In addition to their considerations of weather and game times, baseball's moguls quickly realized that a longer series of games was essential if participants held any hope for financial success in future championship play. From 1885 onward, the World's Championship games were always more than three-game sets, and they were never played in only one city. Never again did the hometown fans of a pennant-winning team face a situation where their heroes played a championship series entirely on the road.

Another feature arising from the New York–Providence series was the tacit agreement among owners and executives of the American Association and National League that the playoffs were to be an ongoing feature of major league baseball. No one boldly proposed a sanctioned means of arranging future playoffs or suggested that such series ought to be regulated by the leagues' presidents or some other duly constituted authority. Major league baseball's leadership adopted a laissez-faire attitude concerning championship play, and future postseason encounters were to be governed largely by the whims of the owners of the pennant-winning teams. But there certainly would be more championships.

CHAPTER FOUR

Chicago and St. Louis

The Years 1885–1886

Major league baseball's championship playoffs following the Providence–New York series in 1884 were elevated to a new intensity in 1885, when the Chicago White Stockings won the NL pennant and faced the new, rapidly maturing power, the St. Louis Browns. Spalding's White Stockings were among the pioneers who created the National League, and for a decade the Chicago team was one of the stalwarts in the League's crusade to establish itself as the purveyor of quality, professional baseball. Founded in 1876 by Hulbert, the driving force in the creation of the National League, the White Stockings immediately dominated. Hulbert was typical of the sort of hard-driving businessman produced by the city of Chicago as it grew from a frontier settlement early in the century to the dominant midwest city at century's end. To fulfill his goals, Hulbert lured Anson from Philadelphia and Spalding from Boston to anchor his White Stockings in 1876. Anson (later known as "Cap" from his many years as Chicago's field captain and manager), Spalding, and their teammates responded immediately to the challenge and led the White Stockings to the first NL pennant in 1876.

For the next decade Chicago was the team to beat. Spalding pitched 528 innings for the White Stockings in 1876, winning forty-seven games and losing only twelve. Then, in 1877, he shifted to the infield and played first base, second base, and third base while pitching only eleven innings. Following the 1877 season Spalding needed more time to supervise his fledgling sporting goods business, and he retired at the age of twenty-seven after two seasons with the White Stockings. He accepted the post of secretary of the club, and when Hulbert died abruptly on April 10, 1882, Spalding succeeded him as president of the White Stockings. Abetted by John T. Walsh, a powerful Chicago banker, Spalding soon gained control of the White Stockings.[1] From this point onward, Spalding rose to the position of principal NL leader, and as such, he heavily influenced baseball until his death in 1915.

Spalding was born on September 9, 1850, in the little farming community of Byron, Illinois, not far from the burgeoning Chicago where he made his fortune. When he was a youngster, his widowed mother relocated the family to Rockford, Illinois, and there young Albert matured into manhood and perfected his skills as a ballplayer. His mother was comfortably situated for income, and Albert, while he endured many of the anxieties of youth, enjoyed the benefits of middle America's prosperity and optimism about the future of the nation. Albert remembered himself as a shy youngster, and that baseball provided him some relief from his worries. As Spalding matured into manhood, he soon attracted local attention for his competence at the game. In 1871 he joined the Boston team in the National Association where he quickly made his mark as a pitcher. Then, at Hulbert's urging and seeing real opportunity in Chicago, he jumped to the National League in 1876 and became the pitching mainstay for the White Stockings.

He was a fine pitcher, but Spalding had higher ambitions in life. While serving as the secretary of the Chicago White Stockings, he simultaneously launched a career in selling sporting goods that eventually made him a wealthy man. His was the American dream: A small-town boy worked hard, saved his money, earned his fame, and prospered throughout life because of his thrift, industry, virtue (and, some might insist, ruthlessness). Horatio Alger Jr. could not have invented a better character for his American success stories so dearly loved by nineteenth-century Americans.[2] Although he did not rise from actual rags to riches, Spalding dramatically improved his position in life, and Alger's readers would have been enchanted by a story modeled on his achievements.

The National League and the White Stockings were originally Hulbert's enterprise, but Spalding led them to fame both as player and as team executive and owner. His achievements totally eclipsed those of Hulbert. Along with the notoriety generated by his successful sporting goods business, Spalding's name is synonymous with the national game for generations of Americans who long since have forgotten Hulbert and the others of his generation who founded the National League. In 1885 the White Stockings were the most dreaded team in the NL, and Spalding stood on the threshold of establishing himself as baseball's unofficial overlord. Few baseball fans were surprised when Chicago won the League pennant in 1885, their fifth in the League's first ten years of competition. Boston occasionally won the NL pennant, upstart Providence won two, but the reigning power was the White Stockings. Now they had the opportunity to compete for the World's Championship, a title coveted by Spalding.

If Spalding's White Stockings were the dominant team in major league baseball, Christian Von der Ahe's St. Louis Browns emerged as a powerful challenger. Like Spalding, Von der Ahe was a baseball pioneer. He was among the men who founded the American Association, and he also sought to elevate his team to undisputed dominance in the exciting,

A young Albert Goodwill Spalding posing for a picture
during his playing days with Boston in the National Association.

(National Baseball Hall of Fame Library, Cooperstown, N.Y.)

sometimes nasty wars in baseball. Of a personality totally different from Spalding, Von der Ahe, using the astute advice and on-the-field leadership of his manager and first baseman Charles Comiskey, quickly built his Browns into an estimable club.

Contrasts between Spalding and Von der Ahe are stark. Spalding was a native-born American who first gained fame as a pitcher and won 252 games for the Forest City Rockfords in his hometown of Rockford, Illinois, for Boston in the National Association, and for Chicago in the fledgling National League.[3] After his playing days ended, Spalding became the epitome of the sturdy, tight-buttoned, relentless businessman who dominated a large part of post–Civil War America's commercial and industrial growth. A stern moralist, a sharp-eyed businessman, nearly always in control of the people who fell into his orbit, Spalding compulsively asserted his views and values. When he could not control a man, Spalding took drastic measures to eliminate him. Michael "King" Kelly, who in Spalding's estimation was a bad influence on the White Stockings, suffered this fate. The King was a stylish ballplayer equally at home as an outfielder and as a catcher, and wildly popular with Chicago's baseball fans. Notorious for his flashy lifestyle, late hours, and frequent visits to the gamier parts of Chicago, the King was a constant source of irritation to Spalding. Chicago's cranks, especially those of Irish nativity, loved him, but Spalding did not approve Kelly's nocturnal habits.[4] By the end of 1886 Spalding finally realized he could never tame the irrepressible King, so in early 1887, he sold Kelly to Boston for the then astonishing sum of ten thousand dollars. Kelly, having refused to conform to Spalding's dictates, was banished from the powerful White Stockings. Spalding did not long tolerate opposition to his Victorian sensibilities or personal ethics.

Christian Fredrick Wilhelm Von der Ahe, on the other hand, represented Spalding's antithesis. Accounts of his nativity vary, but it seems he was born in Halle, Germany, around 1852. Most accounts agree that he arrived in the United States in 1870 and soon settled in St. Louis where he rose from being a grocery clerk to proprietor of a grocery store, to owning a popular saloon named the Golden Lion, and finally to the august status of owner of a major league team. He was a fun-loving, improvident man who never seriously played baseball and never mastered the game's finer points.[5] Quite untroubled by the Association's scheduling games on Sundays, selling alcoholic beverages in ballparks, and lowering the admission prices to attract a broader base of patrons, Von der Ahe prospered as one of baseball's premier baseball magnates in the 1880s.

Despite his achievements, the Browns' owner was often the target of ridicule. He spoke English with a heavy accent, and his malapropisms were noted routinely in the press. He often seemed out of place among his peers. On one occasion, for example, observing a good-sized throng at a game, he allegedly stated, "Vot a fine pig crowd."[6] Once, when he wanted to acquire a player for the Browns, Von der Ahe was reminded that he previously had released the player on two or three occasions. Chris thought for a moment and then replied, "That is right, a rolling moss never catches a stone."[7] His public utterances were the stuff of which legends were born, and the newspapers, the Chicago press in particular, never tired of lampooning his hapless use of English. To men like Spalding, Von der Ahe demeaned major league baseball, but whatever Spalding and his NL peers thought of the Browns' owner, they privately must have marveled over his often shrewd (albeit sometimes comical) marketing of his team's popularity.

During the 1880s Von der Ahe, "der Boss president" as he liked to label himself, stood near the pinnacle of the baseball world, but unlike Spalding, he did not maintain his grasp on fortune and fame. He was forced out of baseball at the turn of the century after suffering a series of reverses. In 1897 and 1898 he endured a bitter divorce, which negatively affected his finances, and on April 16, 1898, a fire destroyed his ballpark.[8] From 1898 forward Von der Ahe's financial status and his personal life declined, and by the time of his death from cirrhosis of the liver in 1913, he had become dependent on old friends for financial assistance. An obituary noted that he had been a generous and sometimes naive man who "never lacked a numerous array of flatterers and hangers-on who would clap him on the back and tell him what a wonderful magnate he was—and drink the wine and smoke the cigars for which he paid."[9] Nevertheless, for a brief period in his life, his Browns' successes earned him celebrity status.

Spalding's distaste for the upstart AA and Von der Ahe's methods of marketing his team caused a natural rivalry between the two owners. In Spalding's view, Von der Ahe and the St. Louis Browns fulfilled his early apprehensions that the new league would erode hard-won reforms elevating baseball from the mire of its earlier difficulties. Von der Ahe sometimes seemed the clown, but his Browns played solid baseball, soon dominated the AA, and rose to a position where both they and their AA colleagues legitimately challenged the NL for dominance. One of Spalding's long-enduring goals was to rid baseball of Von der Ahe and his unorthodox influences, an objective Spalding lived to see fulfilled.

In addition to the tensions between Spalding and Von der Ahe, another factor colored the playoffs between the White Stockings and the Browns in 1885 and 1886. Chicago and St. Louis were natural rivals for recognition as the Midwest's most dominant city. Each city's ruling clique sought to finesse the other city's leaders and demonstrate civic, commercial, and cultural superiority. In the mid-1850s, for example, most of the commercial traffic on the Ohio River was usually destined to reach either St. Louis or New Orleans. Chicago merchants and entrepreneurs encouraged and backed the creation of the Illinois Central Railroad, stretching from

Christian Von der Ahe.
(Used by permission, State
Historical Society of Missouri,
Columbia, all rights reserved)

Chicago to Cairo, Illinois, at the mouth of the Ohio River. Cairo offered the potential of siphoning goods from the river traffic that normally bypassed Chicago. A rail line to Cairo obviously offered Chicagoans new fields for trade and profits. When the Illinois Central line, the first land-grant railroad, went into operation in 1856, it quickly diverted a good portion of the trade that formerly had gone to St. Louis or New Orleans. Chicago's growing network of railroads and its substantial lake transportation facilities, its growing grain storage centers and commodities market, and its huge meat-packing industry, all made it an attractive option for farmers who shipped their produce to Chicago on the newly created Illinois Central. By using the new railroad, farmers in the Ohio Valley gained quicker access to profitable markets in the East. In consequence, the Illinois Central dramatically altered the flow of commodities normally confined to the slower river routes. The Illinois Central immediately prospered, and smug Chicagoans referred to the railway as the "St. Louis Cutoff." Not only did the railroad feed Chicago's prosperity, it fed the egos of Chicago's leaders who always enjoyed an opportunity to demonstrate their city's vitality at the expense of St. Louis.[10]

St. Louis was the older of the two cities, and its history reached back into the days prior to the nation's existence. Born out of the trade on the Mississippi, Missouri, and Ohio Rivers, St. Louis was tied historically to the activities of legendary explorers and fur traders such as Pierre Laclede Ligueste and Auguste Pierre Chouteau. As the gateway to the Missouri River, St. Louis dealt with inland commerce beyond the pale of civilization. It was tied to the Santa Fe Trail trade launched first from Franklin, Missouri, and later from the site of the future Kansas City, Missouri. For more than a century St. Louis had been a jumping off place for the wild interior. When Meriwether Lewis and William Clark passed through St. Louis on their epoch-making trek across the newly acquired Louisiana Territory, Chicago did not exist. Populated by a mixture of Creoles left over from the days of French and Spanish occupation, and recently arrived Americans, St. Louis projected the image of a frontier yet cosmopolitan city situated on the natural arteries to the interior of North America. New Orleans and St. Louis ruled the river trade in the newly acquired western territories of the rapidly growing republic. Each city was a queen of the river, and each held a prominent place in the minds of informed Americans who knew something about the West. Thomas Jefferson, for example, was quite familiar with the basic history of each city, but he probably was unfamiliar with "Chicago," although he would have known something about Fort Dearborn, standing on the site where Chicago was to be born. St. Louis's dominance of the West was destined to change.

A decade after Lewis and Clark and their Corps of Discovery (as President Thomas Jefferson styled them) passed through St. Louis on their roundtrip expedition in search of a northwest passage to the Pacific Ocean, the real founding of Chicago was launched. Although the point where the Chicago River emptied into Lake Michigan was inhabited by French fur traders and their Native American clients prior to 1763 (when Great Britain claimed the area after the Seven Years' War), it remained a remote and somewhat inaccessible post. Later (when the western shore of Lake Michigan became American territory after the Treaty of Paris of 1783 ended the American Revolution), the area destined to become Chicago remained a raw, unhealthy site where fur trappers and Indians coexisted, and where U.S. Army personnel did lonely frontier duty. To historically minded Americans, its most famous event was the massacre of the military personnel and civilians who evacuated the post after a siege by the Potawatomis during the War of 1812. Until the 1820s Chicago was a river, not a city.

Then, all this changed. One of the first events was the appearance of John Jacob Astor's American Fur Company. Astor was bent on opening trade to the hinterland. The Chicago River offered a usable port from which men could portage trade goods to the Des Plaines River, and thence continue to the Illinois River, the Mississippi, and the heartland of the nation. A lucrative fur trade beckoned, and Astor's decision to penetrate the interior of the continent via the Chicago River gave impetus to the beginnings of a substantial settlement. In 1818 a fleet of bateaus under the command of Antoine Deschamps departed the Mackinac headquarters of the American Fur Company, paddled along the coast of Lake Michigan, entered the mouth of the Chicago River, and formally inaugurated the company's fur trade interests in what was to become Illinois. One of the bateaus carried sixteen-year-old Gurdon Saltonstall Hubbard, destined to become one of the titans in the founding of the city of Chicago.[11]

Hubbard eventually left the dying fur business and became the first insurance underwriter in Chicago. By the mid-1850s, he owned several local insurance companies and had established himself as one of Chicago's most influential citizens. Hubbard lived to see the swampy lowlands turn into a city. In his lifetime he witnessed Chicago develop from a harsh frontier settlement populated by rootless people, rogues, and criminals into America's second-largest city, and (in the last two years of his life) see it play host to the world's championship playoffs. Hubbard was an anchor to which the city's history was fastened. His fame later was outstripped by men such as George Pullman, Potter Palmer, Marshall Field, and other merchants and industrialists who made their fortunes in Chicago, but Hubbard's name was linked to that bygone time when the city was born. One man's lifetime and one city's lifetime were synonymous in 1885 when the World's Championship playoffs first came to Chicago.

After its founding, Chicago grew wildly, in spite of the great fire that consumed it in 1871. Growth, often unplanned and unchecked, reigned supreme. By 1880 Chicago was the fourth-largest city in America, with a population of 503,185, surpassed only by New York City, Philadelphia, and Brooklyn. A more sedate, more traditional St. Louis ranked sixth in population among America's largest cities in 1880. Chicago's growth was explained in part by its being securely tied to the vast railway network binding the nation together. St. Louis, although not unacquainted with the railroads, remained more a river city than a railroad hub, and Chicago, favored by its position on Lake Michigan and the web of railroads leading to the city, experienced astonishing growth in the 1880s. By 1890 Chicago far surpassed St. Louis as the largest and most powerful city in the West as its population soared from a little over one-half million residents to a staggering 1,099,850. In the meantime St. Louis was experiencing significant growth, but nothing comparable to Chicago's explosive expansion. St. Louis's population increased from approximately one-third of a million to 451,770 by 1890.[12]

The disparity in size and influence between the two cities steadily widened, and by the turn of the century few outside St. Louis denied that Chicago was the premiere city of the Midwest. Chicago and St. Louis, however, remained rivals in commerce, culture, civic boosterism, and in baseball. Thus, when the White Stockings and the Browns simultaneously became champions of their respective leagues, a playoff between them involved more than baseball's highest honor. It also seemed a test of the two cities' virtues. By the 1880s successes in baseball gave municipalities national recognition, and Chicago and St. Louis hungered for the celebrity of a world's championship—especially if it could be taken at the other's expense.

The 1885 Season

The 1885 pennant races in the American Association and the National League differed dramatically. In the AA the St. Louis Browns ran away with the pennant. They had clinched the championship by midsummer. They eventually compiled a record of seventy-nine wins and thirty-three losses for an impressive winning percentage of .705, sixteen games ahead of the second-place Cincinnati Reds. The Browns averaged six runs per game and their pitchers amassed an impressive earned run average of only 2.44. St. Louis managed only 206 extra base hits in 112 games, and the team batting average of .246 was fifth best in the league. Pitching made the difference for the Browns. Bob Caruthers and Dave Foutz combined for a total of seventy-three of St. Louis's seventy-nine victories while pitching 890 innings and allowing only 781 hits. Speed and pitching were trademarks of Browns' baseball.[13]

Aggressive base-running was another of St. Louis's traits. There are no reliable statistics until 1886 concerning stolen bases in the AA, but well before scorekeepers began noting them, the Browns were notorious for stealing bases and for taking an extra base on errant throws or mental lapses. Walter Arlington "Arlie" Latham was chief among the Browns for running the bases with daring and speed. Arlie, who proclaimed himself the "Freshest Man on Earth," was born in Lebanon, New Hampshire, in 1860 and came to the Browns in 1883.[14] Latham was a mediocre hitter, but his defensive skills at third base were noteworthy. For seven years while playing for St. Louis, Latham set the standard for third basemen.

Latham's impact on the Browns was immediate. In his first season, his base-running drew attention. The *New York Clipper* observed, "He is one of the fastest and best base-runners in the profession, excelling even in that respect all of his St. Louis comrades, whose success this season is mainly due to base-running—a most important factor in a team's composition. In running the bases he couples excellent judgment with a wonderful bit of speed." Charles Comiskey, Yank Robinson, Curt Welch, and Hugh Nichol also contributed to St. Louis's reputation for stealing bases and for swiftness on the base paths. Although no statistics on stolen bases were recorded in 1885, the following three seasons the Browns stole 1,385 bases in 414 games for an average of 3.34 per game.[15] Opponents tried to restrain them, but the Browns would not be denied. In addition to being a fine base-runner, Latham also enjoyed his reputation as a "kicker," fighting the umpires' decisions, and as a relentless heckler. One historian described him as a "fierce competitor, a cheerleader for the fans, and a merciless heckler. He would badger opposing players and encourage the fans to do the same. Latham often roamed the coaching lines to steal signs. The crowds loved him; he was a clown and a prankster, and an accomplished tumbler who incorporated acrobatics into the game on more than one occasion."[16] Raucous and sometimes vile, Latham personified the relentlessly aggressive baseball that was the trademark of the Browns.

Charles Comiskey, who came to the Browns in 1882 and promptly displayed his talents as a player and leader, served as the team's manager after the 1884 season. Comiskey was in many ways a reflection of Cap Anson. He did not hit as well as Anson, but he played first base, and he drove his teammates incessantly. During the Browns' successful days in the 1880s, Von der Ahe (who, it must be remembered, knew little about baseball) relied heavily on Comiskey for the savvy needed to propel the team to its prominence.[17]

Outside their fine pitching, the Browns were not the most talented team in the American Association, but they always found the means to win games. Von der Ahe loved the Browns' style and encouraged it. Winning was important, but Von der Ahe also knew that his concessions at the games prospered when the fans turned out to be entertained by the Browns. If the players were fined, Von der Ahe paid the fines. His attitude was that boys will be boys, and he knew that the fans wholeheartedly approved his support of his players. The rowdy Browns provided not only good baseball but also good vaudeville. St. Louis fans loved their Browns; the fans on the road hated them.

The 1885 National League pennant race was a tight one all season. Chicago and the New York Giants dominated the League in 1885 and compiled some impressive statistics. The White Stockings finally prevailed with a record of eighty-seven wins and twenty-five losses for a winning percentage of .777, an impressive feat. This was a high standard, but the Giants were equally impressive. New York won eighty-five games and lost only twenty-seven for a winning percentage of .759. They finished only two games behind Chicago. Among the other six teams in the League, only the Philadelphia Quakers finished above .500, whereas the other five teams did poorly. World's champions Providence finished in fourth place with a record of fifty-three wins and fifty-seven losses, and the remaining teams in the NL never were competitive in the pennant race. Four of the teams—the Boston Beaneaters, the Detroit Wolverines, the Buffalo Bisons, and the St. Louis Maroons—finished more than forty games out of first place.[18]

Unlike the St. Louis Browns, who depended largely on stellar pitching, defense, and speed to win games, the Chicago White Stockings relied mainly on hitting to defeat opponents. Chicago's pitching was by no means shoddy, but once the season's statistics were compiled, the White Stockings led the NL in runs scored, doubles, home runs, bases on balls, on-base percentage, and slugging percentage. Chicago's capacity for scoring runs was especially noteworthy. In 1885 the White Stockings scored 834 runs and in that category led both major leagues by a wide margin. Only Philadelphia in the AA scored more than 700 runs that season. Ten of the sixteen teams in the AA and NL scored fewer than 600 runs. New York led the NL in hits with 1,085 and posted a team batting average of .269 whereas Chicago finished second with 1,079 hits and a team average of .264. Although New York finished first in team batting average, the Giants scored 143 fewer runs than the White Stockings. Part of Chicago's advantage was because their home ballpark was a small one, which favored power hitting, but overall the White Stockings were blessed with the talented bats of Cap Anson (the first major leaguer to record three thousand hits in a career), King Kelly, Abner Dalrymple, George Gore, and power-hitting Ned Williamson who terrorized opposing pitchers.

In addition to remarkable offensive statistics, the White Stockings also featured more than adequate pitching. Their pitching staff (largely composed of John Clarkson, who won fifty-three games, and Jim McCormick, who won twenty) posted an impressive record in 1885. Clarkson led the league in wins, innings pitched, complete games, and strikeouts. Nearly all the other important categories defining effective pitching were dominated by the New York Giants' Mickey Welch and Tim Keefe.[19] But when combined with their offensive firepower, the White Stockings' excellent pitching was formidable. As the NL's exciting race between Chicago and New York drew to a close and as baseball fans considered the prospects of a World's Championship series between the White Stockings and the Browns, a playoff, at first and superficial glance, seemed to offer a spectacle of Chicago's hitting against St. Louis's pitching, defensive skills, and fleet-footedness. Partisans had their theories concerning the relative merits of the two teams, but few disagreed with the notion that the White Stockings–Browns would be a superb series.

As the season came to an end, Spalding and Von der Ahe commenced negotiations to arrange a championship series between the two leagues. After witnessing the Providence–New York debacle at the ticket window, the owners chose a different format for the series in 1885. Instead of playing on three consecutive days in only one city, Spalding and Von der Ahe agreed to a twelve-game set in seven cities over an eighteen-day period. The agreement called for the series to open in Chicago with one game and then move to St. Louis for three games. Then the series would continue with one game in Pittsburgh, two in Cincinnati, one in Baltimore, two in Philadelphia, and two in Brooklyn, where the event was to terminate on October 31, 1885. Two features now seem curious. First, a twelve-game set left the potential for a tie in games won and lost. The teams faced the possibility of playing the final contests with one of the clubs well ahead in the series, a possibility that would negatively affect ticket sales on the East Coast. Second, nearly all the games were slated for AA sites. Instead of a decisive format, Spalding and Von der Ahe seemed more in search of an exhibition tour.[20] Each owner also agreed to contribute five hundred dollars to a purse to be claimed by the winner. Spalding and Von der Ahe attempted to eliminate the flaws of the 1884 New York–Providence series, but their efforts were to fail miserably.

The first game in Chicago was a portent. A disappointing crowd of only two thousand turned out to see the game and the festivities preceding it. Several players from both teams entered contests such as ball-throwing (Chicago's Ned Williamson won by throwing the ball a little over 133 yards) and base-running (Fred Pfeffer of the White Stockings won by circling the bases in 15.75 seconds) to amuse the gathering crowd. The game finally started at half past three and ended in a 5–5 tie, after Chicago scored four runs in the eighth inning. The late start and the slow game, with a total of sixteen errors, caused the game to end indecisively in the evening darkness. One Chicago sportswriter lamented the poorly played game but asserted that, had it gone another inning, the "Chicagos would doubtless have won, as they had just begun to play when the game was called." The first game was unimpressive as a display of major league baseball, and the small, rather passive crowd rendered the inaugural effort somewhat listless and pedestrian. After the game the teams departed by rail for the next three games in St. Louis.[21]

All was not well with the White Stockings as they departed for St. Louis. A contentious lot, some of them had strained relations with Spalding, scarcely a lovable man, and nearly all of them sooner or later clashed with Cap Anson, their first baseman, captain, and manager. Cap took his duties seriously. His career spanned twenty-seven years, including nineteen years at the helm of the White Stockings, and during his tenure, he frequently thrust himself into the middle of controversies with his teammates. Born in Marshalltown, Iowa, Cap began his major league career in 1871 with the Rockford club in the NA, and then played four seasons with the Philadelphia Athletics (NA) before bolting to the Chicago White Stockings (NL) in 1876. Cap performed well for the Philadelphia club in the doomed NA, but he found stardom and fortune with the White Stockings. He was a

The redoubtable Cap Anson.

(National Baseball Hall of Fame Library, Cooperstown, N.Y.)

large man, a fearsome hitter, Spalding's willing lieutenant during most of their relationship, and (many charge) a racist.

Anson has often been portrayed as the architect of baseball's color line, but this is not a sustainable allegation. He did not take kindly to African Americans, but to assert he was the sole force behind their exclusion from

major league baseball oversimplifies too complex an issue. Racism in baseball reflected the mood of the nation in the 1880s. The emerging ban on
black players was more a mutual tacit agreement among owners and players than the product of a movement led specifically by any one person.
Cap certainly condoned the appearance of Jim Crow in baseball, as is revealed in his book, *A Ball Player's Career,* published in 1900.[22] No one
doubted Anson's skills on the diamond, and few doubted his dedication to
the game. Few of his contemporaries failed to realize that Anson was a
volatile, complex man, but none ever asserted he was the principal architect of the segregationist movement in major league baseball.

When the White Stockings departed for St. Louis, Anson left his regular
center fielder, George Gore, behind. Gore, a consistent .300 hitter, was in
his seventh season with the White Stockings, and Cap concluded that his
lackadaisical play in the opener game merited suspension. Anson accused
Gore of indifferent play in the first game and of overindulging in alcoholic
stimulants the night before.[23] Cap was a teetotaler and a fitness fanatic
who was regularly appalled by some of his teammates' nocturnal habits.
Cap had his flaws, but these did not include either alcohol or living the ri-
otous nightlife of Chicago's notorious saloons, gambling houses, and
brothels. Nevertheless, Anson's disciplinary action against Gore cast a pall
over the White Stockings, who had enough to worry about as they faced
three games with the Browns in St. Louis. Gore was not reinstated during
the remainder of the series, and young, fleet-footed William "Billy" Ashley
Sunday replaced him in the outfield.[24] Although Sunday had been a member of the White Stockings' roster since 1883, he had seen limited service
on the diamond. Between 1883 and the close of the 1885 season, Billy
played in 103 games, amassed 402 times at bat, and made 96 hits for a batting average of .238.[25] Sunday did well in the playoffs, but his bat was not
as potent as Gore's. Billy Sunday was, however, destined for fame far
greater than any he earned in baseball. After the 1890 season, he left major league baseball at the relatively young age of twenty-eight to pursue a
career as a nationally famous evangelist. Evangelism elevated Sunday to
fame well beyond any he earned on the diamond.

Neither Spalding nor Von der Ahe was in Chicago for the series' opening game; in fact, neither saw a single contest. They were in New York City
attending a conference of NL and AA team owners. The leagues' owners
and executives assembled to deal with the aftermath of the recent war
with the deceased UA. After the regular season closed, the triumphant
owners appointed a committee to curtail spiraling salaries and to iron out
other problems affecting the relationships between the surviving major
leagues. The "peace conference," as some of the newspapers styled the
meeting, convened in the Fifth Avenue Hotel in New York City on October
17, 1885, and quickly went to work on the more pressing problems faced

by the leagues. A number of issues were addressed, but the conference's principal objective was to limit salaries. And to this end, the conferees suggested a salary cap of two thousand dollars per season beginning in 1886; the committee also recommended that no player in the major leagues should receive less than one thousand dollars per annum.[26] All of the owners' complicated deliberations led to the creation of a new National Agreement, which ended what little leverage the players had enjoyed in negotiating contracts while the UA existed.[27]

All the players in the World's Championship series knew why their owners were absent. All understood that the purpose of the meeting was to reassert the owners' grip on major league baseball. Some of the players, especially on the White Stockings roster, already had uneasy relationships with Spalding and were not highly motivated to do their best while owners colluded to strip them of hard-won gains in salary. Many of the Browns and the White Stockings probably realized that the "peace treaty" carefully being crafted in New York City by the owners constituted the beginning of war between management and labor.

Unbeknownst to the men on the Chicago and St Louis rosters and to most other major league players, a movement had already begun to counter the owners' offensive against the ballplayers. While the owners met in the Fifth Avenue Hotel and drafted an accord to control salaries and reaffirm their grip on players' destinies, John Montgomery Ward, the renowned shortstop of the New York Giants, and eight of his teammates, including pitcher Tim Keefe and catcher Buck Ewing, were also meeting in New York City, and on October 22, 1885, they formed the first local of what they termed the Brotherhood of Professional Base Ball Players.[28] Ward and his associates at first attempted to keep the Brotherhood a secret organization, as they prepared to challenge the might of the owners who dominated baseball, but by 1886 their efforts to enroll other players publicly revealed its existence and purposes. The Brotherhood sought to protect players from the owners' more egregious practices and to lend them some leverage in negotiating with the lords of baseball. Ward fully understood the task that stood before major league players and, recognizing its enormity, wished to have a few months to prepare for the owners' inevitable onslaught. By the end of the 1886 season, the Brotherhood's activities made secrecy no longer possible or necessary, and the players' union gave the official version of its birth to Francis Richter, the sympathetic editor of *Sporting Life*.[29]

As the Brotherhood matured, it attracted a good deal of attention among emerging labor organizations. Terrence V. Powderly, the fiery leader of the Knights of Labor, for example, attempted to align the Brotherhood with his Knights. Ward understood the value of public opinion, and he steadfastly refused to refer to the Brotherhood as a union. He also refused to consider affiliating the Brotherhood with the Knights of Labor despite repeated invitations. Labor organizations, anarchist societies, and other reformist agencies were sprouting across the United States as it neared the turbulent 1890s, a decade marked by labor unrest and violence. Ward did not want the fragile Brotherhood crushed by larger and dissimilar workers' protests. Baseball was America's game, and he feared that identifying the Brotherhood with a labor movement would alienate many Americans. Victorian Americans seemed to believe that the labor movement was derivative of European unrest, and that organized workers offered nothing but potentially disastrous prospects. Ward realized the players needed to protect themselves from the owners' aggressive policies, but he also understood that the Brotherhood must move quietly and with carefully chosen rhetoric. Had they known of the Brotherhood's birth at the time they were involved in the 1885 World's Championship series, most of the Browns and White Stockings would have applauded Ward's courage and foresight. Within a few months nearly all major league players were contacted and solicited to join the Brotherhood. Of all the stars in the 1885 series, only Cap Anson, a dedicated and invested tory, remained aloof to the Brotherhood. Between 1885, when the Brotherhood was born, and 1891, when it was finally defeated, baseball experienced five or six of its more turbulent years. The Brotherhood not only pitted players against owners, it also pitted players against players and created some tense moments in the world of major league baseball.

When the teams arrived in St. Louis to continue the series, they arrived in the midst of the city's annual Exposition. The Exposition began as the Agricultural and Mechanical Fair in 1855 and gradually developed as the city's premiere cultural event. Each autumn it was held on what is now Fairground Park and eventually covered more than one hundred acres of pavilions devoted to the arts and sciences, a zoological garden, and a race course. It eventually became internationally famous and attracted European royalty, American presidents, and throngs of visitors from all parts of the United States.[30] St. Louis was in a festive mood as the city basked in the glory of early autumn. Thousands of visitors came to the city to visit the Exposition, local merchants profited from the event, citizens enjoyed the opportunity to display their city's charms, and Browns' fans anticipated seeing their beloved heroes gain the upper hand over Chicago in a three-game set scheduled for October 15–17 at Sportsman's Park. Victories over the White Stockings offered the prospect of enhancing the city's ongoing celebration by embarrassing nearby Chicago.

Between two and three thousand fans attended the second game of the series (estimates varied, as usual), and for those who liked to see turmoil on the field, it was an interesting game. Umpires from either the NL or the AA were not assigned to officiate the series' games. Instead, Anson and

Sportsman's Park as it would have appeared in the 1880s.

Comiskey consulted prior to a contest and mutually agreed on one man to call the game. This helter-skelter technique produced some serious reactions during the entire series, but none more severe than the first game in St. Louis. David F. Sullivan, an NL umpire who happened to be in St. Louis attending the series, was selected by Anson and Comiskey to handle the duties behind the plate. Sullivan drew the crowd's wrath when he decided several close plays in Chicago's favor in the early innings. Irate fans mercilessly heckled the beleaguered umpire, and in the sixth inning the game broke up in an ugly incident. With St. Louis holding a 4–2 lead, Chicago came to bat in an atmosphere already poisoned by earlier incidents. Billy Sunday led off the inning with a double. Mike Kelly followed with a ground ball to shortstop where Bill Gleason fielded it cleanly, threw it to first base, and beat Kelly by about ten feet. In the meantime, however, the umpire focused his attention on Sunday who rounded third base and scored, then he turned to first base and declared Kelly safe. All accounts seem to agree that Sullivan was wrong (the one-umpire system often produced such results). Sullivan's declaration that Kelly was safe produced a fifteen-minute quarrel in which Comiskey threatened to take his Browns off the field in protest. Sullivan bravely warned Comiskey that such action would cause a forfeit to the White Stockings, and finally, after heated debate, Sullivan's decision stood: Kelly remained on base, and the game resumed. Kelly, no slouch at base-running, went to second on a wild pitch and then scored on Anson's single to center field, tying the score at 4–4 before an enraged home crowd. Anson was erased in a force play at second base, but Chicago's Fred Pfeffer, who forced Anson at second, remained on first base and proceeded to steal second base. After Pfeffer took second base and advanced to third on a passed ball, Ned Williamson, Chicago's hard-hitting third baseman, proceeded to trickle the ball down the first base line. According to accounts, the ball bounced first in foul territory and umpire Sullivan loudly shouted "foul ball." But the ball then slithered into fair territory where first baseman Comiskey fielded the ball and tossed it to the second baseman covering first, but Williamson beat the throw. In the meantime, Pfeffer scored and Chicago took the lead 5–4. Comiskey immediately argued that although he fielded the ball in fair territory, the umpire had declared it foul. Sullivan, Comiskey loudly declared, must require Williamson to return the plate to hit and Pfeffer's run did not count. He convinced Sullivan of the justice of his cause, but Anson and Kelly descended on the umpire and heatedly persuaded him to reverse his decision, whereupon pandemonium broke out. About two hundred fans swarmed onto the field, the White Stockings armed themselves with bats, Comiskey pulled his team off the field, and the umpire was escorted from the field to safety. Since the inning was incomplete, the official score appeared to leave St. Louis ahead by a score of 4–2. Later that evening, from the safety of his hotel, Sullivan ruled the game a 9–0 forfeit to Chicago.[31] The next day's issue of the *St. Louis Post-Dispatch*, trying to make the best of the previous afternoon's fiasco, declared:

> Many specimens of poor umpiring have been seen here this summer, but that of Sullivan yesterday certainly takes precedence for out-and-out robbery. Not only in single instances were his decisions palpably in Chicago's favor, but his conduct was continued straight through the five and a half innings played, and Comiskey, seeing that Sullivan was determined to have Chicago win, wisely determined to withdraw his men from the field, as forfeiting the game was much more acceptable than playing nine innings only to be robbed.[32]

Game one ended in a tie, game two ended in a row—an inauspicious beginning to the 1885 series. One can only imagine the scene if Spalding and Von der Ahe had been at the game to offer their sage advice to the embattled umpire. Since neither attended the game, the team captains, Anson and Comiskey, were in complete control of their teams' activities, and neither was noted for his taciturnity. For the moment at least, the White Stockings were gratified by the outcome of game two, and the Browns and the St. Louis fans were outraged.

Spalding and Von der Ahe were fully informed concerning the events in St. Louis, and although their teams were dangerously quarreling, confronting umpires, and provoking strident reactions from the fans, the owners remained in New York to carry out their duties in the peace conference underway. Some sportswriters reporting the meeting at the Fifth Avenue Hotel decided to dupe Von der Ahe into believing that events in St. Louis had gotten out of hand. The writers knew that Von der Ahe was especially concerned about the turbulent events in St. Louis. He had expressed his concerns to one of the sportswriters who subsequently filed a story with *Sporting Life* quoting Von der Ahe as declaring: "Py golly! anf dem fellers cut up some mongey shindels mit dot gem tomorrow, I hobe dey got in der lock-oop, de whole gang ov 'em. Vat you dink, will dey have some more row about id?"[33] Seeing a chance to toy with the naive and trusting Von der Ahe, the writers contrived to have a fake telegram delivered to Spalding while the committee meeting was in session. The telegram read:

> St. Louis, Mo. Oct 16—A. G. Spalding, Fifth Avenue Hotel, New York: Sullivan commenced to umpire. Anson objected. Comiskey insisted that he should which provoked Anson. From words they came to blows. Anson unhurt and Comiskey badly used up. Both arrested and now in jail. Will try to bail Anson, but may not succeed as feeling is strong against him. Advise me what to do. Think you better tell Von der Ahe and Brown [Von der Ahe's assistant].

Spalding, who was in on the joke, received the telegram, read it, and then passed it to Von der Ahe. The Browns' owner was completely taken in by the gimmick, and he bolted from the room before Spalding could reassure him that the telegram was a fake. Four sportswriters pursued Von der Ahe to the telegraph office where, as one wrote, it took "fifteen minutes to convince him that the whole thing was a joke and it cost him the seltzers all around. We always manage to enjoy life when Chris is around."[34] Von der Ahe was relieved and took the prank with good humor. Writers enjoyed making Von der Ahe look the fool, but none was opposed to a free seltzer once the fun was over.

Sunny weather and about three thousand fans greeted the teams on October 16, 1885, as the players took the field for game three of the series. Prior to the game, Anson and Comiskey, both unfettered and unscathed, met to agree upon an umpire, and they finally chose Harry McCaffrey, a St. Louis resident and a baseball player on local teams. The outcome of the game was decided in the first inning. Chicago scored one run in the top half of the inning, but St. Louis scored five in the bottom of the first and never surrendered the lead, winning 7–4. Chicago made twelve errors in the contest, and this, coupled with the Browns' timely hits, decided the game. John Clarkson, Chicago's fifty-three-game winner in 1885, pitched well, but he could not overcome the shoddy support of his infield, which committed nine of the White Stockings' twelve errors. McCaffrey earned praise for his umpiring effort from the *Chicago Tribune,* which reported that "Harry McCaffrey, a local ball tosser, was selected to do the umpiring, and he gave very fair decisions."[35] After two controversial games, game three went off without serious incident.

Game four was not so fortunate. Prior to the game, Anson was introduced to William Medart, another local who was a ballplayer and a Browns fan, and Cap apparently found Medart's pre-game manner acceptable since he and Comiskey selected Medart to call the game. St. Louis won the game 3–2 after the Browns scored two runs in the bottom of the eighth inning and held the White Stockings scoreless in the ninth. Compared to some of the earlier games, the contest was well played, but the Chicago press was outraged over what appeared to be partisan umpiring:

> Chicago was robbed of today's game by the umpire who narrowly escaped violence at the hands of Sunday and McCormick [Chicago's pitcher]. This morning Anson was introduced to a ball crank named William Medart, who is an ardent admirer of the home team. The Chicago captain did not know this, and upon the advice of several acquaintances concluded to allow him to umpire the game. The results were disastrous. Every close decision was given in favor of the home team until even the audience, whose sympathy was mostly with the Browns, became disgusted with the robbery and cried out against it.[36]

Another interesting facet to game four occurred when Anson made a surprising change in his team's composition just before the game. He decided to rest catcher Silver Flint who caught the first three games of the series but was not hitting well. King Kelly, who had played in the outfield in the first three games, replaced Flint behind the plate, and Anson, short on outfielders since Gore was not with the team, inserted James "Bug" Holliday, a local amateur, in right field. Apparently, Cap wanted to rest some of his pitchers rather than use them in the outfield, but the choice of Holliday puzzled many spectators. In the 1884 series and again in 1885, managers employed players who were not members of their season-long rosters, and no one seemed to think ill of the practice. Chicago sportswriters noted that the White Stockings were somewhat lethargic in their play, and maybe Cap was attempting to goad some of his players to greater intensity.[37] Even though the game was a close one, the White Stockings appeared to be in disarray and disgruntled. After four games, St. Louis had the advantage with two wins to Chicago's one victory by virtue of a forfeit, and one game tied.

Chicago's performance in the first games of the series certainly appeared lackluster, and several Chicago sportswriters were appalled by the White Stockings' display:

Before last Wednesday the impression prevailed in baseball circles that the American Association nines were second-rate agglomerations of rejected material from league clubs and promising amateurs in no way fit matches for the league nines. The relative difference between the quality of baseball furnished to spectators by the two associations was thought to be represented by the charges of 50 and 25 cents made for the privilege of witnessing their respective games. The league clubs played a half dollar game, the association a quarter dollar game. But the stock of the league clubs did not take as severe a tumble in the pool-boxes after the games of Wednesday and Thursday, as did the public estimation of the relative strength of the clubs.[38]

Anson and his squad failed to crush the Browns as everyone expected, and Chicago fans and their newspapers were dismayed over the prospect of St. Louis embarrassing the White Stockings and the National League.

Before moving on to Pittsburgh to continue play, the series paused briefly while the Browns met the St. Louis Maroons (NL) in game one of a three-game series designed to decide the city's professional baseball championship. The Maroons were the remnants of the club Lucas fielded in the UA in 1884, and they were, at best, a hapless team. In 1885 the Maroons finished forty-nine games out of first place and finished last in nearly all team statistics. The Maroons pitching staff—featuring such men as Charlie Sweeney, John Kirby, Henry Boyle, Hugh "One Arm" Daily, and John J. "Egyptian" Healy—compiled an earned run average of 3.37 for the season, the second-highest in the NL. The Maroons scored fewer runs than any other club in the NL and compiled a dismal record of thirty-six wins and seventy-two losses. They were no match for Von der Ahe's high-flying Browns, but St. Louis fans were interested in a match between them as part of the Exposition's events. After winning the opening match with the Maroons on October 19, Von der Ahe's club then moved on to Pittsburgh to continue the series with Chicago.[39]

Game five was played in Pittsburgh on October 22, and the Chicago White Stockings won by a score of 9–2. Compared to earlier contests, it proved a fairly uneventful game. Only five hundred spectators attended the game.[40] Cold weather and poor attendance signaled that the series was in serious difficulties, but the traveling baseball show moved on to Cincinnati for two games where the teams played game six before a disappointing crowd of only fifteen hundred. Chicago again won by a score of 9–2. The White Stockings and the Browns expected a better turnout in Cincinnati, which enjoyed the reputation of a rabid baseball town, but the players now realized the series' attraction was lukewarm outside their hometowns. Adding to the problem of fan indifference, the weather was conspiring against the teams. Early autumn cold surely contributed to the small turnouts. The evening before the second Cincinnati game, rumors began to circulate that the series, which was tied at two wins apiece for each team, one tie, and one disputed game, might end on the morrow. Only twelve hundred spectators came out to Cincinnati's League Park on October 24 to see the seventh game.

At this point in the series another controversy was born. According to the *Post-Dispatch,* before the game "it was agreed that the game forfeited to Chicago in St. Louis would be called off. This left the clubs with two games each. It was agreed that the game would decide the series for the Championship of America."[41] A formal agreement may not have been concluded between the two teams, but Cap Anson, feeling a bit confident after two easy victories in the last two games, allegedly made the statement, "We each have two victories now and the winner of today's game will be the winner of the series."[42] Cap may have been guilty of anticipatory hubris, but he did not have the authority to alter the series format without Spalding's approval. Either some of the sportswriters present in Cincinnati misinterpreted Anson's remarks, or they accepted others' accounts of Cap's bluster without carefully corroborating their information. Some who intensely disliked Anson may have seized upon poorly communicated information to embarrass the White Stockings' captain.

Whatever the problem many sportswriters, especially those from St. Louis, believed the series was ending with game seven, and that the championship was on the line that afternoon. The St. Louis press certainly adopted this point of view after St. Louis easily won the game by a score of 13–4. The St. Louis interpretation of the status of the series was echoed in the *New York Times,* which reported, "The game today between the St. Louis Browns, champions of the American Association, and the Chicagos, champions of the League, was the decisive one in the series between the two clubs for the championship of the world, and resulted in an easy victory for the St. Louis team." *Sporting Life* also took the stance that the Browns won the series in Cincinnati, and in its 4 November 1885 issue ran a story headed by the caption "The St. Louis Club Wins the Series and the $1,000 Stake from the Chicagos." A disputed and contentious series came to an unsatisfying conclusion accompanied by substantial confusion concerning its outcome.[43]

Once the games in Cincinnati were completed, the scheduled games in Philadelphia and Brooklyn were cancelled because of worsening weather and fan apathy. When Spalding heard the results of the seventh game, accompanied by the assertions that the series had been decided in St. Louis's favor, he reacted immediately. He declared that the disputed second game of the series must count in the record, and that no one had the authority to make such an agreement. The series, Spalding stated, was tied.[44]

For several weeks after the series' conclusion, Spalding adamantly denied that the Browns had won the championship series. He and Anson denied that Cap had made a statement that the second game in Cincinnati would decide the playoffs. If baseball fans expected some sort of resolution of the ongoing issue as to who rightfully claimed the championship, they were soon disabused of that notion. When the National League held its annual meeting in November 1885, Spalding and his peers assembled to conduct League business, amend rules, and perform the usual chores such meetings engendered. No mention of the tied series occurred on the floor of the two sessions held in the Fifth Avenue Hotel in New York City, and no committee was appointed to determine the question. Two weeks later the American Association conducted its annual meeting, and again, nothing officially was done to address the tied series. Most of the AA's meeting was consumed with the struggle brought on by an unsuccessful attempt to expel Erastus Wiman's New York Metropolitans from the Association's roster of teams. While there must have been plenty of unofficial conversation among the owners who attended the league meetings, the leadership in both leagues officially seemed unconcerned about the indefinite status of the ill-fated World's Championship event.[45]

When the Arbitration Committee created by the recent National Agreement convened in Philadelphia on December 8, 1885, it had a full agenda. Its basic task was to deal with the agreements concluded at the peace conference the previous October, and to reconcile differences among owners in the NL and the AA. A number of outstanding questions demanded attention—such as defining the new terms of contracts to be issued to players, the limits on salaries, the relationships among professional leagues. No mention of the controversial end to the Browns–White Stockings championship series came before the Arbitration Committee. Although some modern sources claim an owners' committee officially declared a tied playoff, there is no evidence that the league meetings or the deliberations of the Arbitration Committee delegated such authority to any investigative agency with power to decide the fate of the playoffs.[46]

This does not mean that the debate ended concerning the outcome of the White Stockings–Browns games. *Sporting Life* continued to agitate the issue, and one can only imagine how the paper's editor, Francis Richter, must have enjoyed chaffing Spalding. An item in Richter's paper stated that, "Chicago does not like the recent defeat by St. Louis, as it is the first time in the history of the game that Chicago has had to play second fiddle to the Mound City." Curiously enough, Von der Ahe remained aloof to the arguments concerning the series. Spalding did not; he continued to insist the series ended in a tie.[47]

On balance, the 1885 championship series was none too successful. One game called owing to darkness, one declared a forfeit, and five other games often played with obvious rancor and umpire-baiting before disappointing numbers of sometimes unenthusiastic spectators rendered the series something less than a stellar event. Attendance figures, based on simple estimates supplied by reporters covering the contests, barely exceeded thirteen thousand. Neither Spalding nor Von der Ahe issued statements concerning the financial outcome of the series, but it was commonly believed that the sometimes improvident Von der Ahe did not clear expenses.[48] At a time when the owners were conspiring to limit players' salaries, it was an inopportune time for either Von der Ahe or Spalding to discuss profits, if they earned any, but the likelihood they did seems poor. The players got nothing for the time they spent in the series, and if the owners netted a profit, they wisely remained silent. By any standard, the series was an inconclusive failure.

The 1886 Season

The Chicago White Stockings and the St. Louis Browns personnel did not appreciably change during the winter of 1885–1886, and each remained a strong contender for their own league's pennant. The Browns continued to rely on Comiskey, Latham, and the men who had led St. Louis to the AA championship in 1885. Only one change of any consequence occurred in the Browns in 1886. James Edward "Tip" O'Neill, a young Canadian, emerged as a premiere outfielder and hitter in 1886. O'Neill joined the Browns in 1884 and for his first two years played in only 130 games as both pitcher and position player. In 1886 Tip was installed in the outfield, played in a team-leading 138 games, and led the team with a .328 batting average.[49] O'Neill's first full year as a regular was an auspicious one, and he went on to greater accomplishments after 1885 (including hitting .435 in 1887).[50] Other than Tip's emergence as a star and the Browns' new uniforms, St. Louis entered the 1886 pennant campaign an identical team to the previous year's.[51]

Spalding's 1886 White Stockings team was identical to the team he fielded in 1885. George Gore and Anson made their peace, and Gore returned to his usual place in the outfield in 1886, playing 118 games, nine more than he played in 1885. As the White Stockings prepared for the 1886 campaign, Spalding's determination to win the NL pennant and the subsequent World's Championship became immediately apparent. He decided to send the team to Hot Springs, Arkansas, and train them in Arkansas's warmer weather, away from Chicago's distractions. Speaking of his decision to send the White Stockings to Hot Springs, Spalding declared, "I boil out all the alcoholic microbes which may have impregnated the systems of these men during the winter while they have been away from Anson and me. If that don't work I'll send them to Paris next year and have 'em inoculated by Pasteur. But it will work and we will win the championship again this year."[52] Spalding obviously believed his team members were equal to the challenge of winning another pennant, if he could get them in good physical condition, eliminate dissipation, and focus their energies to on-the-diamond activities. As events proved, Spalding and Von der Ahe had assessed their teams well: Each repeated as champions of their respective leagues.

The White Stockings battled the newly refurbished Detroit Wolverines all summer for the NL pennant. Detroit had entered the NL in 1881 and floundered about in the NL standings through the 1885 season. Then in the summer of 1885 Frederick Kimball Stearns, the owner of the Wolverines, purchased the faltering Buffalo Bisons (NL) for a mere seven thousand dollars.[53] Stearns did not want the Buffalo team. He wanted four of the Bisons for his Wolverines. Dennis "Dan" Brouthers, John Rowe, Hardy Richardson, and James "Deacon" White were fine hitters mired on a hapless team, and by transferring them to the Wolverines, Stearns planned to bolster his team and challenge the White Stockings. Other NL owners, Spalding among them, raised an uproar of protest over the proposed transfer, and Stearns's plan was frustrated. After the season ended, however, NL leadership finally sanctioned his maneuver, and Stearns was able to add four effective hitters to the Detroit Wolverines' roster.[54]

Once the "Big Four" reported to Detroit for the 1886 season, the Wolverines became serious contenders for the NL pennant and finished only two and one-half games behind the White Stockings. Chicago again relied on hitting to win the pennant. The White Stockings led the NL in runs scored, doubles, triples, bases on balls, base percentage, and slugging percentage; they tied with Detroit for the most home runs by a team.[55] The Wolverines amassed a team batting average of .280, winning that statistical category from the White Stockings, who hit a collective .279. It was an exciting race, but the White Stockings' veterans managed to deny Detroit's first serious bid for the pennant.

In the American Association, the St. Louis Browns easily won their second pennant. Von der Ahe's team outclassed all of its competition in 1886 and finished a comfortable twelve games ahead of second-place Pittsburgh. The Browns led the AA in runs scored with 944, and in hits, doubles, and team batting average, but their trademark speed on the bases remained their most disconcerting offensive tool. St. Louis stole 336 bases, leading the AA by a wide margin in that category. Four other AA teams stole more than 240 bases, but St. Louis's closest competitor, Philadelphia, finished second with fifty-two fewer stolen bases. Only two NL teams—Chicago with 213 and Philadelphia with 226—surpassed two hundred stolen bases for the season. Collectively the teams in the AA stole nearly six hundred more bases than their NL counterparts.[56]

Daring base-running and stolen bases were routinely associated with the Browns' attack. The Browns' running, stealing, and sliding proved so noisome to AA rivals that all worried about it when they faced Comiskey's rowdy group. One team unsuccessfully employed a strategy to brake the Browns on Decoration Day. When the Browns arrived in Philadelphia for an early season series with the Quakers, St. Louis had already begun their reign of terror on the base paths. Philadelphia attempted to alter the playing field in order to retard St. Louis's freewheeling base-running. According to *Sporting News*, "In the opening games in Philadelphia with the Browns, to prevent the latter from sliding to bases, they sprinkled rough gravel around the base paths. The Browns instead of taking the bluff, got brooms, swept the gravel away and then went in and ran the bases as they pleased." The Browns, probably somewhat antagonized by rocks and pebbles, stole twelve bases that afternoon. Nothing stopped the Browns from running when they saw an advantage in doing so, and their feats chilled opponents. It was a great tactical weapon, and it also furnished them a fine psychological lever.[57]

Although the White Stockings did not officially claim the NL pennant until October 7, when they defeated Boston at home by a score of 8–4, Von der Ahe set in motion a challenge to Chicago on September 26, 1886.[58] He opened the negotiations for a championship series with a telegram to Spalding that read:

> The championship season is fast approaching an end, and it now seems reasonably sure that the Chicago White Stockings and the St. Louis Browns will win the championship of their respective associations. I therefore take this opportunity of challenging your team, on behalf of the Browns, for a series of contests to be known as the World's Championship Series. It is immaterial to me whether the series be composed of five, six, seven, or nine games. I would respectfully suggest, however, that it would be better from a financial standpoint to play the entire series on the two home grounds, and not travel around as we did last season. I would like to hear from you at your earliest convenience, in order that the dates and other details may be arranged.[59]

Von der Ahe's communication to Spalding was perhaps a little premature. Two weeks remained in the regular season, and Chicago faced a grueling road trip while holding a slim two-game lead on Detroit, but Von der Ahe hungered for a return match with Chicago. He at least appeared confident that Spalding's team was destined to win the NL pennant. Von der Ahe, so often pilloried in the press for his lack of understanding of baseball, addressed some of the botched aspects of the 1885 playoffs. A home-and-home format, he believed, would boost attendance and offer greater hopes for the proposed series to prosper. Chris may have been lacking in fundamental baseball knowledge, but his marketing sense was unerring.

The next day, September 27, Spalding, who was in New York City, addressed a letter to Von der Ahe and stated that if the Browns and the White Stockings did in fact win their respective titles, he accepted the challenge to another championship series. Spalding proposed a nine-game series consisting of four in Chicago, four in St. Louis, and a ninth, if necessary to break a tie, in a neutral site. He further proposed that the winner take the gross receipts from all of the games minus the umpires' salaries and expenses. Each club should, Spalding suggested, pay its own expenses and hometown advertising for the games, and in case of a disputed outcome, the quarrel should be submitted to the Board of Arbitration for final and binding disposition. Spalding's reply to Von der Ahe concluded by stating, "In view of the several misunderstandings that occurred in our series last season, I deem it wise to have all conditions agreed upon and understood."[60] A flurry of communications immediately followed Spalding's response as he and Von der Ahe negotiated the details of another series.

By October 9, 1886, the basic discussions governing the World's Championship Series were completed. Spalding telegraphed Anson, his team captain still in Boston finishing the final series of the regular season, and officially informed Anson and the White Stockings they were booked for another championship series with the Browns. In his telegram to Anson, Spalding both praised and enticed his team while stating:

> You have claimed the pennant in great style. Knew we could depend on the old war horses in a finish. You have won the League championship; now come home and win the World's Championship. As a token of my appreciation, I herewith tender each man a suit of clothes, awaiting their order, and the team collectively one-half the receipts of the coming series with St. Louis. Accept my hearty congratulations.[61]

Spalding wanted to win the title as badly as did Von der Ahe. Generosity was not one of Spalding's more notable character traits, and yet he publicly committed himself to awarding his players one-half the income of what might well prove a financial bonanza. Ultimately, however, the crafty, hard-driving monopolist gave his players nothing other than a new suit of clothes. A new suit of clothes to a team of veterans who clinched their second successive pennant was scarcely a lavish reward, but to the parsimonious Spalding, a free fitting at a haberdasher may have seemed ample reward. If the White Stockings won the championship, he retained half the proceeds; if they lost, Spalding had no financial obligation to his players other than to pay their traveling expenses. For Spalding it was a cheap way to earn some of the celebrity he coveted while entailing few risks other than his team's prestige.

Spalding and Von der Ahe compromised and agreed to a seven-game format. They set the series to begin with three games in Chicago and then to shift to St. Louis for three games. The series was scheduled to begin on October 18, and the games were to occur on consecutive days ending on October 23. If necessary, a seventh contest was to be arranged at a time and place mutually selected by the owners. The winner was entitled to the gross gate receipts minus the umpires' salaries and expenses. Mindful of the umpiring problems of their 1885 games, Von der Ahe and Spalding devised an improved system to select umpires for 1886. Each man agreed to choose three umpires from his league and present the list to his rival who then was required to designate two for service in the series. Spalding and Von der Ahe eventually selected John McQuaid and "Honest John" Kelly of the AA and Grayson Pearce (often referred to as "Grace" in box scores) and Joseph Quest of the NL as umpires for the series.[62]

Joseph Quest holds a unique place in baseball history. Quest enjoyed a short career as a major league player, and he allegedly was involved in an incident that elevated him to a special position in baseball lore. In 1882, the story goes, Quest was a member of the Chicago White Stockings, and one afternoon he and several of the players attended the horse races at a Chicago track. The players had a tip that a horse named Charley was a sure thing in one of the races, and most of them placed bets on Charley. Quest refused to do so, and when Charley took an early lead, Quest's companions chaffed him severely. As the horses rounded the final turn, Charley went lame and all the horses passed him. Legend has it that Quest looked at his tormentors and said, "Look at your old Charley horse now." Then (according to legend), the White Stockings were playing the Giants the next afternoon, and Quest was coaching third base. He relayed the steal sign to George Gore who promptly set out for second base in good fashion, but about half way Gore pulled a leg muscle and was easily retired. As Quest hurried to Gore's assistance, he supposedly looked at the players on the bench and yelled, "There's your old Charley horse—he'd have made it all right if it had not been for that old Charley horse."[63] Quest's actual words, if any, will remain unprovable, but all competent baseball trivia experts know that Quest coined the term for a pulled leg muscle. Quest never publicly claimed credit for minting one of baseball's prime linguistic tidbits. His reticence to do so may have been influenced by the fact that, later in life, he was employed in the city clerk's office in Chicago, and after being implicated in an embezzlement scandal he disappeared. The date and place of his death are unknown. No one ever seriously suggested Quest was a dishonest umpire, but his subsequent life and his reputation for honesty did not fare so well.

The concluding sections of Spalding and Von der Ahe's agreement declared that umpires would be selected by lot, prior to each game, and that Kelly, Quest, Pearce, and McQuaid were designated the Board of Umpires. Each umpire was guaranteed one hundred dollars in salary plus travel and hotel expenses for the entire series.[64] And finally, Spalding and Von der Ahe consented to a stipulation that, if a dispute arose over the series' outcome, the Board of Arbitration created by the recent National Agreement should examine the facts and render a binding judgment on the contestants. Von der Ahe and Spalding carefully sought to avoid the mistakes of the 1885 debacle.

The first game, in Chicago, was plagued by bad weather. All morning of October 18, 1886, the city was drenched in rain, and by the time of the game, although the rain had slackened to a fine, drizzling mist, the temperature was quite cool. Spalding and Von der Ahe held a meeting in Spalding's office before noon to review the details governing the series and then adjourned for lunch, prior to going to the ballpark for the three o'-clock start. In spite of the poor weather conditions, an estimated three to five thousand spectators assembled to watch the teams go through their pre-game exercises. Each team was given about a half-hour for the players to loosen their muscles prior to the game, and when it came time for the White Stockings to do their pre-game drills, they marched onto the field to the accompaniment of a brass band. They were accompanied also by their mascot, Willie Hahn, dressed in a resplendent facsimile of the player's distinctive uniforms. Hahn took his place on the Chicago bench while the White Stockings spread out on the field and prepared minds and bodies for the upcoming contest with the Browns.[65]

Just before play began the umpires drew lots and determined that McQuaid (many accounts of the series misspelled McQuaid's name, rendering it McQuade) would call the first game. Anson won the coin toss and elected to reserve the last at bat for his team, the Browns came to bat and were retired in order, and the 1886 World's Championship Series was under way. Chicago's pitcher, John Clarkson (who had won thirty-six games in the regular season in 1886), proved masterful. He was opposed by St. Louis's Dave Foutz, a forty-one-game winner, but Foutz and the Browns managed only five hits off Clarkson, and with the paucity of base-runners and the damp field, the Browns were unable to run to any advantage and were shut out 6–0.[66] The first game proceeded without incident, and even though the weather remained threatening all afternoon the teams played a full nine innings. McQuaid apparently performed satisfactorily as umpire, and unlike several of the games of the previous year, no quarrels occurred on the field. One Chicago report declared:

> It was a good game, well played by both clubs, and chiefly remarkable for the coaching of Latham, a sawed-off Brown with a voice that would put to shame the most ambitious fog-siren on the lakes. His incessant howling and jumble of catch phrases was funny for about fifteen minutes. Then it grew tiresome, and before the fourth inning he was universally conceded to be the worst nuisance ever inflicted upon a Chicago audience.[67]

It was impossible to ignore Latham, and the Chicago press even in victory vented its spleen on the noisy third baseman. Although the weather remained inhospitable throughout the afternoon, the Chicago fans were warmed by their team's relatively easy victory over the Browns, as they witnessed a highly satisfactory outcome in the first game.

The second game reversed the fortunes of the previous day. The day was warm and sunny, and St. Louis defeated Chicago by a score of 12–0. St. Louis's Bob Caruthers, a thirty-game winner in 1886, limited Chicago to only two hits. The Browns hit well in the second game, and they were aided by nine Chicago errors. Caruthers became something of a one-man team. He was a far better than average hitter (in addition to his pitching duties, he played in the outfield and second base during the 1886 season, amassing 317 times at bat and posting a .334 batting average) and along with Tip O'Neill, who hit two home runs, led the Browns' offensive attack with three hits apiece.[68] An innovative umpiring change proved the most interesting aspect of the game. Spalding and Von der Ahe agreed to experiment with one of Spalding's pet ideas on how to improve umpiring by using what the press called the "three umpire system." The three-umpire system involved selecting one umpire as the "referee," then using a second umpire to call the game while his league's team was at bat, and a third while his league's team took its turn at bat.

Immediately before the second game the umpires gathered to draw lots, and John Kelly was designated the referee. Chicago drew McQuaid and St. Louis drew Quest to serve as the umpires. Kelly stood behind the pitcher but moved back of second when runners reached base. When Chicago was in the field, Quest called balls and strikes and plays on the field, and when St. Chicago came to bat, McQuaid assumed the umpire's duties behind the plate. According to the pre-game agreement, the "out" umpire could appeal his opposite number's decisions on balls and strikes, fair or foul balls, and plays at bases. In this case the referee issued the final, binding decision. Team captains were also authorized to call times out if they had questions on rules.[69] The experiment worked fairly well; there were no serious challenges to either umpire during the game.

On October 20, 1886, Chicago and St. Louis played the last of the games in Chicago on a rainy day before an estimated six thousand onlookers. St. Louis won the coin toss, elected to reserve the last at bat, and immediately allowed the White Stockings two runs in the first inning. After six full innings the White Stockings led by a score of 6–4, but Chicago proceeded to score five runs in the seventh and eighth innings and won the game 11–4. Although clouds, cold, rain, and gathering darkness caused the game to be called after the completion of eight innings, the Browns did not complain about the shortened contest. Nothing remarkable happened during the game. Only one umpire, "Honest John" Kelly, called the game, and he was not seriously challenged by either team. Compared to the first two games there were fewer players' errors, and all in all, the White Stockings out-

The St. Louis Browns posing before the scoreboard in Sportsman's Park.

played the Browns while taking a lead in the series two games to one.[70]

Game four took place in St. Louis on October 21 in Sportsman's Park before at least ten thousand enthusiastic spectators who, naturally enough, heavily favored the Browns.[71] The weather, according to the *Post-Dispatch,* "seemed a trifle cold for ball-playing and the spectators, buttoned up in overcoats, shivered in their seats."[72] The fans, in a jolly mood, ignored the less than ideal conditions and cheered their Browns, who won the game by a score of 8–5. The first game in St. Louis, even though it was called at the end of seven innings, was one of the better games of the entire series. Chicago took an early lead, which then changed hands three times in a neatly played contest. Joseph Quest umpired the game, and he performed his duties without a serious challenge as the Browns evened the series at two games apiece.[73] On the following day the White Stockings and the Browns again met in Sportsman's Park for the critical fifth game, and a crowd equal to that of the day before assembled to witness the contest.[74] Eager Browns' fans realized the importance of the game; they also knew that the innovative three-umpire system might be introduced to St. Louis that afternoon. In both cases the St. Louis partisans were gratified. Kelly, McQuaid, and Quest repeated the experiment first performed in Chicago, and the assembled crowd thoroughly approved the umpires' conduct of the game as the Browns scored seven runs in the first three innings and won the contest 10–3. Darkness forced suspension of play after six innings, but the Browns had the upper hand when the umpires decided the gathering gloom was too great for further play.[75] Now the Browns led the series three games to two, and Von der Ahe and his faithful and voluble patrons sensed a monumental victory over Spalding's highly vaunted White Stockings.

As the series slowly swung in St. Louis's favor, many fans proved unable to credit the Browns' performances against Chicago. The White Stockings were the heavy favorites at the outset of the playoffs, and now Chicago stood on the brink of disaster. At this juncture, rumors that the White Stockings were "hippodroming" some of the games swept through St. Louis. *Hippodroming,* in the parlance of the 1880s, meant deliberately losing games. Apparently many fans could not reconcile themselves to Chicago's poor position in the series, and they concluded that the White Stockings were allowing St. Louis to win in order to prolong the championship games and generate greater receipts. Attendance in St. Louis far exceeded the turnout the series had enjoyed in Chicago, and rumors floated about that the White Stockings were allowing the series to turn to the Browns' favor, before winning game six and forcing a decisive seventh game. If this were true, as many fans suspected, the White Stockings were fattening the purse prior to the kill. It was common knowledge that several of the White Stockings, especially King Kelly, were on bad terms with Spalding, and some fans believed the players were using the series to enrich themselves at Spalding's expense. The rumors became so intense that Spalding and Von der Ahe publicly denied that any of the players were involved in hippodroming games. The *Post-Dispatch* directly addressed the question on October 23:

> In view of the fact that the cry of "hippodrome" in connection with the base ball games for the World's Championship has become universal, Messrs. Spalding and Von der Ahe have declared themselves ready to do all in their power to prove to the public that the games are played on a perfectly square basis. Mr. Von der Ahe said last night that the last thing for him to do was to make an affidavit that the games were not hippodromed and that he was only too willing to do that. Mr. Spalding said that any man with a grain of sense in his head who had witnessed the games will know without being told they were played for blood, and know on the strength of many things which caused the cry, that the games are on the square.[76]

Some of the Chicago sportswriters were suspicious, however. The day before Spalding and Von der Ahe's views appeared in the St. Louis papers, one of the Chicago sportswriters approached Anson and asked him for his views on the growing controversy. Cap's response did little to dispel rumors of manipulated games when he was quoted as saying: "I know the receipts of the Chicago games are deposited in the First National Bank. I was present when the agreement was made in Spalding's office and I heard all that passed. If we win the series the Chicago players get half the money, and that is what we are playing for."[77] No evidence survives to suggest the Chicago team fixed any of the games, but the White Stockings' performances in St. Louis aroused suspicions as the series gradually tilted to the Browns' advantage. For the first time in World's Championship competition, the specter of hippodroming—or gamblers' unwanted influence on games—presented its ugly countenance. Sports fans in the 1880s probably were a bit more cynical than their modern counterparts, and to many cranks the Browns seemed either to be playing well beyond their popularly recognized potential or they had received assistance from an unexpected source. The first assumption was probably true; the latter was not. Nevertheless, the rumors of tainted games persisted.

At half past two in the afternoon of October 23, on another rain-threatened day, Grayson Pearce, making his only appearance as an umpire in the series, called "play," and the game that decided the World's Championship commenced, but it did not begin without controversy. The day before game six, Spalding announced that Mark Baldwin, a recently acquired pitcher, would pitch for the White Stockings. Baldwin, a young left-handed pitcher, played for Duluth in the Northwestern League in 1886, and he was a youngster with great promise. In one game he struck out nineteen batters, and in others he routinely overpowered hitters. Spalding saw real potential in the young pitcher, and on October 20, the day of the last championship game in Chicago, he announced he had signed Baldwin to a White Stockings' contract.[78] Baldwin presumably was signed for the 1887 season, but he immediately began working out with the team. When the series concluded in Chicago, Baldwin accompanied the team to St. Louis and continued his training with the White Stockings. By that time observers understood that the wily Spalding had a scheme. Upon learning that Spalding intended to use the recently signed Baldwin in game six of the playoffs, Von der Ahe immediately protested. Although non-roster players had appeared in games in earlier playoffs, Spalding's attempt to use Baldwin carried the potential of heavily affecting the series' outcome. Anson's use of an unknown outfielder in 1885 or New York's use of a rookie and unknown pitcher in the already decided championship series of 1884 were trivial in comparison to Spalding's blatant attempt to insert Baldwin into the series at this critical juncture. Although he was untried against major league hitters, Baldwin certainly held the potential to revive the White Stockings while resting the pitching staff for a seventh game should one become necessary. An intense argument between Spalding and Von der Ahe over Baldwin's eligibility preceded the game. Spalding's effort to revitalize his pitching staff with Baldwin did not violate any of the rules that he and Von der Ahe had defined three weeks earlier, but the Browns argued that Baldwin's late arrival on the White Stocking's roster violated the spirit of the games. Finally, Spalding capitulated, and Baldwin did not appear in game six, but according to one Chicago writer Spalding was "wrathy" over the incident.[79]

The crowd of eight thousand fans at Sportsman's Park sensed history in the making when Pearce called for the first hitter to step to home plate. Destiny seemed to favor their beloved Browns. Caruthers started the game for St. Louis, and John Clarkson pitched for the White Stockings. Prior to game six, Clarkson made three appearances in the first five games, and he had pitched twenty-four innings in only five days. At first, on October 23, it appeared Clarkson would get another day's rest and be ready for a possible seventh game; but when the Baldwin quarrel ended, Clarkson was chosen to replace Baldwin, and he resolutely took the pitcher's box. Caruthers, St. Louis's starting pitcher, was better rested than Clarkson when he drew the assignment for game six. Caruthers pitched games two and three for the Browns and allowed the White Stockings only two hits and no runs in his first appearance, and twelve hits and eleven runs in his second, while winning one game and losing one to Chicago.[80] Because Caruthers was a fine hitter, he was active in the series in capacities other than pitching. He started in right field in games one, four, and five, and contributed a .250 batting average to the Browns' assault on Chicago pitching.[81] Caruthers, who had rested his pitching arm for two days prior to game six, would face Clarkson. Clarkson, on the other hand, had only a single day of rest before he was called upon to oppose Caruthers in what proved to be the series' finale. Neither man was unacquainted with frequent appearances in the pitcher's box, but Caruthers seemed to have a slight advantage.

Chicago scored a run in the second inning, and another in the fourth as rain began to fall. In the fifth inning, as the rainfall intensified, Comiskey requested that play be halted until the rain ended. Anson objected. As a discussion ensued involving Comiskey, Anson, and Pearce, a portion of the crowd surged on the field, and a crisis appeared in the making. Police quickly deployed on the diamond to maintain order while the game's fate was under discussion. Finally, as the rain slackened and stopped and Pearce called for play to resume, the fans drifted back to their seats, and the game continued. Chicago scored another run in the fifth inning and led by a score of 3–0. Finally, the Browns produced three runs in the bottom of the eighth and tied the score.[82] At the end of nine innings the score was tied at 3–3. After Chicago did not score in the top of the tenth inning, Curt Welch led off the tenth for St. Louis, singled to center field, and advanced to second when Dave Foutz playing right field hit a ground ball to Chicago's Ned Williamson at shortstop and got on base when Williamson made an error. Yank Robinson sacrificed the runners to second and third, and the stage was set for the most exciting play of the series. With Doc Bushong hitting, Welch broke for the plate, and Clarkson's pitch sailed over King Kelly's head. Welch was safe at home. The Browns were the world's champions. Delirious fans rushed out of the stands and bodily carried the Browns off the field.[83] King Kelly later tried to explain what had happened with Clarkson's final pitch: "I signaled for a low ball on one side and when it came it was high on the other. It struck my hand as I tried to get it, and I would say that it was a passed ball. You can give it to me if you want to. Clarkson told me that it slipped from his hands."[84]

King Kelly was not the sort of man to avoid responsibility for his actions on the field, and he manfully declared that the play was a passed ball rather than a wild pitch, although he did mention that Clarkson suggested the ball slipped when he delivered the pitch. Whatever the situation may have been, Welch, who scored, was billed as the man who made the fifteen thousand dollar slide since his play ended the series and enabled the Browns to claim the gross gate receipts. As Robert L. Tiemann has pointed out, "there is no contemporary evidence that Welch actually slid across the plate."[85] Nevertheless, Welch's "fifteen thousand dollar slide" persists in baseball's lore, even though the series grossed only about fourteen thousand.

Spalding left St. Louis in an angry mood and according to legend refused to pay his players' expenses to return to Chicago.[86] Four of the White Stockings' stalwarts (King Kelly, Ned Williamson, George Gore, and Silver Flint), unaffected by Spalding's behavior, seized the opportunity and stayed several extra days in St. Louis. Led by Kelly, whose sybaritic reputation was widely acknowledged, the players passed the time agreeably, and the *Sporting News* reported that four nights after the series concluded the foursome were seen enjoying an evening in St. Louis's Union Club House.[87] Spalding's reaction to some of his players' lingering in St. Louis and celebrating is unrecorded, but his opinion of Kelly undoubtedly was affected by the King's post-series activities. Later in the year Spalding decided to sell King Kelly, and early in 1887 he sold him to Boston for the considerable sum of ten thousand dollars.[88] Although Kelly's baseball skills were never doubted, he frequently clashed with Spalding on a variety of issues; the relationship between the two men was tenuous at best. In Spalding's opinion Kelly was a bad influence on the White Stockings, and he believed Kelly's nocturnal habits partly caused the debacle in St. Louis.

Several years later Anson echoed Spalding's viewpoint in his *Ball Player's Career,* asserting that dissipation contributed to Chicago's setback in St. Louis: "We were beaten, and fairly beaten, but had some of the players taken care of themselves prior to these games as they were in the habit of doing when the League season was in full swim, I am inclined to believe that there might have been a different tale to tell."[89] In any event the series was done, and now the St. Louis Browns' partisans gloated over the undisputed World's Championship their heroes had brought to the city. The *Sporting News,* headquartered in St. Louis, effectively voiced local sentiment when it carried a short item:

> The World Series not only proves that St. Louis has a better base ball club than Chicago but . . . it is a better base ball town. For years Chicagoans with their characteristic blow and bluster have claimed that the only time St. Louis could turn out a crowd to a ball game was on Sundays. The games of the World's Series, however, were played on week days and they not only drew crowds twice as large as those in Chicago, but more money was taken in at the games here notwithstanding the fact that twice as much was charged to see the games in Chicago as was charged here. Facts cannot lie.[90]

According to *Sporting News,* the receipts for the three games in Chicago produced $6,554.25, and the final three games at Sportsman's Park yielded $7,365.85, which totaled to a grand figure of $13,920.10.[91] Unlike Spalding, Von der Ahe had not committed himself to awarding half the gross to his players prior to the series, but in the euphoria of victory, he did. The Browns received $6,960 as their part of the receipts, and when the money was divided among the twelve men on the roster, each man earned a tidy $580. Each player's share roughly equaled a working man's annual salary in the 1880s. St. Louis was ecstatic with its newfound notoriety as home of the world's champions of baseball; Von der Ahe's fame and popularity as a major league owner reached its zenith; and the Browns, who faced a short exhibition schedule once the playoffs were concluded, prepared to winter with fattened wallets and contented hearts. The winter of 1886–1887 was a good time for St. Louis baseball fans.

The World's Championship series of 1886 surpassed the previous year's experience in all categories. First of all, it proved decisive. No one doubted its outcome. The Browns won the series. Although he evidently harbored the notion that some of his players did not take the games seriously enough, that they caroused excessively, and that Kelly and others were spoiling apples who ruined the entire barrel, Spalding publicly acknowledged that the Browns were the world's champions.[92] Second, attendance for the 1886 games certainly outstripped the first Chicago–St. Louis encounter. In 1885 newspaper writers' estimates of attendance at the first

Chicago–St. Louis series suggested that approximately thirteen thousand fans witnessed the games. The 1885 attendance figures are a blend of estimate and guess, and though they are useful it must be remembered that the journalists who knew the ballparks' capacity squinted at the gathered fans and guessed a figure to include in their accounts. A better standard of measure, although not foolproof, emerged in the 1886 championship games. Gross receipts for the Chicago-based games were $6,554.25. The White Stockings charged the NL admission of fifty cents per game, and this would mean that approximately 13,108 fans paid to see the first three games. When the series moved to St. Louis, the Browns charged the AA's usual twenty-five cents per ticket, and since the games in St. Louis yielded $7,365.85, the last three games attracted at least 29,463 paying patrons. Not counting the inevitable complimentary tickets for the friends and business associates of Spalding and Von der Ahe, and the uncounted people who deftly managed to slip in to the ballparks, at least 42,500 witnessed the 1886 World's Championship of baseball. Using the formula of dividing gross receipts by local ticket prices, the figures suggest that attendance in Chicago averaged 4,369 per game whereas the St. Louis games each drew 9,821. Average attendance for the seven games in 1885 had probably fallen below two thousand per game, once the series moved to its listless conclusion in Pittsburgh and Cincinnati and those pathetic figures are factored into the attendance statistics.

In addition to the success at the ticket window, the 1886 playoffs, when compared to the previous years' games, were not marred by frequent, ugly quarrels among players or between players and umpires. Two factors probably contributed to this improvement. First of all, the umpires chosen for the games were selected by the owners prior to the beginning of the series, and each of the four men had major league experience in calling games. In 1885 an umpire often first met opposing captains just moments before a game began. Anson and Comiskey frequently relied on the advice of friends when selecting an umpire in 1885. In 1886 the umpires were a known commodity and they were chosen by lot. Players occasionally became upset in the 1886 series, but none seemed to believe that he was being "homered" by an umpire. None of the journalists covering the 1886 games filed reports complaining of umpire-committed robbery. Other than the quarrel over calling game six as rain threatened, the 1886 games were relatively placid, especially when contrasted with some of the vitriolic arguments of the previous year's games.

Second, Spalding and Von der Ahe attended all the games in 1886. Their presence undoubtedly exercised a calming influence on the series. Anson and Comiskey were combative souls who often excited their teammates in the first series in 1885; with their owners looking on, they were less prone to provoke quarrels. As team captains and managers, Anson and

Comiskey carried heavy burdens, but in 1886 they relied on their owners to solve procedural disputes. Spalding and Von der Ahe scarcely were soul mates, but each had a vested interest in reconciling differences and in promoting a certain amount of decorum on and off the diamond as the games progressed.

Without a doubt the 1886 championship was the most competitive and financially successful of the first three playoffs between the NL and the AA. Spalding and Von der Ahe demonstrated that a properly managed and well-played set of games could reflect creditably upon major league baseball, produce a profit, and unquestionably decide the "World's Championship" of professional baseball.

CHAPTER FIVE

The Browns and the Wolverines

The Year 1887

Von der Ahe's Browns faced a new rival in the postseason playoffs in 1887 when the Detroit Wolverines deposed the Chicago White Stockings as National League champions. Detroit's entry into the National League in 1881 arose from unusual circumstances. After the NL formed in 1876, cities usually gained memberships in the League after franchises failed. Between 1876 and 1881 the usually eight-team NL placed franchises in fourteen different cities.[1] As newly organized teams formed and failed, ambitious entrepreneurs elsewhere watched the game of musical chairs and dreamed of bringing a major league team to their municipalities. NL leaders were always vigilant in seeking new venues for their brand of baseball, and Detroit soon attracted their attention. As was the case with other cities in the Midwest, Detroit grew rapidly in the 1880s. It opened the decade with a population of 116,340, and ten years later the 1890 census recorded that Detroit's population had grown to 205,876, an increase of 76.96 percent.[2] From the NL leaders' viewpoint Detroit grew into an ideal site for a franchise. It was located at a strategic point beyond the League's northeastern clubs and amid the teams in the Midwest. Railway connections to Detroit were excellent, the city was the gateway to the upper Great Lakes, and long before the automobile created the metropolis of Detroit, the NL owners realized the city was destined to become one of the more important U.S. centers of manufacturing and commerce. Detroit was a natural site for a baseball team.

Detroit's opportunity to join the National League in 1881 did not come from a failed franchise. Cincinnati had been expelled from the NL the previous year. The Cincinnati Red Stockings club president, Justus Thorner, did not agree with the League's ban on Sunday baseball and the sales of alcohol at games. Thorner asserted that Cincinnati's heavily German American population had no bias against Sunday ball and they expected beer and whiskey sales at games. Despite repeated warnings from the NL leadership, the Cincinnati club continued its much-criticized policy of renting the Reds' grounds to local teams for games on the sabbath and routinely profited from the sale of strong drink, especially beer, to thirsty fans. So Cincinnati was expelled from the NL, and Detroit was presented the opportunity to join the roster of major league cities.[3]

The newly formed Detroit Wolverines entered the National League in 1881 and managed a fourth-place finish with forty-one wins and forty-three losses. After that they marched steadily to the League's cellar and arrived there in 1884, fifty-six games out of first place. In the club's first four years, they won 151 games and lost 226 for a .400 winning percentage. They featured an anemic offense, a porous defense, and a woefully inadequate pitching staff. In 1884, for example, they finished first in games lost; finished last in runs scored, team batting average, and earned run average; and tied last in fielding average.[4] Detroit fans suffered mightily in 1884.

The following year the Wolverines fared slightly better, rising to sixth in the NL standings. Only the Buffalo Bisons and the dismal St. Louis Maroons lost more games than the Wolverines. The Maroons were the remnants of Henry Lucas's UA-pennant-winning team in 1884, and they proved a hapless entry in the National League. The St. Louis Maroons were not up to the NL's standards, and in August 1886, after nearly two disastrous seasons, Lucas became discouraged and sold his franchise to a group of St. Louis businessmen who later sold the club to Indianapolis.[5] The Buffalo Bisons, on the other hand, were only slightly more inept than the Detroit Wolverines. In 1885 the Bisons managed to lose seven games more than the Wolverines, who were promoted into sixth place when the season ended. The Maroons were beyond redemption, but the Bisons had several talented players who, while they could not overcome the odds facing their squad, did possess major league talent.

As the Bisons floundered during the 1885 season, Frederick Kimball Stearns, the president of the group of investors who acquired the Wolverines in 1885, grasped an opportunity to purchase the Buffalo franchise in September. Stearns had no interest in saving the Bisons from extinction. Instead, he intended to transfer Dennis "Dan" Brouthers, John "Jack" Rowe, Hardy Richardson, and James "Deacon" White from the Bisons to the Wolverines to infuse his team with new life. Brouthers was a burly, hard-hitting first baseman who hit .359 his last year with the Bisons; Richardson was a second baseman who hit .319 in 1885; and Jack Rowe, a shortstop, and Deacon White, a third baseman, each hit in the .290s in their final seasons with Buffalo. The "Big Four," as the press labeled them, drove in 212 runs for the Bisons. The starting infield for the Wolverines, by comparison, drove in only 89 runs in 1885.[6] In Stearns's mind, players the caliber of the Big Four were a siren's call. They obviously had the potential to invigorate Detroit's anemic batting order.

Since there was no rule against any owner operating two major league teams, Stearns carefully watched as the Bisons' ownership faltered and the team sank into seventh place in September. Sensing an excellent opportunity, Stearns initiated contact with the Buffalo team and immediately engineered the purchase of the Bisons for only seven thousand dollars.[7] Stearns's strategy was innovative and daring. The Wolverines, who first appeared to have acquired a moribund team, overnight gained the rights to at least four players of unquestioned ability. On September 17, 1885, the owners of the Detroit and Buffalo clubs signed an agreement that called for the Bisons to finish the season with their roster minus the Big Four, who were to join the Wolverines on September 19.[8] Rival NL owners, fearing the immediate consequences of a fortified Detroit roster, cried out in protest and collectively restrained Stearns from immediately moving the Big Four to the Wolverine's roster. Consequently, Detroit did not enjoy the benefits of Stearns's bold maneuver until 1886. When the Bisons' purchase was announced, *Sporting Life* observed prophetically:

> The sale of the Buffalo Club and the transfer of the big four to Detroit naturally created the greatest excitement among baseball men, especially in League circles. Perhaps no club in the League had, or ever had, four men who, as a quartette of players, have as wide a reputation as that of Rowe, Brouthers, White, and Richardson. In batting alone they are a tower of strength, three of them left-handed hitters and they will, together with the other heavy hitters on the Detroit team, make the club the greatest batting aggregation in the country and a formidable factor in the next year's pennant race.[9]

Stearns's bold perspicacity impressed a good many of baseball's most knowledgeable figures. Everyone expected the Wolverines to be a major factor in the NL's 1886 pennant race.

Aside from the acquisition of the Big Four, there were other factors that also promoted the Wolverines' development. Early in 1886 Detroit purchased Fred "Sure Shot" Dunlap from the St. Louis Maroons. Dunlap was a dependable hitter and an even better second baseman. He and Hardy shared duties at second, and when Dunlap was inserted in the starting lineup, Hardy usually played in the outfield where he excelled.[10] St. Louis's baseball sage Al Spink often asserted that Dunlap was the greatest second baseman he ever saw. After Dunlap joined the Detroit club in 1886, he saw action in fifty-one games for the Wolverines, and the following season, although hampered by a leg injury, he managed to play sixty-five games at second base.

Not only did the Wolverines add hitting power to the roster, but two pitchers blossomed in 1886. Charles Busted "Lady" Baldwin and Charles H. "Pretzels" Getzien flourished when the Big Four and Dunlap supplied them runs in unprecedented numbers. From 1881 through the 1885 season, the Wolverines averaged 4.7 runs per game, but after Brouthers and company joined the Wolverines, the team averaged 7.1 runs per game.[11] Baldwin and Getzien obviously profited by the surge in runs scored and responded by winning 114 games for the Wolverines in 1886 and 1887.[12] Backed by the new bats in the Wolverines' attack and reinforced by the steady defense furnished by the renovated team, Baldwin and Getzien enjoyed the best years of their careers during the sudden emergence of their team as a potent force in the NL. Detroit's renaissance was remarkable. In 1884 they were the NL's doormat; two years later, thoroughly rejuvenated, they challenged the mighty White Stockings, and then replaced them as League champion in 1887.

Frederick Kimball Stearns was unlike either Spalding or Von der Ahe. At the time he entered the baseball business, he was an extremely wealthy man who looked upon the game more as an avocation than a vocation. He played baseball in college where he developed a passion for the game. Stearns made a fortune manufacturing pharmaceuticals in the early 1860s, and in 1867 he participated in the creation of Park, Davis and Company, which became one of the nation's largest and most profitable pharmaceutical corporations.[13] By the 1880s he possessed great wealth, social position, and a restless soul that carried him into other fields. As he sought to invest his money in areas where he saw profit potential, Stearns chose to form the group who purchased the Wolverines. He had the wealth, social position, and clout to attract financial supporters, and he consequently entered baseball in 1885. By the time he gained entry into the hurly-burly of professional baseball, Stearns carried with him an almost patrician-like presence.[14] In contrast to Stearns, Von der Ahe's eccentricities appeared even more comical, and Spalding, a man still on the make in the 1880s, appeared far below Stearns's gentlemanly standards. Stearns, Von der Ahe, and men such as Spalding reflected the complex nature of America's fluid yet stratified society. Under normal circumstances the three men had nothing in common. Baseball, however, drew them together. Few other enterprises in late-nineteenth-century America could have created the bond that briefly held them together.

The St. Louis Browns basked in the glory of their title during the winter of 1886–1887 and opened the 1887 season for all practical purposes unchanged. Comiskey, O'Neill, Latham, and the usual cast of characters formed the nucleus of the Browns' roster. Other than the appearance of Charles Frederick Koenig on the pitching staff, Von der Ahe's "poys" were established St. Louis heroes. Koenig grew up in St. Louis, and in 1886 he played briefly for the doomed Kansas City NL franchise. During the winter of 1886–1887 nineteen-year-old Koenig, whose surname the press now translated as "King," signed a contract with the Browns and immediately developed into a formidable pitcher. Known as "Silver" for his extremely fair hair, King won thirty-two games for the Browns in 1887 as they won their third consecutive pennant.[15] Combined with Bob Caruthers and Dave Foutz, King gave St. Louis three excellent pitchers. Many major league teams used what amounted to a two-man pitching rotation, but the Browns featured three excellent pitchers who flourished in 1887.

A deeper pitching staff, as baseball experts regularly declare, is always an asset, but in the 1880s a wealth of pitching was essential in the ever-growing American Association. In 1882 the AA played an 80-game schedule, and as the Association gained strength and popular support, it steadily expanded successive seasons' play. By 1885 the number of sanctioned games rose to 112, and by 1887 AA teams faced a 140-game schedule. Two men might manage an 80-game schedule, but at least one more regular starting pitcher was required when teams faced a 72 percent increase in regular season games. With the arrival of Silver King, the Browns had their third reliable starter. St. Louis won a record 95 games in 1887, and King, Foutz, and Caruthers registered a total of 86 wins that season. In addition to their pitching feats, King, Foutz, and Caruthers made other contributions to the Browns' record-making season in 1887 that are often overlooked. They played a total of 150 games in the outfield and 39 games at first base. They collectively had 1,009 times at bat and made 327 hits for a composite batting average of .324.[16] In contrast, Yank Robinson was the only regular position player who pitched for the Browns in 1887, and this was for a measly three innings. King, Foutz, and Caruthers obviously were fine, overwhelming pitchers, but they also added a dimension to the Browns that few teams could approach. Not only were the Browns a talented team, they also, by late-nineteenth-century standards, had an unusually flexible roster of versatile players. The Browns were on the cusp of becoming a dynasty.

Rule changes notably altered the game's configuration in 1887. In an effort to standardize rules and improve baseball, the NL and the AA held a conference committee in Chicago in 1886. A variety of issues were considered, but the two changes that most affected the game were those governing pitchers and those that benefited hitters. To begin, steps were taken to limit pitchers' deliveries and deceptive practices. Prior to 1887 the pitcher's box measured seven feet deep and four feet wide. With such a large working space, pitchers developed the custom of hiding the ball behind their bodies and usually taking two steps forward in the box before delivering a pitch. Such action obviously made it difficult for the hitter to see the ball until the moment it was released, and the pitcher's motion further distracted a batter. In 1887 pitching rules were changed in three ways. First of all, the pitcher could no longer hide the ball behind his back; the ball had to be in sight as the pitcher began his delivery. Second, the pitcher's box was reduced to five feet six inches in depth while remaining the standard four feet in width. The most important change in the pitching regulations was the section that anchored the pitcher. He could no longer take what amounted to a run at the hitter as he delivered his pitch. As the *Sporting News* described the altered rule:

> the pitcher is now required to keep his right foot—his left, if a left-handed pitcher—standing on the rear line of his position, and he is not allowed to lift his feet until the ball leaves his hand. In reality he can not pitch or throw the ball unless this foot is on the ground; and it is from the pressure of this foot on the ground that he derives the power to give the lasting impetus to the ball in delivering it. He is also required to hold the ball so that it can be seen in his hand by the umpire.[17]

Prior to 1887 pitchers often used what could perhaps best be described as a "cricket-like" delivery, but now they were denied that advantage.[18] In addition to altering delivery style, the conference committee also ruled that five pitches outside the strike zone constituted a base on balls, and the committee also raised the number of strikes from three to four to retire a hitter. Providing the hitters with an extra strike certainly aided them and partially accounted for the rise in batting averages in 1887.

Another rules change in 1887 had another profound effect on baseball. The conference committee decided to count a base on balls as an official time at bat and as a hit.[19] Many hitters prospered with the new rule. Based on a hundred times or more at bat, three NL players and six AA hitters recorded averages of .407 or better in 1887. The Browns' Tip O'Neill compiled an amazing .485 batting average with bases on balls factored as hits.[20] Although many of the more feared hitters enjoyed inflated averages, team batting averages did not soar, however. In 1886 team batting averages in the NL and the AA were .251 and .243 respectively, and in 1887 the averages rose to .269 and .273 respectively.[21] The following year, after the leagues decided not to count bases on balls as hits and as the pitchers adjusted to the new rules governing deliveries to batsmen, team batting averages returned to pre-1887 levels. Individual hitters faced a sharper decline in batting averages in 1888. O'Neill hit .335 in 1888, for example, and Cap Anson (who hit .420 in 1887 and led the NL) hit .344. By 1890 the NL and AA clubs recorded team averages of .254 and .253 respectively, which closely mirrored 1886 statistics. Modern chroniclers who compile record books usually compute 1887 batting averages without bases on balls counted as hits, but in 1887, the bonus hitters added a bit of statistical spice to the season.

Von der Ahe's St. Louis Browns took an early lead in the race for the AA pennant, and by the end of May, they led second-place Cincinnati by four games. As the season wore on, the Browns steadily widened their lead on the Cincinnati Red Stockings and won the pennant by a comfortable fourteen games. St. Louis fans relished their Browns' successes, but there was little suspense in the pennant race. Perhaps the most exciting issue experienced by the Browns' fans in 1887 was a series of unsubstantiated reports that Joseph Pulitzer, publisher of the *New York World,* had offered Von der Ahe one hundred thousand dollars to transfer the Browns to New York City. Reports floated about that Von der Ahe and Pulitzer held a meeting in New York City to discuss the details of either moving the Browns east and letting them continue to dominate the AA, or perhaps moving the club into the NL. Worse yet, rumors abounded that Von der Ahe might sell the club to Pulitzer. Von der Ahe and George Munson, the Browns' secretary, quickly scotched the rumors. Von der Ahe publicly proclaimed that he would not sell or remove the team; not even, he declared, for twice the sum allegedly involved in the phantom negotiations. Other than the usual shenanigans by Latham and his cohorts, the season proceeded without serious incident, and the Browns again dominated the AA.[22]

The NL pennant race was a tight one in 1887. At the beginning of September, Detroit was in first place in the NL, but only by a slim four games over the Chicago White Stockings and by five games over third-place New York. By season's end the Wolverines, who won twenty-two of their final thirty-two games, claimed the NL championship.[23] Both Chicago and New York faltered in the last month of the season, and Philadelphia passed them to finish second in the NL race, only three and one-half games behind the Wolverines. Although the Quakers waged a fierce late season rally, their challenge came too late for them to overtake the Wolverines, and Stearns's daring purchase of the Buffalo Bisons and the subsequent transfer of the Big Four to Detroit paid huge dividends to Detroit's baseball fortunes. In the final month of the season, the Wolverines, now taken much more seriously than at the beginning of the season, continued to play steady baseball and became the experts' choice to win the League pennant. Perhaps the only surprise in Detroit's march to the pennant was outfielder Sam Thompson's productivity. The Big Four were acquired to drive in runs, and they did so in 1887. Collectively, they batted in 366 runs, but no one anticipated Thompson's leading the Wolverines in runs batted in. Sam was a fine young outfielder playing in only his second full year in the major leagues, and he blossomed into an awesome hitter. Surrounded by the hard-hitting newcomers, he drove in 166 runs in 1887.[24] "Big Sam," as Thompson was nicknamed, was no fluke. Not counting a brief return to baseball with the injury-riddled Detroit club in 1906, Sam played fourteen seasons in the major leagues, eight times driving in a hundred or more runs. Fortunately for the Wolverines, Big Sam had the best year of his career in 1887 and contributed mightily to Detroit's championship season. The Big Four plus Thompson drove in a combined 532 runs out of Detroit's total of 969 runs scored. Opposing pitchers found no soft spots in

The 1887 world's champion Detroit Wolverines.

(National Baseball Hall of Fame Library, Cooperstown, N.Y.)

the Wolverines' batting order, and with the improved defense provided by the Big Four, the Detroit team was never severely challenged in 1887 after it found its stride midseason and repeatedly manhandled its opponents.

By the end of August, as his Browns dominated the AA, Von der Ahe began musing about a championship playoff in 1887. At the outset of the year, Von der Ahe and his players expected either Chicago or New York to win the NL pennant. Everyone understood that Detroit would be a factor in the pennant race, but Chicago, even without Kelly and McCormick, still appeared likely to repeat as League champions. Baseball pundits also expected New York, stocked with veteran players who had been teammates for several seasons, to do well in the 1887 pennant race. Tradition and experience, the experts judged, would for the time being overcome Detroit's raw talent. As the season progressed, however, the experts soon realized they were wrong: Detroit was an immediate challenge. As the NL pennant race unfolded and three teams competed for the title, a reporter asked Von der Ahe if he preferred playing Chicago or Detroit in a World's Championship series. Never one to avoid a question or to anticipate a controversy, Von der Ahe foolishly responded that he would rather play Detroit than Chicago: "I would rather play them because I think they are an easier team to beat than the Chicagos. Besides that St. Louisans have never seen the Browns play the Detroits so that the games would be more of a novelty than those with Chicago."[25] In one utterance he annoyed Spalding, ignored the New York Giants, and gratuitously antagonized the Wolverines, who eventually thoroughly embarrassed him and caused his tactless remark to haunt him.

As the 1887 season neared its completion and Detroit emerged as NL champion, after Philadelphia was finally eliminated, Stearns initiated contact with Von der Ahe in a letter dated September 23, 1887, and issued a challenge to the Browns. Stearns suggested a fifteen-game series incorporating some of the format of the 1885 playoffs between the Browns and the White Stockings. Stearns wanted the games to be played in several cities. He suggested only that no more than one game be played in each city, other than Detroit and St. Louis. Stearns further suggested that he and Von der Ahe make up a purse so that the players on the winning team should each receive one hundred dollars, and that the owner of the winning team receive 75 percent of the net proceeds. Stearns furthermore asked Von der Ahe to agree to the selection of two umpires (one from the NL and one from the AA) prior to the series, and that the umpires serve alternately during the course of the games.[26] Stearns's proposal, which at first glance appeared to mirror the 1885 games between St. Louis and Chicago, was unique in the history of the playoffs in the 1880s. He visualized a series that would last well in excess of two weeks, and one that, if Von der Ahe accepted the fifteen-game concept, meant that baseball's World's Championship was destined to appear in nearly a dozen cities; nothing so ambitious had before been proposed.

Von der Ahe's response was prompt and positive. He offered only two amendments to Stearns's proposed guidelines for a series. First, he accepted the fifteen-game format, but he wanted to exempt St. Louis, Brooklyn, and Philadelphia from the one-game limit and apply it in all other sites. Second, he suggested that any fines imposed by the umpires during the championship games be donated to a worthy charity.[27] Other than denying Detroit more than one game in the series and playing a total of four in Brooklyn and Philadelphia, Von der Ahe accepted Stearns' basic concept for a World's Championship. Now the negotiations could begin.

Stearns and Von der Ahe quickly compromised and agreed to a format that called for three games in St. Louis, two games in Detroit, two games in Brooklyn, two games in Philadelphia, and single games in Pittsburgh, New York, Boston, Washington, D.C., Chicago, and Baltimore.[28] "Honest John" Kelly, who managed the Louisville club (AA) in 1887, and John Gaffney, who managed the Washington Statesmen (AA) for part of the 1886 season and in 1887, were selected to officiate the series. Each man was a respected baseball personality. Kelly, a colorful figure in his own right, later became a partner to Michael "King" Kelly in the operation of a saloon, "The Two Kels," located on Sixth Avenue and 30th Street in

Manhattan, which became a popular rendezvous for players, actors, and others of less savory reputation.[29] No one ever seriously suggested that "Honest John" was anything other than an upright and impartial umpire. The Kellys operated a saloon that capitalized on the King's celebrity, and in the 1880s few, if any, sports fans viewed their activities as inappropriate. Gaffney was perhaps less colorful than Kelly, but he left an indelible mark on the umpiring profession. He began his umpiring career calling games for Harvard, Yale, and Brown and then joined the NL as an umpire in 1884. After his stint as manager of the inept Washington club, Gaffney returned to umpiring and remained active in both major and minor league baseball until 1900. Many of his contemporaries thought him the most efficient umpire of his era. In addition, Gaffney was an innovative man. He was the first umpire to wear spiked shoes for better traction, he invented a special blouse to store extra baseballs, and he invented a cork pad for protection while behind the plate.[30]

Gaffney and Kelly were widely approved in Detroit and St. Louis as the series' umpires. As the series prepared to begin in St. Louis, the local paper assured its readers that "Both men are eminently satisfactory to all parties as Kelly will not care to favor the Browns or Gaffney the Detroits. Neither is dependent upon his abilities as an umpire for a living and will therefore have no cause whatever to play favorites with either team." According to the agreement concluded between Stearns and Von der Ahe, the umpires' starting roles would be decided by the pre-game coin toss. The team captain who won the coin toss had the right to reserve the last at bat if he felt this was the appropriate strategy. So, when the Browns were at bat, Gaffney, the AA umpire, was to call balls and strikes while Kelly was responsible for decisions at the bases. When the Wolverines took their turn at bat, Kelly was to move behind home plate while Gaffney judged play on the bases.[31]

After the series' first two games, however, the umpiring plan was modified. Instead of alternating behind the plate inning-to-inning, Kelly and Gaffney alternated game-to-game. Kelly and Gaffney proved highly effective umpires. Near the series' conclusion, the *Detroit Free Press* reported that the players approved of the umpiring throughout the games and that "Kelly and Gaffney are to be presented with medals by the Detroit and St. Louis clubs in recognition of their fine umpiring. It has been superb, there not being a single genuine kick in any of the games." Only the ownership and management remained skeptical of the system and balked at employing two umpires in regular season games. Baseball experts who opposed the idea of a second umpire on the field did so on the grounds of fiscal concerns; an additional umpire, the game's savants declared, promised intolerable expenses.[32]

Ticket prices were, as usual, governed by the owners. Stearns and Von der Ahe, hoping to increase receipts, elevated admissions above the 1886 level. Admission to the series' games in 1886 had been either twenty-five cents in St. Louis or fifty cents in Chicago. In 1887 Von der Ahe and Stearns agreed to offer three levels of ticket prices. Regular seats would cost fifty cents, reserved seats one dollar, and upper-level, chair sections a dollar and a half.[33] Even though they effectively doubled the price of admission to the 1887 World's Championship games, Stearns and Von der Ahe attempted to counter criticisms that they were unduly exploiting baseball fans by offering choices of ticket prices. Even so, for St. Louis fans, for example, tickets at least doubled in price when compared to the 1886 series. Stearns and Von der Ahe were not unmindful of public opinion, but they also intended to play a majority of the games away from their home crowds. They were, perhaps, not as concerned over the feelings and pocketbooks of fans in Brooklyn or New York.

Rather than pledge a portion of the net proceeds to the players, Stearns and Von der Ahe chose to create a twelve-hundred-dollar purse to be divided equally among the men on the roster of the winning team.[34] Von der Ahe in particular was unenthusiastic about sharing proceeds from the series with his players. In 1886 he gave one-half of the net proceeds to his Browns as a reward for their performances, and as he later explained during the 1887 playoffs, "Last year I gave them $625 each, and they used the money against me and refused to sign contracts."[35] Von der Ahe believed the bonus his players garnered from the World's Championship victory in 1886 enabled them to hold out for more money in 1887. His generosity, Chris maintained, had been poorly answered by ungrateful players. Von der Ahe was especially annoyed with Bob Caruthers and Doc Bushong whom he viewed as the ringleaders of his players in the demands for increased salary. Two weeks before the 1887 playoffs began, rumors surfaced that Caruthers and Bushong would not be members of the Browns' roster in 1888. When questioned by the press, Von der Ahe confirmed that he intended to rid his team of Caruthers and Bushong to the highest bidder.[36] Caruthers, a noted pitcher who often was in disfavor with Von der Ahe, eventually was sold to Brooklyn for $8,250 where he performed well for another three years, and Bushong, who shared the Browns' catching duties with Jack Boyle in 1887, was released to Brooklyn in 1888.[37] Caruthers's and Bushong's departures from the Browns were yet in the future when Von der Ahe publicly confirmed suspicions that the St. Louis club was in disarray, but to astute students of baseball, the Browns were not the team they had been the previous year. Von der Ahe did designate one hundred dollars for each man as a reward for playing in the World's Championship, but above and beyond that, he was not about to reward players he planned to sell or enrich those he felt were disloyal. If the Browns were to reap additional income from the upcoming series, they had to win the

World's Championship and claim the twelve-hundred-dollar prize Stearns and Von der Ahe pledged as an incentive to the winning team. The Browns felt resentful and viewed their owner's parsimony as vengeful; they had won another pennant for Von der Ahe, and now he refused to share the bounty of postseason play with them. Although the Browns enjoyed a record-setting season in 1887, they entered the World's Championship series poorly motivated and quarreling openly with their owner.

Stearns, in part, emulated Von der Ahe. He and his partners indicated that they harbored no intention of dividing the bulk of the championship's receipts with their club, although, prior to the World's Championship games in 1887, the owners set aside a sum of money that rewarded each Wolverine four hundred dollars for his pennant-winning season. Players on the losing club were not to share in the purse created by the owners. The St. Louis Browns, making their third consecutive appearance in the World's Championship, felt themselves slighted and faced the prospect that, if the series went badly for them, they each would reap only the measly hundred dollars Von der Ahe awarded them for winning the AA pennant.[38] Even if the Browns triumphed in the playoff and received the additional one hundred dollars per player, they would still have only half of what the Wolverines had already received. From the Browns' point of view, neither sum was sufficient reward for their accomplishments during the past three seasons. While neither club rewarded its players generously, the Browns, compared to the Wolverines, were far more negatively affected by the treatment they received from their owner. Many of the Wolverines remembered their days with inferior clubs and dreadful records, and the prospect of competing in professional baseball's premiere event motivated them even though the financial returns were perhaps less than they would have preferred. As events proved, the 1887 championship games pitted an energetic contingent of newcomers against a disgruntled, three-time participant rendered restive and lethargic by its acidic relationship with the owner.

When the Wolverines arrived in St. Louis and registered in their hotel, they caused quite a sensation. Newspaper accounts stressed that the Wolverines were a physically large team, and one that seemed confident and relaxed as they gathered in the lobby of the Southern Hotel. If the Wolverines were at all harried by the Browns' reputation and the attention the World's Championship brought to them, they masked it well. One factor, however, seemed against the Detroit club: It entered the series minus Dan Brouthers. Brouthers was the Wolverines hard-hitting first baseman who drove in 101 runs in the regular season, and in a meaningless, season-ending NL game in Indianapolis, he severely sprained his ankle stealing second base.[39] Brouthers's ankle was so badly damaged, he played in only one of the fifteen games. He managed to get two hits in his one-game appearance; he could swing the bat, but he could not run.

Consequently, big Dan was a spectator for nearly the entire series.

St. Louisans awoke on October 10, 1887, to an unpleasant, rainy morning. The series was to open that day at half past two in Sportsman's Park, and early in the morning Stearns and Von der Ahe feared the rain might force a cancellation. By mid-morning the heavy rain abated and became a fine mist, although the temperature remained uncomfortably cool. Von der Ahe and Stearns had agreed to a parade through St. Louis on the morning of October 10 to publicize the game and to enthuse local fans. There was little real need for a parade. Every baseball fan in St. Louis, Detroit, and elsewhere already knew the details of the upcoming series. What the parade really offered was an opportunity for Chris to be seen in public with his team as they led the Wolverines to the slaughter. Von der Ahe always enjoyed the pre-game, on-the-road festivities and often led the vanguard of his players when they traveled from their hotel to the ballpark in a rival city. The parade, scheduled to begin at ten o'clock, was to follow a circuitous route through St. Louis to Sportsman's Park. When the time arrived for the players to gather in the lobby of the Southern Hotel to begin the parade, the Wolverines balked. Intermittent rain, cool temperatures, and a long boring carriage ride caused the Detroit players to decide they would rather stay in the warm dry hotel until just before game time. Von der Ahe was upset. He wanted the parade. It was his moment to preen in local society, gather applause, and bask in the glory of his team's achievements. So, Chris pressed his case. Finally, after two hours of bickering, the Browns and the Wolverines boarded their carriages about noon and an abbreviated version of the parade got under way. Because of sudden downpours of rain and delays in getting the carriages to the Southern Hotel, the parade departed in disconnected segments. The numerous, enthusiastic spectators patiently waiting were treated to a disjointed spectacle. A portion of the cavalcade would pass by, then there would be a hiatus of a few minutes, and then more celebrities would come into view. Others, not informed that the route had been altered, saw nothing. It was not the sort of review that Von der Ahe had visualized, but he had his moment in the sun, albeit on a cloudy, rainy day.[40]

When the players and the dignitaries arrived at Sportsman's Park, they found a large, raucous crowd awaiting them. Attendance figures for the first game are imprecise, as for all fifteen games of the series. Most figures are the estimates sportswriters included in their accounts. In game one, for example, the *Detroit Free Press* claimed that seven thousand fans crowded into the St. Louis ballpark, whereas the *St. Louis Post-Dispatch* estimated that four thousand cranks witnessed the opener.[41] When the Wolverines took the field for their pre-game exercise and drills, they were watched closely by the local fans. This was Detroit's first appearance in St. Louis, and the Browns' partisans carefully measured the Wolverines' apparent skills, their demeanor, and their style in an effort to reassure themselves that the Michigan team was merely another challenger, not a new force the Browns could not manage. If their beloved Browns could defeat the White Stockings, the St. Louis cranks told themselves, the Wolverines presented no greater challenge.

The results of the first game surprised no one. The Browns jumped out to a two-run lead in the first inning, and scored four more in the fifth. Bob Caruthers held the Wolverines to one run and allowed them only six hits while he contributed three hits to the Browns' sixteen-hit attack. Even though the weather was disagreeable, the St. Louis fans were obviously warmed by the Browns' mastery of the Wolverines. The *Detroit Free Press* informed its readers that St. Louis's treatment of the Wolverines had "thrashed them out of shape, pounded them back into form again and finally stepped on them with both feet and crushed them into the Mound City mud—outbatted, out fielded, and demoralized, razzle-dazzled, and subjugated them."[42] Oddsmakers favored the Browns at the opening of the series, and their optimism appeared justified. The Browns played errorless baseball, whereas the Wolverines committed five errors and collected a few scattered hits. The umpiring went well, the fans proved enthusiastic and orderly, no quarrels emerged on the field, and the receipts for the game were substantial. Neither Von der Ahe nor Stearns could want for more, although Stearns's evening meal may have proved rather tasteless as he contemplated the day's carnage.

The next afternoon the Wolverines and the Browns met in game two. Between seven and eight thousand fans gathered at Sportman's Park on a clear, cold, windy day to witness the spectacle. This time the tables were turned, and the Browns' seven errors enabled Detroit to carry off a 5–3 victory in nine innings. Heavy attendance in St. Louis garnered nearly one-half the series' projected expenses, and with thirteen remaining games, the profit potential for the World's Championship appeared rosy.[43] Only one incident marred the second game. A fan named John Gutterman was fatally injured. His accident was not reported fully in the newspapers, but eleven days after the first game, the *Post-Dispatch* reported that Gutterman "died this morning at his residence, No. 3620 North Grand Avenue, from injuries received at the baseball park on the 11th inst. His leg was broken and he was internally injured, and he has been under the treatment of Dr. Standing ever since."[44] Gutterman apparently fell from one of the stands. None of the newspaper accounts mentioned any rowdiness or disturbances among the crowd that might have contributed to the incident. Apparently, Gutterman was one of those luckless souls who fall victim to freak accidents.

At seven o'clock in the evening, the teams boarded a special train at Union Station for the overnight trip to Detroit. The train, appropriately decorated to advertise the World's Championship games, was made up of sleepers and a dining car for the teams, the owners, and the staff and press that accompanied them.[45] Throughout the series, the special train carried the traveling baseball show to its destinations and became a home on the road for all except in the cities where the series paused for more than one game. Players and their traveling companions had access to a dining car, and they used their accommodations for both rest and recreation. Card games and other diversions occupied them during travel hours, and when fatigued, they retired to their berths for rest. Because of the intimate quarters, newsmen were afforded a microscopic view of the interactions between the teams and their teammates. After the entourage boarded the train for the trip to Detroit, the Browns' lackadaisical attitude toward the series, their hostility toward Von der Ahe, and the tensions among them became apparent to the press. Some of the writers quickly sensed that the St. Louis club was not in a frame of mind conducive to good performance.

After an overnight journey, the special train arrived in Detroit just before noon. The weather was bright, clear, and cool. By game time the sky was overcast but no rain fell, and, apart from the fans being uncomfortable in the chilly air, the game got under way on time before an estimated five thousand Wolverines partisans who had gathered at Recreation Park to witness the historic event.[46] The first appearance of championship baseball in Detroit treated the crowd to what was probably the best contest of the series. Caruthers drew the starting assignment for St. Louis and locked into a memorable pitching duel with Charlie Getzien. St. Louis scored a run in the top of the second inning, and Detroit tied the game 1–1 in the bottom of the eighth. Then, for the next five innings, Caruthers and Getzien pitched shutout baseball until Caruthers finally gave up a run in the bottom of the thirteenth inning, allowing the Wolverines to claim a 2–1 victory. Getzien, who pitched brilliantly all afternoon, scored the winning run for Detroit. After he singled, he advanced to second on a bobbled double play, went to third base on a ground out, and scored when third baseman Yank Robinson fumbled a ground ball, recovered, and threw it to Comiskey at first base who dropped the ball and allowed Getzien to score. It was an ignominious ending to an otherwise titanic struggle.[47]

Several aspects of the game are unusual. The game was played in only two hours and fifteen minutes.[48] The Browns outhit the Wolverines 16–7 but offset their hitting advantage by committing seven errors to Detroit's two. The Browns' lapses in fielding puzzled everyone. Known for effective defensive work, St. Louis played error-free baseball in the opening game, then committed fourteen errors in the next two games while the Wolverines registered only three. The Browns' defensive lapses indicated that perhaps they were not as focused on their game as were the Wolverines. No one suggested that the Browns deliberately faltered, but everyone understood that poor fielding boosted Detroit's successes in games two and three.

Morale in the Browns' camp was low and tempers high when the teams departed Detroit for the overnight run to Pittsburgh, the site of the next game. The Wolverines retired early, but some of the Browns got up a poker game. About eleven o'clock at night a fight broke out between second baseman Yank Robinson and outfielder Curt Welch. No one had noticed the poker players consuming alcohol, but the *Post-Dispatch* reported:

> Robinson and Welch became imbued with an overflow of spirits. They were very noisey [sic] and began quarreling over the cards. One hot word led to another, and finally Welch hit Robby, and Robby countered on Welch's already bruised nose, which thereupon assumed a more livid complexion. It should be explained that Welch had been nursing a bruised probo [sic] as the result of a previous encounter. The fighting "champs" were pulled apart before any further damage was done.[49]

Von der Ahe did not witness the exchange of blows, and all present conspired to conceal the incident. Chris learned of the altercation when the newspapers reported the fight. Even had he known earlier, he probably could not have rectified the situation and rallied his club. Personal animosities among the Browns, their quarrels with Von der Ahe, and their poor performance in the series combined to divide and dispirit the club. In addition, the Browns had little incentive to play well. At very best they stood to garner two hundred dollars for winning their third consecutive pennant and the championship match with the Wolverines. The Browns were apathetic about the series' outcome. Oddsmakers who initially preferred the Browns switched their allegiance after the third game and declared the Wolverines a 10–8 favorite.[50]

The Browns' decline continued in Pittsburgh. Lady Baldwin held St. Louis to only five hits and shut them out 8–0. Detroit scored four runs in the top of the first inning, and St. Louis was essentially out of the game before the Browns had their first turn at bat. In addition, the Browns committed six errors, which did nothing to aid their cause or soothe Von der Ahe's emotions as he watched his club lose its third consecutive game to the Wolverines.[51] Attendance was respectable and the tour made more than expenses by stopping in Pittsburgh, but the World's Championship contingent experienced some exploitation by local entrepreneurs. The *Detroit Free Press* carried a report that declared, "The World's Championship aggregation is considered fair game for all. At Pittsburgh to-day they were squeezed to the extent of $90 for carriages and $57 for a band. The carriages were shaky, which also was the ailment of the band."[52] Even so, the Wolverines and the Browns departed for Brooklyn after having performed before an estimated four to five thousand spectators, which probably helped salve the irritation Von der Ahe and Stearns felt over the high prices of carriages and bands in Pittsburgh.

When Stearns and Von der Ahe had negotiated the sites and dates of the championship games, they deliberately constructed the schedule so that the teams would arrive in the New York City area on Friday and play in Brooklyn that day and in the Polo Grounds on Saturday. Weekends were always times of heavy attendance since more fans could get to the ballparks, and New York City, Brooklyn, and outlying towns and villages constituted a potential bonanza in ticket sales. Game five took place in Washington Park, Brooklyn, on a clear, windy, cool afternoon. Estimates of attendance varied as usual, but it seems nearly seven thousand fans braved the cool weather and watched the Browns come to life and defeat the Wolverines 5–2. Neither team played particularly well. They committed a total of nine errors, but none of the muffs substantially affected the outcome.[53] One Detroit writer informed his readers that their beloved Wolverines may have been jinxed on the way to the ballpark. Both teams lodged in the Grand Central Hotel in New York City and took carriages to the ferry, which carried them over to Brooklyn. When the Wolverines arrived at the river and boarded the ferryboat for Brooklyn, the Detroit club and its entourage discovered that a funeral cortege was on board. "The Detroit party went to the ball ground with a fear and foreboding which was fully realized. . . . [Perhaps] these omens did exert a malevolent influence on the Detroits and bring defeat to them, and then again perhaps it was the combination of timely hitting by the Browns, wonderfully good fielding by the same individuals and wild pitching on the part of Mr. Conway that lost the game for the league champions."[54] With tongue in cheek the Detroit writer made light of the day's play in Brooklyn and apparently saw something of a renaissance in the Browns as they appeared to return to form; it was, as the next four games proved, a brief renaissance.

The next day in the Polo Grounds, the Wolverines resumed their mastery of the Browns. About six thousand fans, mostly wearing overcoats, braved a keen wind to witness game six. One St. Louis writer observed that the Polo Grounds was a "dirty looking place."[55] It proved a dreary day for St. Louis. Charlie Getzien drew the pitching assignment for the Wolverines. The Wolverines scored six runs in the first two innings, St. Louis made seven errors total, Detroit added another three runs in the top of the ninth, for a decisive 9–0 victory.[56]

Bill Gleason's fielding in the Polo Grounds earned Von der Ahe's ire. The St. Louis shortstop made three errors and significantly contributed to the Browns ragged performance. Normally a fairly steady player, Gleason inexplicably faltered. After playing errorless ball in game one, St. Louis made twenty-eight errors in the next five games, and Gleason was charged with ten of that total. He was not the sole cause of the Browns' slump, but

John Montgomery Ward looking debonair and confident. (National Baseball Hall of Fame Library, Cooperstown, N.Y.)

he was a handy scapegoat for Von der Ahe and the press. So much so that manager Comiskey took Gleason out of the lineup in the next game. When the Browns departed for Philadelphia to continue the series, they trailed the Wolverines by two games, were playing poorly, and seemed nearly beyond resuscitation.[57]

After observing the National League's ban on games on the sabbath, the teams resumed the series on Monday, October 17, in the Philadelphia Baseball Grounds.[58] The Browns, minus Gleason, surely had their backs to the wall as they prepared for the contest. A good crowd, maybe sixty-five hundred, turned out to see the game on a warm clear day. John Montgomery Ward, the Giants' star, and Helen Dauvray, the noted actress, were among those witnessing the pre-game activities, and their presence added luster to the afternoon. Ward and Dauvray were recently married, and their appearance at the game caused something of a sensation that afternoon.[59] Ward was one of the superstars of his era, a leader of the baseball Brotherhood that promised to challenge the major league baseball cartel, and an idol of thousands of cranks across the nation. He was handsome, a college graduate, accomplished, urbane, often gallant, though somewhat egotistical. Helen Dauvray, a celebrity in her own right, was a prominent actress on the New York stage and a noted baseball fan. She was breathtakingly beautiful and, in addition to being an accomplished actress, for a brief time also operated her own theater in New York City.[60]

Ward and Dauvray attended the game for two reasons. Ward naturally wished to see some of the championship play, and he and his spouse also wanted to see the Dauvray Cup, which was on display before the game. Earlier in the year, perhaps anticipating that Ward's Giants would win the NL pennant and the World's Championship, Helen had donated a sterling silver cup estimated to be worth five hundred dollars to commemorate the series. She stipulated that the winning team should retain possession of the trophy until another team claimed it. She further stipulated that should any team win the World's Championship three times, that team could keep the Dauvray Cup forever. The sterling silver cup caused quite a sensation in the baseball world. Its front featured a right-handed hitter at bat beneath flying pennants, with two baseballs and a catcher's mask above the hitter's head. Crossed bats formed the cup's handles, and on the reverse side it carried the inscription:

THE DAUVRAY CUP
Presented by
MISS HELEN DAUVRAY
TO THE PLAYERS WINNING THE
WORLD'S CHAMPIONSHIP

In addition to the cup, Dauvray also had gold medals struck for the first year of the cup's existence. Each member of the winning team, as Dauvray specified, was to receive a medal when the team took possession of the cup. The medals were awarded only once, and each of the original winners took permanent possession of his medal.[61]

As the Wards sat in their private box and watched the players prepare

A likeness of the Dauvray Cup. The drawing appeared in the *Kansas City Star* on October 8, 1893, after the Boston Beaneaters, who that year won the National League pennant for the third consecutive year, took permanent possession of the cup. The fate of the cup is unknown.

for the upcoming contest, the Dauvray Cup was placed on home plate so that all the fans could get a glimpse of the trophy. The *Detroit Free Press* reported, "The Wolverines were very careful not to hit it with the ball. They naturally did not desire to injure any of their personal property. The Browns regarded the property with wishful eyes."[62] Although the Wolverines were playing well and the Browns seemed hopelessly dispirited, the Detroit reporter may have been a bit premature in claiming the cup for Detroit with only six games completed. Nevertheless, the Wards intrigued the fans, and the display of the Dauvray Cup added a measure of novelty to the game.

Although Detroit's domination of the Browns continued, the Philadelphia game was one of the better of the series. Detroit scored three runs in the bottom of the second inning and, behind Lady Baldwin's commanding pitching, held the lead and finally won the game 3–1. The weather was good, the ballpark was in excellent condition, and the teams committed a total of only three errors, the fewest in any game of the playoffs.[63] After the game, the teams boarded their special train and departed for Boston where they were scheduled to play next. With nearly half the scheduled series completed, Detroit now held a three-game lead on the Browns, and while no one was yet prepared to write an obituary on St. Louis's championship hopes, fans, reporters, and many of the players sensed imminent doom.

The World's Championship traveling baseball show arrived in Boston at half past eleven on the morning of October 18 for game eight of the series. South End Grounds, the home of the Boston Red Caps (NL), served as the site for the contest. The ballpark had been in service since 1871 when it opened as the home field of the Boston Red Stockings (NA).[64] South End Grounds over the years had fallen upon hard times and was in sore need of upkeep and expansion. According to the *Post-Dispatch,* South End Grounds presented a shabby appearance, and it was the worst ballpark in the major leagues.[65] Boston baseball fans, nevertheless, were some of the more enthusiastic in the country, and Detroit and St. Louis played to packed stands. Although Gleason returned to the St. Louis lineup and played errorless ball, Caruthers allowed the Wolverines seventeen hits and nine runs while his teammates earned only two runs off Charlie Getzien. Detroit took a commanding 6–2 lead in the series that afternoon and needed only two victories in the remaining seven games to claim the World's Championship.

After the appearance in Boston the Wolverines and the Browns turned south and played a second game in Philadelphia the next day. Detroit extended its winning streak, defeating the Browns 4–2 in a well-played contest before slightly more than two thousand fans.[66] The second appearance in Philadelphia gave the Wolverines their seventh victory in the series, and with six games remaining on the schedule, the Browns though not yet interred were moribund. Although the series so far had not been as competitive as the owners may have wished, the World's Championship had so far been financially successful. Receipts after the second Philadelphia date totaled $34,680.[67] Expenses for the series had long since been defrayed, and Stearns and his associates and Von der Ahe were obviously relieved of any fear that the playoffs might cost them money. Von der Ahe was distressed by his team's poor showing, but so far as the financial aspects of the playoffs were concerned, he had no immediate concerns.

When the teams arrived in Washington, D.C., for the next game on October 20, 1887, the weather turned uncooperative. A light rain fell all day, and the game was postponed until half past ten the next morning. The schedule already called for a game in Baltimore the next day. So, on October 21, the teams for the first time had to play a doubleheader. St. Louis won the morning game in Washington, D.C., and after hastily leaving the capital, Detroit decisively won the afternoon contest in Baltimore by a score of 13–3. Thus Detroit claimed the World's Championship.[68] Von der Ahe's mighty Browns had lost eight games to the upstart Wolverines and forfeited their status as world's champions. Worse yet, the Browns had to face another four games with Detroit. Stearns wanted the games to showcase his team and to enlarge the receipts. Von der Ahe's attitude was ambivalent. He was downcast over his club's failure in the series, but he also felt compelled to honor his agreement with Stearns, and he always en-joyed appearing in public as the "Boss President" of his club.

Late on the afternoon of October 21, 1887, news of the Wolverines' vic-tory in Baltimore reached Detroit via telegraph. Mayor Marvin H. Cham-berlain immediately appointed a committee, chaired by Colonel Walter G. Seeley, to plan a homecoming celebration.[69] Seeley and his committee had hurried work to do. The Wolverines and the Browns were scheduled to play another game in Detroit on October 24, as the championship tour made its way back to St. Louis for the final game. Undaunted by the short time available, Colonel Seeley opened a subscription to raise funds and quickly raised one thousand dollars to fund the celebration of Detroit's first world's champions.[70] Plans for the Wolverines' homecoming devel-oped rapidly, and by October 23 the *Sunday News* informed its readers that "All the arrangements . . . have been completed. Over $1,000 has been subscribed and both teams will be wined and dined to their hearts content before and after the game. A band and 60 carriages will meet them at the Wabash Depot on their arrival at 10:00 A.M."[71] Detroit baseball fans, city leaders, and the public in general demonstrated their joy over the Wolver-ines' successes, which all believed reflected favorably on the city, enhanc-ing its burgeoning image as an economic crossroads for the American economy. Even before automobile manufacturing bestowed immortality upon Detroit, the city was coming into the foreground of the industrial revolution underway in America, and the World's Championship, in the minds of the city's residents, announced Detroit's new status as a city on a par with the powerful municipalities represented in the NL and the AA.

While the Detroit city fathers feverishly prepared to toast their heroes, the World's Championship tour trudged back to New York City for a sec-ond game in Brooklyn's Washington Park on Saturday, October 22. By game time the weather was bitter cold. As the *Post-Dispatch* put it, "The wind was blowing a hundred miles an hour from forty different direc-tions. The weather was absolutely frigid." The players wore cardigan jack-ets to shield themselves. According to the *Detroit Free Press*, a "blizzard howled around Washington Park today and a dizzy crowd of 800 people turned out."[72] St. Louis defeated Detroit by a score of 5–1 in a shortened game that was marked by Dan Brouthers's only appearance in the World's Championship.

Dan's ankle still troubled him, but after the Wolverines clinched the championship, he asked to be inserted into the lineup. Brouthers managed to get two hits and fielded his position at first base cleanly, but he clearly could not run.[73] The effort he made in Brooklyn had its consequences. Two days later, when the Wolverines took the field in Recreation Park in Detroit before their adoring cranks, Dan was again not in the lineup. His ankle was, if anything, worse. Nevertheless, he took one opportunity to play, even though it was an afternoon in Brooklyn in weather scarcely congenial to a sprained ankle, and the decision probably cost him the chance to play before hometown fans when the series returned to Detroit on October 24, 1887. Knowledgeable baseball fans realized that his absence from the Detroit batting order heightened the already impressive achievements of his teammates. Had he been available for the entire series, the Wolverines may well have routed the Browns even worse. *Sporting News* probably summed up St. Louis fans' feelings concerning Brouthers's absence from the lineup: "Brouthers did not play. Thank God."[74] After an hour and twenty minutes of play in the swirling wind and bitter cold, the game was called at the end of the seventh inning; it was too frigid to continue play as the sun dropped lower in the sky. Many of the nearly frozen fans quit the ballpark long before the seventh inning, and further play seemed pointless.

As usual the World's Championship paused on Sunday, and then the next day, October 23, both teams boarded their special train and departed for Detroit for the thirteenth game. The Wolverines and the Browns were scheduled to arrive at ten o'clock the next morning to participate in pre-game and post-game festivities prior to leaving for Chicago for the next-to-last game on the tour. Detroit was prepared to greet the Wolverines in grand style, and Mayor Chamberlain, Colonel Seeley, and a host of local dignitaries were scheduled to meet the train at the Wabash Depot and lead a parade of sixty carriages carrying the players, Stearns and Von der Ahe, and other members of the World's Championship entourage to Russell House for a reception and breakfast prior to the afternoon game.

All the plans were set, and no one expected what finally happened: The train carrying the teams arrived two hours early. When the train pulled into the station, the depot was empty. Stearns, realizing that his contingent had arrived earlier than anticipated, ordered his players to stay aboard the train, posted guards so they could not slip away, and dispatched an urgent message to Mayor Chamberlain. At about nine o'clock in the morning, sixty carriages—some of them transporting Mayor Chamberlain, Seeley, and other hastily assembled dignitaries—converged at the depot, and after a few short speeches welcoming the Wolverines home, the crowd was transported to Russell House for a formal reception.[75] After speeches praising both teams for their heroic tour and especially lauding the Wolverines for their splendid play in the World's Championship, the spent but good-natured travelers were served an elegant breakfast. Once the ceremonies and the meal were finished, the teams prepared to travel out to Recreation Park for game thirteen of the World's Championship tour. Von der Ahe was genial all morning, and a local newspaper, mimicking his accent, reported that he observed: "Der cidy is vild. I never seen der like. I bed we blay ter a big busyness dis afdernoon. Dot was von immense recepshoon."[76]

As the teams made their way to the ballpark, enthusiastic crowds gathered along the streets, anxious to catch a glimpse of the local heroes. Repeated cheers, applause, and obvious demonstrations of affection buoyed the spirits of the weary players, and when they finally arrived at Recreation Park, the Wolverines and the Browns were raucously welcomed by four thousand excited fans. Pre-game festivities featured, among other things, rewards for some of the Wolverines. Dan Brouthers was presented a commemorative bat by A. G. Spalding's sporting goods company; Charlie Ganzel's admirers gave him an elegant gold watch; Charlie Bennett's fans brought a wheelbarrow loaded with 531 silver dollars out on the field as a gift to him. Getting into the spirit of the occasion, Bennett pushed the wheelbarrow around the bases, trailed by a fifer and drummer playing "Yankee Doodle."[77] The Wolverines were equal to the festive spirit in Detroit and handily defeated the Browns 6–3. After the game the players returned to Russell House for more good food, more praise, and more speeches. Then later that evening the World's Championship tour entrained for Chicago for another match prior to returning to St. Louis to complete the series.[78]

Even though the Wolverines had departed, Detroit residents continued to bask in the glow of their newfound status. Detroit was home to the world champions! Never mind the somewhat hubristic and vicarious connection, Detroit and its citizens were now associated with the best baseball team in the United States and, by implication, the entire world. The celebration in Detroit briefly united ethnic groups and economic classes in a collective display of civic pride. Everyone loved the Wolverines, and for the moment, many of the growing divisions in local society were set aside as Detroit fans feted their champions. Never mind that the bulk of celebration included only the city's elite, and never mind that the ordinary citizens were as usual mere onlookers. Nearly everyone who took notice of the official reception for the Wolverines and Browns was caught up in the unifying delirium fostered by associating with a championship ball club. It was heady stuff for a city lately come to the forefront of major league baseball. The Dauvray Cup was placed on display in the window of Roehm and Sons Jewelers located at Grand Circus Park and Woodward Avenue, and the public was invited to view the trophy. According to the local press, the window at Roehm and Sons displaying the cup attracted many proud and curious pedestrians pausing to gaze at Miss Dauvray's gift to baseball.[79]

Cold weather continued to stalk the series in game fourteen in Chicago. The contest was held at Loomis Street Park rather than West Side Park, the Chicago White Stockings' home, and about "600 V.S.C. (very select cranks) braved the hard weather" to watch the Wolverines defeat the Browns 4–3.[80] Von der Ahe must have been disappointed by the meager attention Chicago fans gave the game. Chris and his Browns were back in Chicago, and even though recently dethroned as the reigning world's champions, they were in the series and the Chicago White Stockings were not. This realization must have been some balm to Von der Ahe's troubled soul. He had been forced to witness the Browns' dismal performances in the series, but at least, for a moment, he took his seat in the stands, smiled, and issued pronouncements to the Chicago press. Few in Chicago seemed interested in the game.

The series finally staggered to its conclusion in St. Louis on October 26, 1887. By now, the weather was winterlike, and only seven hundred fans came out to Sportman's Park to see the final game, which the Browns won by a score of 9–2.[81] After seventeen days, many miles, and a good deal of anguish, the 1887 World's Championship was completed. Although it purported to be a national journal, *Sporting News,* published in St. Louis, favored the Browns in its coverage of the World's Championship, and Spink's weekly declared, "Detroit has whipped us, and whipped us fairly. That point is settled and excuses and crawfishing are now out of order."[82] Von der Ahe's assessment of the series was not quite so generous to the Wolverines. His feelings concerning the series emerged when he stated:

> We were in no condition to play ball with any club, much less the Detroits. We had only one pitcher, Caruthers, and they knocked the life out of him every time he went in the box. Foutz's thumb was hurt, and he could not curve a ball to save his life. Gleason was no good; he was sick and broke up, and he lost three of the games for us. Besides, the Detroits had great luck. We outplayed them in several games, and still we were beaten. They played the best games of their lives—they admit that themselves—and the men individually wanted to win the series, both for the glory and the money. Our boys wanted to have the same arrangement as last year made with them, that I should give them half the receipts, but once is enough to do that. I pay them double salary, and that is enough. I don't think they tried as hard as they might to win. Just wait until next year. We will have a new short-stop and a couple of pitchers that will make things hum.[83]

Although Detroit "whipped" the Browns, the statistics for the games were relatively close in most vital categories. Detroit outhit the Browns 157 to 151, a margin of only six hits; outscored St. Louis 73–54; and surprisingly, led the Browns 33–20 in stolen bases, perhaps the most telling category in the series. The Browns were widely renowned for their defensive skills, yet they committed sixty-seven errors to Detroit's forty-nine.[84] By modern standards neither team played exemplary defensive baseball, but the Browns averaged more than four errors per game, and many of these profoundly affected the series' outcome.

Although cold weather and waning interest in the series contributed to diminishing proceeds in the final stages of the series, profits from the games were substantial when compared to previous World's Championship events. After eleven games were completed and Detroit had won the title, the *Post-Dispatch* informed its readers that the series had garnered $35,320 in gate receipts.[85] Neither the Browns nor the Wolverines released official totals once the series was completed, but *Sporting Life* estimated the gross income at forty thousand dollars.[86] Receipts for the first eleven games averaged approximately $3,200, and for the final four games, after the intense cold weather set in and the Wolverines claimed the title, ticket sales yielded about $1,200 per contest. The figures for the final four games included the homecoming game the Wolverines played in Detroit. At least four thousand of the Wolverines' faithful fans, who probably would have endured a blinding blizzard to celebrate the event, attended the contest. Had Detroit not been scheduled in the final four games, the total receipts for the last segment of the series would have been substantially less. Estimated expenses for the championship games was set at $15,000 for an average of $1,000 per game; had the series played to the average of the final four games, Von der Ahe and Stearns would have netted virtually nothing.[87] As it was, however, they stood to divide about $25,000; a point many of the players must have noticed and fretted over. Had Von der Ahe shared his proceeds with his players, they would have earned a sum roughly equivalent to the previous year, but now they gained nothing for two weeks of work, stress, and embarrassment.

Although it proved financially successful, the 1887 format for a World's Championship was not repeated by subsequent contenders. Fifteen games proved too many for several reasons. Fans lost interest in the games as the troupe went from city to city attempting to lure patrons to the ballparks. After the Wolverines took a commanding lead and cold weather set in, the World's Championship lost its allure to cranks. In Brooklyn, for example, game five garnered an estimated $5,500 in gate receipts, but when the teams returned for game twelve, waning interest in a decided series and frigid weather reduced the gate proceeds to a minuscule $275.[88] Except for the homecoming game in Detroit on October 24, only one of the final six games sold enough tickets to defray expenses. Hometown crowds avidly bought tickets, players responded positively to their faithful friends in familiar ballparks, and games in Detroit or St. Louis, with the exception of game fifteen in St. Louis, were better-played games than those on the road. A shorter schedule of games played before more enthusiastic hometown fans, which also reduced travel expenses, became the norm for future series.

The 1887 World's Championship was a combination of title play and exhibition baseball. Von der Ahe and Stearns and his associates turned a profit, but they also paid a price in that the players, especially the Browns, became disgruntled with the format, and relationships between the own-

ers and some of their players were harmed irrevocably. Just as the 1884 series with its three-game format in one town was too restricted in concept,
so the fifteen-game schedule in ten towns was too open-ended. Owners,
and Von der Ahe among them, realized that a fifteen-game format where
all games were played regardless of games already won or lost was a poor
concept. Baseball's leadership did the best it could to develop a concept of
a World's Championship series. With no precedent to guide them, baseball magnates groped their way through the task of forming playoffs, gen-
erating profits, and coping with players' demands. Von der Ahe and
Stearns carried the notion of a series to its outside extreme—one that
would not be repeated.

The New York Giants

World's Champions, 1888

Von der Ahe's Browns opened the 1888 season a vastly altered team. Three years of successes and quarrels had rent the team badly, and Von der Ahe decided to cleanse his club of those players he found particularly troublesome. By opening day, five of the club's mainstays had been eliminated. Pitchers Bob Caruthers and Dave Foutz, who combined to win 198 games for the Browns in their pennant-winning years in 1885, 1886, and 1887, were sold to the Brooklyn Trolley Dodgers (AA), where they proceeded to win 125 games over the next several seasons. Doc Bushong, who had shared catching duties with Jack Boyle, was also released to Brooklyn, where his career went into decline.[1] Of the three Browns who went to the Brooklyn team, Caruthers most distinguished himself by winning 110 games in four years.[2]

In addition to Caruthers, Foutz, and Bushong, Von der Ahe also disposed of outfielder Curt Welch and shortstop Bill Gleason. Welch and Gleason were sold to the Philadelphia AA franchise. Welch's career with the Browns had been a notable one. He led the AA in fielding averages in 1885 and 1886 while hitting .276 during his three-year tenure with the Browns. Welch's nocturnal activities particularly annoyed Von der Ahe, and when the opportunity arose to send him to Philadelphia for catcher Jocko Milligan and three thousand dollars, Von der Ahe quickly disposed of the able but hard-living outfielder.[3] Bill Gleason, a good citizen when compared to Welch, arrived in the major leagues in 1882 as a rookie shortstop for St. Louis and by 1884 had established himself as a regular in the Browns' lineup. He averaged 124 games a year at shortstop during the glory years of 1885, 1886, and 1887 while hitting a composite .271 during the pennant-winning seasons in St. Louis.[4] Gleason played poorly in the 1887 series with Detroit, and Von der Ahe decided to include him in his house-cleaning reform. After joining Philadelphia, Gleason's skills eroded, and by 1890 he was out of the major leagues. Von der Ahe's changes in the Browns' roster were daring and certainly challenged Comiskey's skills as manager and team captain as the club prepared to compete for the pennant in 1888.

As St. Louis fans witnessed the metamorphosis of the Browns, they realized that the 1888 season was destined to be an unusual one. No longer could they depend on the sturdy arms of Caruthers and Foutz, Welch's steady work in center field, or Gleason's workhorse ethic at shortstop. Now the fans had to acquaint themselves with new players with different skills and different personalities. Of all the players Von der Ahe brought to St. Louis to replace those he discarded, Tommy McCarthy was the most notable. McCarthy, who debuted with Boston in the UA, had played in only 119 major league games prior to his arrival in St. Louis, but he quickly blossomed into a fine outfielder and a better-than-average hitter.[5] Harry Lyons, an outfielder who joined the Browns in the latter part of 1887, played in 123 games in 1888 but hit a meager .194 and was dealt to the Giants in 1889.[6]

Two players joined the Browns after the 1888 season began, and each made a significant contribution to the team's final pennant-winning year. When the season opened longtime second baseman Yank Robinson attempted to fill Gleason's spot at shortstop, but the experiment did not go well and Yank was unhappy with his new task. To remedy this Von der Ahe acquired Bill White from Louisville after the season was about one-third completed, and White proceeded to play seventy-four games at shortstop for the Browns. White fielded his position competently while hitting a modest .175, but his presence allowed Yank Robinson to return to his natural position at second base where he excelled.[7]

Pitcher Elton P. "Icebox" Chamberlain was the other player to join the Browns later in the season. Chamberlain possessed one of the more unforgettable nicknames in all of baseball's history. He apparently acquired the name Icebox from his calm demeanor in the pitcher's box. Chamberlain began the season with the Louisville Colonels where, by late August, he had recorded fourteen wins against nine losses. In an effort to bolster his pitching staff Von der Ahe purchased Icebox on September 1, 1888. An item in *Sporting News* entitled "Chamberlain Is Ours" ecstatically reported that Von der Ahe had secured the Icebox from the Colonels and predicted Chamberlain would do well in St. Louis.[8] Chamberlain responded by winning eleven games and losing only two after he joined the Browns. Later in his career Icebox, while pitching for Cincinnati, made baseball history on May 30, 1894, when Bobby Lowe hit four home runs off him in one game; only one other pitcher, William Terry, equaled that feat.[9] In 1888, however, Chamberlain's sudden appearance on the St. Louis pitching staff proved a tonic for the Browns in their efforts to win a fourth consecutive pennant. Chamberlain proved a genuine asset when he distinguished himself again in 1889 with thirty-two wins.[10] Longtime Browns fans may have lamented the departures of Foutz, Caruthers, Bushong, Gleason, and Welch, but the new Browns, combined with the corps of

Jim Mutrie's powerful New York Giants posing for a team picture in 1888.

(National Baseball Hall of Fame Library, Cooperstown, N.Y.)

veterans who remained on the roster after Von der Ahe's purge, carried the club to another pennant. Comiskey met the challenge of leading a rebuilt team, and his efforts as manager and captain were in no small part responsible for the Browns' successes in 1888.

By late June the Browns had played nearly half their schedule, and unlike the previous three years, they did not establish an early lead in the pennant race. As Comiskey labored to shape his team to meet the challenges facing them, the Brooklyn Trolley Dodgers played exceptionally good baseball and by June 30, 1888, followed St. Louis in the standings by only a few percentage points.[11] Throughout July the Browns and the Trolley Dodgers remained only a few percentage points apart in the standings. Then after they acquired Icebox Chamberlain, the Browns began to assert themselves and by season's end captured their fourth consecutive pennant by a comfortable margin of six and one-half games.[12] Although the Browns again won the AA pennant, the team did not dominate the league as it had the three previous years. The Browns won pennants in those years by an average of fourteen games over the second-place teams, and each year they had established an early lead and never faced any serious challenges. In 1888, however, they had to struggle throughout most of the season in order to maintain a first-place standing, and it was not until the arrival of Icebox Chamberlain that they anchored themselves securely in first place. A third starting pitcher made a great difference. Silver King won forty-five games in 1888, and the newly emerging Nat Hudson contributed twenty-five wins once the season ended. In late August, King and Hudson began to show signs of fatigue, however, and when Icebox Chamberlain joined the team and took his regular turn in the pitcher's box, he provided them with an extra day's rest between pitching assignments. They responded well to the breathing space he provided during the last six weeks of the pennant race.[13]

When the season's statistics were compiled, few were surprised to learn that the Browns' hitters led the American Association in home runs (36), tied for first with Philadelphia in team hitting (.250), and led the league in bases on balls (410); their 1,189 hits, 468 stolen bases, and 789 runs scored were second best in the AA. King, Hudson, and Chamberlain won eighty-one of St. Louis's ninety-two victories, and they compiled some impressive statistics. They led the AA in earned run average with an impressive 2.09, gave up the fewest bases on balls, and allowed the fewest hits per game.[14] Pitching had always been one of the Browns' strengths, and even though Foutz and Caruthers were no longer with them, the tradition continued another year. Tip O'Neill, Comiskey, Yank Robinson, Arlie Latham, and the new recruits McCarthy and White hit well, ran the bases with their usual daring, and played good defensive baseball. Good pitching, strong defense, aggressive base-running, and strong hitting were St. Louis trademarks in the mid-1880s. Knowledgeable baseball fans expected nothing less from the Browns, but insightful cranks also recognized that the club was aging and that it was rent by quarrels with Von der Ahe and by personal differences among the players. The Browns were an excellent team, but they were not the dominant force they had been in previous years. Time, disappointment, and injury steadily took their toll. Nevertheless, they again captured the nation's attention as they prepared to compete for the World's Championship of baseball for the fourth time in as many years.

John B. Day's New York Giants won the NL pennant in 1888 after a long and exciting struggle with the Chicago White Stockings. Much as the Browns struggled through the first part of the 1888 season, the Giants battled their NL rivals through the first half of the season before moving into first place on July 28, 1888, and hovering there until they finally clinched the pennant on October 4.[15] The Giants were on the verge of a two-year domination of the National League, and New York fans were delirious with joy over the prospect of World's Championship baseball returning to their city.

The Giants were formed through the efforts of John B. Day, a successful cigar manufacturer in Connecticut, who had moved to New York City by 1880 where he established a cigar factory on the Lower East Side and became a millionaire. Day enjoyed baseball and played amateur ball in the city and with his brother-in-law, Joseph Gordon, became involved in professional baseball in 1880 when they formed the New York Metropolitans. The Metropolitans—a semiprofessional team composed of players from the old Brooklyn Unions and the Rochester, New York, Hop Bitters—competed against local amateur and professional clubs, and in 1881 Day's Mets, as they were popularly styled, joined the newly formed Eastern Championship Association.[16] In the following year, Day rejected an opportunity to place the Mets into the AA as it organized for its maiden season, but after witnessing the AA's successes and perceiving the potential for profit in owning a "major league" team in New York City, he changed his mind, and on October 24, 1882, the Mets were admitted to membership in the AA.[17] At the time he moved his Mets into the AA, Day also purchased the moribund Troy, New York, team, which had joined the NL in 1879. Troy usually finished in the bottom half of the League's standings during its four-year tenure, and the attending financial difficulties led to its demise as a League franchise in 1882. Seeing an opportunity to place an NL team in New York City, Day promptly purchased the franchise and moved it to New York City where the club was admitted to the NL on December 6, 1882.[18] Within the space of only six weeks, Day became the owner of franchises in opposing major leagues.

Known as the New Yorks or the Gothams, Day's NL team had several players of major league ability. When Day purchased the Troy franchise he acquired catcher William "Buck" Ewing, pitchers Michael "Smiling Mickey" Welch and Timothy Keefe, and first baseman Roger Connor.[19] Day also acquired John Montgomery Ward, who was nearing the end of his career as a pitcher and on the threshold of converting to shortstop, from the Providence Grays prior to the 1883 season.[20] Since he owned two teams, Day chose the better players to stock his NL team, soon to be known as the Giants, and assigned the lesser to his AA franchise, the Metropolitans.[21] Day was not infallible in his assessment of talent. He, for example, assigned Timothy Keefe to the Mets where he won a total of seventy-eight games in 1883 and 1884. Day remedied this oversight and moved him to the Giants in 1885 where Keefe, known as Sir Timothy for his courtly behavior, averaged thirty-four wins a season through 1889.[22] Keefe won 342 games in his total career, which ended in 1893, and to this day he ranks among the elite of major league pitchers. Ewing, Connor, Ward, Welch, and Keefe became the mainstays of the Giants in the mid-1880s and led the team to prominence.

Day's New York club opened the 1883 NL season only twenty-three days before the Brooklyn Bridge was inaugurated, and they did poorly their first season, finishing in sixth place with a record of forty-six wins and fifty losses.[23] Undaunted by the club's lackluster performance in 1883, Day set about the task of strengthening his team. He brought untried Danny Richardson to the Giants in 1884, and by 1887 Richardson matured as the team's everyday second baseman and distinguished himself over an eleven-year major league career.[24] James "Orator Jim" O'Rourke, who had earlier proved his abilities in Boston, Providence, and Buffalo, joined the Giants in 1885. "Orator Jim" was legendary for his unusual use of language. A reporter once asked him, "What makes a good ballplayer?" to which Orator Jim replied:

> However desirous and willing I am to yield to my inclination to oblige you, I feel constrained from circumstances to solicit your kindest indulgence in this matter, if for no other reason than in consequence of a conscientious conviction that my modesty would not permit me to swell my egotistical proportions to such limitations as to anticipate that I could talk upon any subject in a manner either entertaining or edifying your publication.[25]

One newspaper observed that fractious reporters were punished by being sent to interview O'Rourke. Whatever his extemporaneous speaking skills, the Orator was a fine outfielder, and he contributed to New York's successes in the late 1880s. Outfielder Michael Tiernan, a twenty-year-old resident of Trenton, New Jersey, debuted as a major leaguer with the Giants in 1887, and "Silent Mike" quickly established himself as a defensive asset and a dangerous hitter.[26] Tiernan, who was once timed at 9.9 seconds in the hundred-yard dash, added useful speed to the outfield and contributed to the Giants running game on the base paths. Mike Slattery, a journeyman outfielder, and Art Whitney, a competent if unspectacular third baseman, were added to the Giants' roster in 1888, and with their arrivals, New York was set for the upcoming campaign, which was to carry the club to the NL pennant.

The 1888 Giants were a talented team, and the core of the club had played together for several years. The Giants' manager, Jim Mutrie, also was a talented man. In 1884 he managed the New York Metropolitans when they challenged the Providence Grays in the first World's Championship series, and when he led the Giants into the 1888 series, he became the first manager in baseball history to guide teams into the World's Championship series from rival major leagues. Mutrie possessed the skills to develop his younger players, keep his veterans relatively content, and cope with the ever-changing baseball environment of the 1880s. Day relied heavily on Mutrie's judgment of talent, and unlike Von der Ahe, Day was disposed to allow his manager a free hand in the daily operations of the club. The Giants, unlike the Browns, were a healthy mix of veteran performers and emerging younger players. It was an impressive club. Everyone expected the Giants to be a contender, and as events proved, no one was disappointed by the team's performance in 1888.

Anticipating that the Giants would eliminate the White Stockings from the NL's pennant race during their series in New York City in early October, Von der Ahe and the Browns' team secretary, George Munson, traveled to New York City to negotiate terms for a World's Championship series with John B. Day.[27] On October 4, 1888, the Giants, behind the capable pitching of Ed "Cannonball" Crane, defeated Chicago by a score of 1–0 and claimed the NL pennant.[28] Later that day Von der Ahe, Day, and their assistants met in the Grand Central Hotel and opened discussions for a playoff between the Browns and the Giants. Von der Ahe and Day quickly agreed to the concept of a series, but several details, such as sites for games and the selecting of an NL umpire, were not completely resolved at the first meeting. George Munson was elected to handle the publicity for the series, and *Sporting Life* observed, "As he [Munson] is a hustler of the first quality he will doubtless repeat the successes he scored as the advance agent for the World's Series between St. Louis and Detroit."[29]

In principle Von der Ahe and Day agreed to a nine-game series featuring three games in New York, three games in St. Louis, and one game each in Boston, Brooklyn, and Philadelphia. Ticket prices for the contests were set at one dollar per seat per game. Shortly after the basic agreement was concluded, Von der Ahe and Munson returned to St. Louis, and almost immediately the preparations for the upcoming World's Championship series encountered difficulties. First, charging one dollar per seat for the games was roundly criticized as pricing many of baseball's stoutest fans out of the ticket market. In response to this charge, Von der Ahe and Day subsequently agreed to use a three-tier pricing system, selling general admission tickets for fifty cents, grandstand seats for one dollar, and choice seats in the grandstand for one dollar fifty cents. Second, the attempt to play one of the games in Boston was foiled. Arthur Soden, the owner of the Boston team, refused to accept a flat fee for the use of his ballpark for one of the series' games; instead, he demanded 25 percent of the gate receipts. Soden's fee was too much for Von der Ahe and Day, so they decided to schedule the planned Boston game in the Polo Grounds. This meant that the Giants' Polo Grounds was the designated location of four of the games. To solve this problem, the owners planned the series as a ten-game event with four games in the Polo Grounds, four in St. Louis, one in Brooklyn, and one in Philadelphia. In the event of a tied series after ten games, the tiebreaker would be played in Cincinnati.[30] Neither owner publicly discussed anticipated rewards for their players. *Sporting Life* reported that "After deducting expenses the receipts of the games will be divided, but whether the players will share in this division, and if so, in what proportion, is not stated."[31] Rumors abounded that bonuses would be handed out once the series was completed, but the Giants and the Browns entered the games with no assurances of any additional income arising from the 1888 World's Championship.[32] In recognition of his manager's performance in 1888, Von der Ahe presented Comiskey with a five-hundred-dollar government bond prior to the opening of the series.[33] None of the Browns other than Comiskey nor the Giants received rewards from their owners for clinching pennants. By late 1888 the activities of the Brotherhood of Professional Base Ball Players had sorely strained relationships between owners and players, to such a point that the atmosphere surrounding the competing parties was poisonous, and men such as Von der Ahe and Day were not in any mood to enrich their players. Everyone expected that the winning owner would reward his players, but few expected either owner to be generous.

Von der Ahe's Browns concluded their season in Cincinnati by splitting two games with the Reds on Sunday, October 14, 1888. Immediately after the doubleheader, the Browns boarded their special train—decorated with flags and banners proclaiming their status as American Association champions—and departed for Columbus, Ohio, where they were joined by a group of traveling companions composed of Mrs. Von der Ahe, Mrs. Comiskey, Arlie Latham's sister, Mr. and Mrs. Al Spink, and a few others. Once the party was assembled in Columbus, the train headed eastward for New York City where the World's Championship series (now routinely referred to as the World Series) was to commence the following Tuesday.[34] Ever the soul of ebullience, Von der Ahe staged a triumphal entry into New York City. He chartered a special train, paid the hotel and traveling expenses for his team and guests who were registered in the Grand Central Hotel, bought new suits of clothing for his players and his guests, and spared no expense to coddle his entourage.[35] Chris's generosity and his love of attention prompted him to spend a sizable sum as he ushered his team and faithful friends into Gotham.

On Sunday evening, while Von der Ahe's special train made its way to New York City, the Giants' fans feted them. Two of their greatest fans, actors De Wolf Hopper and Digby Bell, spearheaded a special tribute at the Star Theatre. The theater was appropriately decorated to commemorate the occasion, and the Giants were presented with three thousand dollars to divide among themselves. A beautiful blue silk banner emblazoned with "Champions 1889, N.Y. B. C." was draped across the stage, and the occasion was formalized with speeches by Congressman Amos Cummings and Senator Jacob A. Cantor.[36] In addition to the gifts to the Giants and the speeches, several actors and actresses entertained the packed house with songs, skits, and other performances, but as usual, Hopper stole the show when he recited "Casey at the Bat."

Unbeknownst to those present, Hopper was carving baseball immortality out for himself in 1888. Two months earlier Hopper, a highly successful actor, had publicly delivered for the first time the poem concerning Casey's disaster. The event took place at Wallack's Theatre on the evening of August 14, 1888, when the Giants and the Chicago White Stockings responded to his invitation and attended a performance of McCaull's Opera Company's rendition of Prince Methusalem on "baseball night." Hopper, along with his close friend and fellow actor, Digby Bell, and most of the cast of McCaull's troupe, including thirty chorus girls, had attended the Giants–White Stockings game at the Polo Grounds that afternoon, and in the evening the players came to the theater to see the operetta. The theater was decorated in a baseball motif, and the Giants sat in balcony seats facing the Chicago team in a balcony opposite them. As the time for the curtain approached, General William Tecumseh Sherman entered the theater to take his seat. He received a standing ovation from the audience. Sherman graciously acknowledged the tribute, took his seat, and the curtain rose. Throughout the play Hopper made sly references to baseball. In the second act when the time came for him to sing "The Dotlet on the I," he delivered the song in his usual elegant style, but he also chose to lace his rendition with allusions to baseball. Just before he delivered his song and his tribute to the Giants, he turned to the White Stockings and declared, "You have had the pennant long enough to stand this."[37] He proceeded to improvise, lauding his beloved Giants.[38] At the conclusion of his song, an usher brought forward to him an immense floral display in the shape of a baseball; it was a gift from the Chicago team, and Hopper was pleased and affected by the thoughtfulness of the White Stockings.

Earlier in the evening Hopper had committed to memory Ernest Thayer's poem "Casey at the Bat," and in honor of the occasion he delivered the poem to the packed house. His presentation of Casey's mighty failure delighted everyone. Reporters observed that General Sherman laughed until tears rolled down his face, and that the audience roared its approval of Hopper's surprise.[39] Little did Hopper suspect what was happening that evening. He was to live a long, full life after his introduction of the poem on the New York stage. He later observed that he probably recited "Casey" at least ten thousand times in subsequent appearances in theaters throughout the country.[40] Hopper did not die until 1935, and by then he was perhaps more famous for Casey's misfortunes than was Thayer who wrote the poem. Hopper's presentation of "Casey at the Bat," during the festivities at the Star Theatre celebrating the Giants' first NL pennant, further associated his name with Thayer's poem, and an important bit of growing baseball lore was reinforced. A. G. Spalding later wrote: "I shall not undertake to determine as to whether the poem made Hopper great, or Hopper made the poem great. As a friend of Hopper, and as an admirer of the poem, I am inclined to the opinion that each owes a good deal to the popularity of the other."[41] Fortunately, Hopper introduced

Casey to the audience that evening in 1888, and children, adults, and baseball fans have delighted to it ever since.

When the World's Championship series commenced on Tuesday, October 16, the fractious Browns were in their usual state of disarray. Two factors unsettled the team. First of all, Nathaniel "Nat" Hudson, one of their pitching mainstays, was not in New York. Nat, along with Silver King, carried the brunt of the pitching duties for the Browns in 1888 and compiled a record of twenty-five wins and ten losses.[42] An enigmatic soul, Hudson left the Browns after the pennant was secured but prior to the season's end and journeyed to Hot Springs, Arkansas. According to the St. Louis press, Nat left St. Louis on October 1 to rest his arm and to prepare for the upcoming series with the Giants. By opening day of the series, Hudson had not rejoined the club, and he did not respond to Von der Ahe's repeated pleas to resume his place in the starting rotation.[43] As a result the Browns' pitching staff was depleted by one-third as they entered the series. The other factor upsetting the Browns concerned money. At the outset of the season, the AA set aside a prize of $1,250 for the pennant-winning club. The Browns presumed the prize would be divided among them, but by the series' opening game, they had begun to suspect that Von der Ahe intended to keep the money in the club's treasury. Several of the Browns nurtured old grudges against Von der Ahe and became disgruntled.[44] Quarrels between Von der Ahe and his players over salaries, bonuses, and shares of playoffs receipts were not news in 1888, but the resentments of the players surely affected their attitudes as they prepared to contest the Giants for the World's Championship.

Rain fell all morning the day the series opened in New York City. About noon the weather cleared, but the Polo Grounds remained soggy and the inclement start to the day probably diminished the ticket sales. Nevertheless, about five thousand spectators had arrived by game time, and they were a fiercely partisan group of Giants fans. The base paths were covered with sawdust in an attempt to improve footing for base-runners, and the Polo Grounds were decorated, adorned with the Giants' new flag proclaiming them NL champions.[45] Each team displayed new uniforms—the Browns in white and brown, the Giants in black and white—and each had a uniformed mascot.[46] John Gaffney and "Honest John" Kelly were engaged to reprise their umpiring triumphs in the 1887 World's Championship series. They took their places on the diamond just before three o'clock in the afternoon, and the first game of the series got under way.[47]

Tim Keefe drew the opening assignment for the Giants, and Silver King opposed him. Each pitched a fine game, and when the contest ended nine innings later, the Giants prevailed by a score of 2–1.[48] The only surprising statistic in the game was that the Browns stole only two bases. St. Louis prided itself on its running game, but the Giants' catcher, Buck Ewing, denied them

Timothy Keefe showing his pitching motion while a member of the New York Giants.
(National Baseball Hall of Fame Library, Cooperstown, N.Y.)

that advantage. The Browns left six men on base and had they stolen more bases the game's outcome would have been different.[49]

On October 17, about fifty-five hundred chilled fans witnessed the second game of the series. The weather remained raw and windy and tested the determination of those who huddled in their seats as the Browns evened the series, defeating the Giants 3–0 behind Icebox Chamberlain's six-hit shutout. Mutrie's men stole four bases compared to none for the Browns and committed fewer errors, but when the Giants had men in scoring position, Chamberlain squelched their opportunities. This game, in spite of less than ideal playing conditions, proved an interesting and relatively well-played contest.[50] The victory in game two apparently relieved the Browns' tensions. Many of them must have felt downcast after the first game as they reflected on the poor start they made in the series, and as their thoughts were haunted by the debacle against Detroit in 1887. According to J. Thomas Hetrick: "That evening, St. Louis players and their fan entourage hoisted beer, wine, and champagne at the Grand Central Hotel bar. Von der Ahe himself celebrated, ordering each of his players to buy a new suit of clothes and send him the bill. The party lasted until the wee hours of the morning."[51] As events soon established, however, Von der Ahe's optimism, while perhaps an effort to instill confidence in his club, proved premature.

October 18 dawned fair and clear, and even though a cold wind continued to blow, the gusts served to dry the field. Between five and six thousand people entered the Polo Grounds to witness game three, and according to one account, there "also was a larger attendance of the fair sex than usual."[52] Tim Keefe and Silver King again faced each other, and Keefe again prevailed by a score of 4–2. Each team got five hits, but the Browns committed five errors and failed to steal a single base while the Giants stole six. After the game, when Comiskey was queried about the cause for the Browns' impotence on the base paths, he replied, "Ewing, Ewing."[53] Catcher Ewing, who controlled the Browns beautifully throughout the series, proved himself equal to St. Louis's running attack and undermined their confidence in the first three games. Keefe also proved magnificent in the opening games; in his first eighteen innings against the Browns, he allowed them only eight hits and three runs. As they for the most part had done in the 1887 series, the Browns' pitchers did well in the first three games, but St. Louis did not hit well, committed damaging errors, and did not unleash the club's vaunted running game. After game three, many probably mused that Von der Ahe's celebrating the outcome of game two may have been the equivalent of whistling in the cemetery. At any rate, game four was set for Washington Park in Brooklyn on the following afternoon, and at that point, the Browns, although dispirited, were not yet ready for a mortician.

Game four in Brooklyn was critical for the Browns. After the contest in Washington Park, St. Louis faced yet another game in the Polo Grounds and one in Philadelphia before the club returned to St. Louis for the final four games of the series. If the Browns hoped to put on a winning streak at home and claim the championship, they could not afford to fall too far behind the powerful Giants who were playing excellent baseball and enjoying effective pitching. Brooklyn was an AA franchise, Washington Park was like a home field to the Browns, and they expected to enjoy some support from the Brooklyn fans who, while they may have tired of St. Louis's domination of the league, probably disliked the Giants more.

Any hopes the Browns entertained that Chamberlain could maintain mastery over the Giants were dashed in the third inning when New York scored four runs and took a 5–0 lead. As about three thousand fans sat in gloomy rainy weather in Washington Park, Cannonball Crane dominated the Browns with his blazing fastball. A *New York Times* reporter wrote that the "rain in the morning and the drizzle in the afternoon made the grounds a quagmire, and the players tramped around in mud and water nearly to their shoe-tops." According to *Sporting Life,* the Browns "stood away from the plate as though in fear lest the ball would hit them, and the big pitcher had an easy time of it."[54] The Browns managed to score a couple of runs against Crane in the eighth inning, but it was too little too late; the score ended 6–3 in favor of the Giants.[55] After the game in Brooklyn, the Browns had fallen behind the Giants by two games and faced another contest in the Polo Grounds the next afternoon.

On Saturday, October 20, the series resumed at the Polo Grounds in what the *Daily Tribune* described as a "Dakota" breeze.[56] Cold and disagreeable weather became the norm for the series during its East Coast phase, and New York fans had their devotion to their Giants tested by the unfavorable elements. They proved equal to the challenge as nine thousand cranks turned out to see the first weekend game. Keefe and King again opposed each other, and the Giants scored a single run in the first inning and held that lead until the third when the Browns scored three runs. St. Louis added a run in the sixth inning, and when the Giants came to bat in the eighth, St. Louis led by a score of 4–1, Silver King seemed in control of the game, and Von der Ahe probably contemplated a fine post-game dinner with his friends and sycophants. But Von der Ahe's dinner plans were ruined when disaster struck.

In the eighth inning, as the cold intensified and growing darkness threatened to end the game, Art Whitney led off with a single to left and gained second when Tim Keefe bounced a ball to shortstop Bill White who momentarily bobbled the ball, elected not to attempt a double play, and retired Keefe at first base. Mike Tiernan then singled, and Whitney scored from second base. Buck Ewing, who had already become a hero to New York fans for his work behind the plate, tripled to the deepest part of the field, and Tiernan trotted home and made the score 4–3. With precious daylight fading, the umpires briefly stopped the game for a few minutes until the cheering of the throng subsided.

When play resumed Hardy Richardson hit a ball back to pitcher Silver

King, who failed to field it cleanly. Richardson reached first base while Ewing scored from third base and tied the score at 4–4, and the Giants' fans again thundered their approval. Umpires Kelly and Gaffney ignored the tumult this time, and Roger Connor promptly tripled and drove Richardson home giving the Giants a one-run lead. John Montgomery Ward then hit a lazy fly ball into center field. When Ward had come to bat, center fielder Harry Lyons positioned himself near the fence, and when Ward lofted the ball toward him, Lyons rushed forward to make the play. Second baseman Yank Robinson looking over his shoulder dashed into center to field the ball, and the two collided knocking each other to the turf. Lyons got by far the worst in his collision with Robinson and had to be carried from the field. He did not return to the lineup for the balance of the series. After the injured Lyons was removed to the St. Louis bench and play resumed, Ward, adding insult to injury, stole second, advanced to third on a throwing error, and scored on a wild pitch. The Giants scored five runs on four hits, three St. Louis errors, one wild pitch, and one collision in the outfield, and took a 6–4 lead over St. Louis. By the time the inning was concluded, the New York fans were delirious with joy and, characteristically, taunted the Browns unmercifully.[57] Yank Robinson came to bat in the top of the ninth in a gloom made festive, in the minds of New York sportswriters, by the electric lamps twinkling in the darkness outside the Polo Grounds.[58] Kelly and Gaffney consulted on playing conditions and ended the game owing to darkness.[59]

Game five was disastrous to the St. Louis cause. The Browns now trailed the Giants by three games, Lyons was eliminated from the series because of injury, and the club's morale was low. Von der Ahe did little to inspire his team when, regarding Lyons's disastrous collision with Yank Robinson, he observed: "If it had not been for Lyons we would have won to-day's game. He will never play on my team again. I will sell him to some minor league if they want him, but I do not think he is the man for this club. I'm sorry he hurt himself, but it is his own fault and he cannot blame anyone but himself." Lyons did not return to the Browns in 1889. Von der Ahe sent him to the Giants during the winter, and Lyons played parts of three seasons in New York and one year in the minor leagues before retiring from baseball in 1894.[60]

Nothing seemed to go to the Browns' advantage. Each game they found new ways to lose. At this point a controversy emerged. Von der Ahe, who rarely governed his tongue, began muttering that "Honest John" Kelly, the NL umpire, was favoring the Giants. The decision to end game five owing to darkness was unavoidable, but Von der Ahe could not bring himself to remain silent. He had to speak out, and he created unnecessary animosities.

In addition to raising the charge of favoritism in the umpiring of the series, Von der Ahe also proved he had learned little or nothing from the

1887 games with Detroit. In 1887, rather than rest his team during the hiatus to observe the NL ban on Sunday games, Chris scheduled a contest with Brooklyn during the off day. He did the same in 1888. While the Giants rested, preparing to leave for Philadelphia to resume the series on Monday, October 22, the Browns played Brooklyn in Washington Park on a bitterly cold afternoon before seven thousand hardy spectators. A patched lineup of Browns took the field in Washington Park. First baseman Charlie Comiskey was in center field, catcher Jack Boyle at first, and amateur Joe Murphy, a baseball editor for the *St. Louis Globe-Democrat*, in the pitcher's box. Brooklyn demolished the Browns by a score of 17–1.[61] Von der Ahe shared a tidy purse with Brooklyn, but his venture did little to improve the Browns' flagging spirits as they departed for Pennsylvania.

Game six took place at the Philadelphia Baseball Grounds.[62] Although cold damp weather continued to plague the series, a crowd of dignitaries, players from both Philadelphia major league teams, many New Yorkers (two hundred fans had accompanied the Giants on the train to Philadelphia), and about thirty-five hundred local baseball fans gathered to witness the contest. Prior to the start of the game, the Giants held a brief testimonial at the Continental Hotel for actors De Wolf Hopper and Digby Bell and presented them with gold-headed canes as tokens of their esteem and appreciation for the actors' unwavering support. Hopper and Bell were certainly pleased and not a little amused by Orator Jim O'Rourke's brief remarks as he thanked the actors for their many kindnesses to the Giants. After the ceremony Bell remarked that Orator Jim had unleashed a flow of pure English that "knocked Gladstone silly."[63] Shortly after the ceremony at the hotel, the Giants and their entourage journeyed out to the ballpark to get on with the series.

Other than Ed Herr, who began the game in center field replacing the injured Harry Lyons, Comiskey fielded his usual team. Icebox Chamberlain drew the starting assignment against Smiling Mickey Welch. St. Louis got off to a good start and, after three innings, established a four-run lead over the Giants, but weariness overtook the Browns. New York scored eleven runs in the final three innings and coasted to a 12–5 victory.[64] In both games five and six, the Giants scored sixteen of their eighteen runs in the final three innings of each game. Fatigue and lack of focus certainly plagued the Browns.

Now the Giants led the series five games to one, and even though St. Louis amassed a reputation of being nearly unbeatable in Sportsman's Park, few expected the Browns to overcome such a deficit and claim the World's Championship. As the Giants and the Browns prepared to entrain for St. Louis, one New York reporter filed a story in which he observed Von der Ahe was "forced to admit that he is no longer the President of the 'der boss gelub' and that distinction now belongs to Mr. John B. Day of New

York."[65] Now, after better than a week of foul weather and intense batterings at the hands of the Giants, the Browns returned to St. Louis with only the slimmest hopes they could reverse the devastating trend they had endured in the East.

Von der Ahe created another tempest as the teams traveled to St. Louis. After the defeats suffered by the Browns, Von der Ahe had muttered darkly about the umpiring, within earshot of several newsmen while the train paused in Pittsburgh. Searching for a story, some of the reporters aboard the train traveling to St. Louis descended on Chris and pressed him on the matter. Von der Ahe allegedly declared his views. He indeed believed the umpiring partly responsible for the Browns' woes, along with the poor work of his shortstop, Bill White, who committed several crucial errors in the first six games.[66] Von der Ahe most likely had decided to rid himself of White before the 1889 season and was probably thinking aloud about the club's shortstop problem; but the allegations of uneven umpiring were far more serious, and they began immediately to haunt him. Von der Ahe's remarks, dispatched from Pittsburgh by the Associated Press, quickly raised a commotion.

When the train reached Indianapolis, reporters accompanying the teams showed John Gaffney the telegram containing the gist of Von der Ahe's remarks, and he reacted immediately. Gaffney, the AA umpire in the series, took greater offense over Von der Ahe's thoughtless remarks than did NL umpire John Kelly, whom, according to the *St. Louis Post-Dispatch*, Von der Ahe accused of betting on the Giants. After reading the contents of the telegram the reporters supplied him, Gaffney stated:

> I am the Association umpire, and in these games I have been umpiring as its representative. I have tried to do all I could to be honest and just and right, and I have not given New York the best of the close decisions. I simply deny it. I appeal to the pitchers and catcher of the St. Louis club for expressions of opinion of the matter, and I'm willing to stand or fall by what they say. I am not a man that can be bought, and I am not a man that will permit his prejudices to run away with him. I have done my duty, and I am sorry that Mr. Von der Ahe has spoken as he has.[67]

Shortly after he issued his terse but dignified statement, John Gaffney resigned as umpire for the series. John Kelly announced he would support Gaffney in the controversy, and so, when the special train carrying the Giants and the Browns arrived in St. Louis, the series apparently had lost its umpiring corps.

Von der Ahe quickly moved to squelch the tempest he had created. When the train arrived in St. Louis, he assembled reporters in the depot and declared that he had been misquoted. Shortly thereafter, Chris, John

Day, Jim Mutrie, George Munson, Gaffney, and Kelly attended a meeting in the Lindell Hotel where Von der Ahe again repudiated the allegations carried in the Associated Press release. Gaffney and Kelly, though probably suspicious, declared themselves satisfied with Von der Ahe's explanation and announced they would continue as umpires in the series.[68] Joe Pritchard, reporting for *Sporting Life,* later wrote that after the meeting he was standing in the lobby of the Lindell Hotel talking to Mutrie and Kelly when Art Whitney, the Giants' third baseman, joined them and stated that he had overheard Von der Ahe's remarks in Pittsburgh and that Chris had not been misquoted.[69] Whitney said no more, and Pritchard certainly implied that he, Mutrie, and the others were disposed to believe Whitney. A potentially embarrassing crisis was averted, but nevertheless, Von der Ahe's unfortunate propensity to speak without considering the consequences managed to place a blemish on the series.

Warmer weather greeted the series in St. Louis. Enough so that the spectators who had witnessed the games on the East Coast discarded their overcoats and enjoyed crisp but comfortable autumn weather in Sportsman's Park. As usual, estimates of the crowd varied; reports of attendance fluctuated between four and six thousand.[70] Whatever the size of the gathering, the St. Louis fans were enthusiastic, and they were rewarded with a Browns' victory. Ed Crane started for the Giants against Silver King. New York scored three runs off King in the second inning, but the Browns tallied four in the third and added three more runs in the fourth, while King protected the lead and defeated the Giants 7–5 in an eight-inning game shortened by darkness. Timely hitting and daring base-running made the difference for St. Louis. According to *Sporting Life,* the Browns "showed their old-time skill in base-running, and to their success in taking every chance while on the bases is largely due their victory."[71] Although the sentence relating the Browns' revival was truly awkward, the writer made his point. The Browns stole seven bases and took several extra bases while running out hits. In addition to losing the game, the Giants sustained several injuries in the contest. First baseman Roger Connor severely wrenched his leg in the seventh inning, so badly that he did not return to his position during the remainder of the series. The worst incident involved Willard Brown who was catching for the Giants in Buck Ewing's place. In the eighth inning Brown took a foul tip on his right thumb off Comiskey's bat. Crane, the pitcher, rushed to home plate to attend to his teammate, and, thinking the thumb was only dislocated, attempted to pull it into position. Crane was covered with a gush of blood for his effort and quickly realized that the thumb was shattered. A physician soon arrived on the field and took Brown to the sideline where he administered first aid prior to taking him to a hospital for treatment. According to one account, "blood flowed so freely that even the players turned away to shut out the painful sight."[72] After the day's work St. Louis garnered only its second win in the series; the Giants led the World Championship series five games to two. As the jubilant St. Louis fans exited Sportsman's Park, the more realistically minded among them fully understood that the Browns were merely delaying the inevitable. Keefe awaited them tomorrow, and the Browns had done little against his pitching. Even if St. Louis managed to beat him tomorrow, Keefe would have at least one more start against the Browns before the series could be tied. As nice as the victory was, knowledgeable fans understood their heroes were probably past redemption.

Game eight decided the championship. Icebox Chamberlain faced Tim Keefe, who so far had won three games against the Browns, and behind Keefe's steady pitching the Giants coasted to an easy victory. Buck Ewing hit a solo home run for the Giants in the first inning and drove home three more with a triple in the third as New York won by a score of 11–3. Pleasant weather lured nearly five thousand fans to the game, but many Browns' partisans must have had a premonition that the Giants would not be denied in game eight. That evening's *Post-Dispatch* probably mirrored their mood when it ran an account of the game under the heading "The Pennant Lost," in which the paper concluded: "The Giants have outfielded them, outbatted them, have stolen more bases, out-thrown them, outrun them, and, all in all have played a better game of ball. Many claim that it was luck but, in the philosophy of baseball, luck seems to be always with the best club and to have a terrible effect on averages."[73] Tim Keefe, Buck Ewing, and the remainder of the New York roster proved too much for the Browns to overcome. New York decisively won the championship. One New York newspaper reported, "St. Louis is gloomy tonight, but it is not entirely due to the muggy mist which hangs over the town."[74]

Even though two games remained in the series, three of the Giants left St. Louis once the championship was settled on October 25. John Montgomery Ward and Ed Crane departed for Colorado where they joined a team of all stars recruited by Spalding to face his Chicago White Stockings in a series of exhibition games in the United States, the Sandwich Islands, New Zealand, and Australia. Roger Connor, whose leg injury rendered him unfit for duty, returned to New York City the next day to tend to personal business.[75] Umpire John Kelly returned to New York City after game eight and left John Gaffney to umpire the final two now-meaningless games alone. Other Giants stars, among them Keefe and Ewing, did not appear in the final games. On October 26, the New York "Colts," as one newspaper labeled the Giants, lost a poorly played game to the Browns by a score of 14–11 in ten innings before less than a thousand spectators, and the next afternoon, the Browns again defeated the Colts 18–7 before less than five hundred paid admissions.[76] In the final two games of the series, the teams scored a total of fifty runs, made fifty-nine hits, and committed nineteen errors, putting a lackluster ending to the 1888 World's Championship series.

After the game on Saturday, October 27, Von der Ahe, in a magnanimous gesture, presented the Giants with the World's Championship flag, which had floated from the flagpole in Sportsman's Park. The pennant commemorated the Browns' victory over the Chicago White Stockings in 1886, and *Sporting Life,* which enjoyed tweaking Von der Ahe, wrote, "What old championship flag? The Browns have had no genuine pennant to float since 1887, in the fall of which Detroit knocked them completely out."[77] Nevertheless, it must have been difficult for Von der Ahe to surrender his treasured, if outdated, flag to the Giants. Later that evening, in a special ceremony at the Grand Opera House in St. Louis, the Giants were formally presented with the Dauvray Cup and the newly minted Hall Cup as symbols of their status as world's champions.[78] After a performance of "Lend Me Five Shillings" starring Nat Goodwin, the curtain came down and, then after a few minutes pause, rose again displaying a stage decorated with flowers and a banner proclaiming "The World's Champions." A table bearing the Dauvray and Hall cups was wheeled onstage, and then the Giants led by Jim Mutrie filed to the stage where John W. Norton, the manager of the Opera House, made a short speech and officially presented the trophies. Mutrie graciously accepted the trophies for New York, thanked Miss Dauvray and Mr. Hall, thanked St. Louisans for their hospitality, and commended the Browns for their play and their manly acceptance of defeat at the hands of his club. He also announced that the Giants were officially disbanded.[79] The Browns probably took little comfort in Mutrie's considerate remarks; they had lost the World's Championship a second consecutive year, and Comiskey and his players found little solace in Mutrie's sportsmanship.

The next afternoon the remnants of the Giants played an exhibition game against the Browns in St. Louis. Since Mutrie had disbanded the Giants, they and the already disbanded Browns were free agents. Since they were no longer under any obligations to their owners, the players scheduled the game to earn some pocket money from ticket sales. Tim Keefe pitched for the Giants, and Silver King, who had faced Keefe three times in the recent series and lost all three, started for the Browns. About twenty-five hundred spectators turned out to see the exhibition game in which the Browns defeated Keefe and the Giants 6–0.[80] As the players gathered to divide the gate receipts, many of the departing St. Louis fans must have puzzled over how, now that the World's Championship was lost, the Browns played an errorless game, hit Keefe freely, and ran the bases with abandon. New York fans believed they had the answer, in that the Giants took the field without Roger Connor, John Montgomery Ward, Buck Ewing, and Art Whitney. Whatever the rationalizations may have been, the Giants, such as their depleted roster allowed, and the Browns finished their encounter with an exhibition game that attracted about twice as many spectators as the combined attendance of the last two games of the series.

Estimates of the income from the World's Championship varied, but the evidence suggested that gross receipts amounted to about twenty-five thousand dollars, and that expenses for both teams amounted to approximately seven thousand dollars. Von der Ahe and Day did not issue public statements declaring the financial matters concerning the series, and they did not inform the public on how they split the proceeds. Early in the negotiations to establish the playoff, the press speculated that the winner would take 60 percent of the profits and the loser the remainder, but once the series was completed, *Sporting Life* reported it was "quite probable, however, that the receipts were divided equally."[81] If the figures reported in the press were anywhere near accurate, Day and Von der Ahe each pocketed about nine thousand dollars after they deducted expenses. If the Giants took 60 percent, Day garnered nearly twelve thousand dollars and Von der Ahe settled for little less than seven thousand. In either case, each man made a tidy profit. Day awarded each of the Giants two hundred dollars for their efforts in the series, but Von der Ahe refused to reward his players out of his share of the receipts. In response to a query as to whether his players received compensation for their work in the series, Chris declared:

> There is no contract whereby I promised to pay my men $200 whether they won or lost the world's series. The whole thing is that I promised them that if they played good ball in the series, no matter how the result of it would be, I would give them $200. This do I not only say they didn't do, but anyone who witnessed the games and knows what they can do will also be of the same opinion.[82]

Von der Ahe did relent a little and agreed to award the $1,250 the AA set aside for the pennant winner. Many of the Browns suspected originally that Von der Ahe meant to keep that money as well, but he really had no legal claim to it, and so the Browns divided the sum between them, which came to about one hundred dollars per player. So far as the players were concerned, Giants and Browns alike, the rewards for participating in the 1888 World's Championship were meager. So far as Von der Ahe and Day were concerned, the returns were satisfying.

The Browns' glory days ended with the 1888 World's Championship. In 1889 they finished second in the American Association pennant race, slipped to third in 1890, and in 1891, the last year of the AA's existence, returned to second place in the final standings. In 1892, after the demise of the AA, St. Louis joined the National League and failed to compete successfully in the League. They finished eleventh in a twelve-team league.

Throughout the 1890s the Browns remained each season in the lower half of the NL standings. The Giants, on the other hand, repeated as NL champions in 1889 and won a second World's Championship. One champion faded while another flared into national prominence led by stalwarts such as Buck Ewing, John Montgomery Ward, Tim Keefe, and other stars in the Giants' roster.

CHAPTER SEVEN

New York and Brooklyn

The Year 1889

As the 1888 championship season closed in St. Louis, baseball fans contemplated the off-season drought they dreaded. Newspapers seem barren without box scores of games; no pennant races to watch unfolding, no day-to-day pleasure in watching the virtuous triumph and the unscrupulous defeated. During the off-season, newspapers supplied baseball-hungry readers the usual information concerning players, their salaries, the owners' ongoing problems regarding franchises and personnel, and the normal gamut of sports gossip, but such fare pales to insignificance when compared to the excitement of the regular season. Winter is a dreary time for baseball fans. During the winter of 1888–1889, however, baseball fans were treated to a series of unusual developments that provided them interesting off-season news to tide them over to spring. Two issues, in particular, captured the ongoing interest of dedicated baseball fans as the nation installed Benjamin Harrison in the presidency in 1889.

First of all, A. G. Spalding made the news when he organized an exhibition tour to feature his Chicago White Stockings and a hand-picked team of major league players named the All Americas. Amid great fanfare, Spalding, the White Stockings, most of the All Americas, and an entourage of spouses, newspapermen, and baseball personalities departed Chicago on October 20, 1888, and launched Spalding's "Australian Tour."[1] Spalding planned to lead the teams from Chicago to California and play a series of games prior to departing for New Zealand and Australia. Games in the United States, in part, were designed to promote baseball, but exhibition appearances in Wisconsin, Minnesota, Nebraska, Colorado, Utah, and California were expected to produce revenue vital to the tour's financial solvency. In Colorado, for example, the baseball tourists played two games in Denver and one in Colorado Springs before large and enthusiastic crowds. An estimated 10,200 fans attended the games in Colorado, and Spalding pocketed an estimated eleven thousand dollars from the three engagements.[2] The purpose of the "Australian Tour" was to promote interest in major league baseball in parts of the United States where it was

Albert Spalding's Chicago White Stockings and the All Americas
posing for a photograph during their World Tour, 1888–1889.
(Courtesy of Jay Sanford, Arvada, Colo.)

unavailable during the regular season, and to interest foreigners in America's game. Spalding genuinely intended to proselytize the game, but he, the owner of a flourishing sporting goods business, also expected to boost sales of baseball paraphernalia.[3]

After reaching Australia by way of the Sandwich Islands and New Zealand, Spalding converted his "Australian Tour" into a "World Tour," and the traveling baseball show crossed the Indian Ocean, played games in Ceylon, India, passed through the Suez Canal, and sojourned in Egypt where the teams visited the pyramids and the Sphinx. After a pleasant visit in Egypt, the tour traveled to western Europe. Spalding's entourage arrived in Europe in the middle of winter and played a few games before small, largely indifferent gatherings of polite onlookers before setting out for the return trip to the United States. On April 6, 1889, they arrived in New York City where Spalding and his teams received a tumultuous welcome. After triumphal parades and appearances in the city, the intrepid world travelers were feted to a sumptuous banquet at Delmonico's famous restaurant. The gala event at Delmonico's attracted many of the city's personalities and politicians plus other notables such as Theodore Roosevelt and Mark Twain.[4]

Spalding's baseball tourists visiting the Sphinx during their World Tour.
(Courtesy of Jay Sanford, Arvada, Colo.)

Once the festivities were concluded in New York City, the Spalding group visited other major American cities as it made its way to Chicago, where another joyous welcome awaited. Not to be outdone by New York City, Chicagoans staged a huge welcome when the tour arrived in Chicago. One hundred thirty organizations, ranging from boating clubs to local baseball clubs, gymnastics groups, and bicycling associations, acted as an escort from the depot to the Palmer House where a lavish banquet was held in honor of the Chicago White Stockings and the All Americas. The honored guests were saluted by ubiquitous politicians, whose speeches commended the gallant world travelers. Local civic leaders likewise praised Spalding and his fellow travelers, and according to one account, "The menu was one that would satisfy the most exacting epicure."[5]

Soon after the tour terminated in Chicago, the White Stockings began their NL season, and the All Americas scattered to rejoin their clubs. Baseball-minded Americans followed the tour's progress around the world with keen interest and partially avoided the off-season doldrums by enjoying accounts of baseball in Colorado or Egypt or other exotic climes. Reports of players trying to throw baseballs over the Sphinx amused their fans at home. Reporters' accounts of various nationalities' reactions to the American national game provided fascinating reading for baseball fans counting the days until baseball season began again, and ethnocentric fans quietly rejoiced over the effort to spread the gospel of baseball among heretofore disadvantaged foreigners. However slight the actual effect Spalding's tour may have had on raising worldwide recognition of baseball as a manly sport, the globe-circling excursion certainly provided excellent off-season diversion to baseball-hungry fans and readers in the United States.

In addition to the "World's Tour" and its attending fanfare, another issue caught baseball fans' attention during the winter of 1888–1889. When the major league owners held their annual meetings after the end of the 1888 season, in addition to transacting the usual business they also agreed to place a salary classification program in effect for 1889. John T. Brush, the owner of the NL's Indianapolis franchise, drafted the bulk of the Salary Classification Plan adopted by the National League in late November 1888. Brush's plan announced the owners' intentions to limit players' salaries.[6] Tensions between players and owners mounted during the 1888 season as there approached a monumental collision between labor and management. The Brotherhood of Professional Base Ball Players intended to challenge the owners' reserve rule, which bound players to their teams, and astute readers of baseball's affairs realized that the acceptance of Brush's plan to control salaries hastened the looming crisis.

Brush, who became the arch villain to the Brotherhood of Professional Base Ball Players, was an interesting figure. He became the owner of the Indianapolis Hoosiers in 1887 and quickly learned hard economic lessons attempting to earn a profit from an inferior team in a relatively small city.[7] In 1888 the Hoosiers languished in or near the basement of the NL standings, and Brush struggled to keep his franchise fiscally viable. At one point in the 1888 season, he toyed with the idea of introducing night baseball in Indianapolis. On the evening of August 21, 1888, two gaslights were erected in center field in Tinker Park, and several of the Hoosiers tested the artificial light to determine if they could see the ball in flight. According to an account in *Sporting Life,* the lights were

> located along the centre field fence about thirty yards apart, being between thirty and forty feet high, have a cross-bar at the top like that on a telegraph pole and about the same length. The cross-piece had burners on the upper side, about six inches apart, and when the gas was turned on it makes a solid flame, say about four feet long. The two burners alone made the park perfectly light, and the ball could be seen as well as daytime. The light is perfectly steady and free from shadows. The gas company is at work fixing things and the other lights will be put up to morrow [sic] or next day. It is the intention to put up sixteen, and if two furnished enough light to play ball by it can easily be imagined what sixteen will do.[8]

Brush viewed night baseball as an expedient to pump financial relief into his franchise, but as events developed, his plan failed. Subsequent experimentation with gaslights to illuminate the Hoosiers' diamond proved the concept ineffective, a waste of time and finances. *Sporting Life* later reported that the experiment was repeated on September 6 and that it "promises to be a failure."[9] Indianapolis did not pioneer the first night game in major league history. The Cincinnati Reds earned that distinction almost a half-century later, when their club installed powerful electric lights in Crosley Field in 1935 and inaugurated night baseball against the Philadelphia Phillies five years after many of the minor leagues had turned to night games to attract patrons. Brush was ahead of his time when he considered the utility of artificial lighting for baseball. But in matters concerning the economics of baseball, he was fully attuned to his peers—he believed, or at least publicly declared, that salaries had escalated to a level that responsible management could not afford.

Alarmed by his desperate struggle to save his Indianapolis franchise, Brush spearheaded the movement to control what he and other owners viewed as dangerously mounting costs. The easiest target was players' salaries. Brush's plan was a curious mixture. It called for players to be graded on their statistics, ability, attitude, personal habits, and temperance. Newspaper writers, owners, and other moralists frequently lamented the libertarian lifestyle flaunted by some ballplayers, and the Brush system opened an avenue of retaliation against men such as King Kelly and others who enjoyed the robust nightlife. In essence, however, the classification program was established to control salaries.[10] Other than allowing extra compensation for a player who assumed a manager's duties or one who functioned as team captain, the salary classification plan set forth five ironclad categories: Class A had the salary of $2,500; B had $2,250; C had $2,000; D had $1,750; E had $1,500. Estimates varied as to how many major leaguers earned salaries in excess of $2,500, but only about twenty to thirty players exceeded that level. NL owners wished to avoid direct and immediately destructive conflict with their stars and club mainstays, so they inserted a clause into the Brush plan that permitted negotiations for players already earning more than $2,500.[11] Players who exceeded the maximum salary had until December 15, 1888, to bargain with their owners and legally maintain their salaries above the $2,500 ceiling. The owners did not actually attempt to lower salaries of the highly paid stars, but they certainly took a decisive step toward limiting salaries for the rising young players.

Thirteen days after the National League announced its classification program, the American Association held its annual meeting in St. Louis's Lindell Hotel. The leaders of the AA shared nearly all the concerns of their counterparts in the NL, and their decision regarding the salary limitations was a foregone conclusion. The AA endorsed and adopted the salary classification system.[12] Baseball fans everywhere realized that the owners had drawn a line in the sand, and that they challenged the players to respond. Wintertime baseball news in 1888–1889 was exciting. Rumors of a strike abounded, some speculated that the players might form their own league, some suggested that ambitious entrepreneurs backed by ample funds were preparing to cooperate with the players. The baseball cartel staggered toward a confrontation between management and labor. Fans anticipated an eventful season in 1889.

When the defending world's champions, the New York Giants, opened the 1889 season, the team was nearly an exact replica of the 1888 club. All the position players returned to the club; the only change in the team's appearance was the emergence of Cannonball Crane as one of the Giants' pitching stalwarts. During the 1888 season, Tim Keefe and Mickey Welch had carried the brunt of the Giants' pitching duties. They had won a combined sixty-one games, and Ledell Titcomb, serving as the third starting pitcher, won an additional fourteen games. In 1889 Crane replaced Titcomb as the third pitcher in the rotation and won fourteen for the Giants while Titcomb's career waned as a major leaguer.[13] The Giants also acquired Hank O'Day from the Washington Statesmen during the 1889 season. O'Day had been laboring with the woeful Washington club since 1886. He was a fine pitcher whose record belied his talent. In three and one-half seasons he recorded only twenty-eight wins against sixty-one losses, but astute observers realized he was a far better pitcher than his record indicated. When he joined the Giants, O'Day was starting off the season with his usual poor record. He had won only two games. After joining the Giants and finding he enjoyed better support, he won nine out of ten games and materially contributed to New York's late season pennant drive.[14] Since Welch and Keefe again led the Giants' pitching staff and won a combined fifty-five games, the Giants to most baseball fans looked an identical team. Ewing, Ward, O'Rourke, Richardson, Whitney, and the other Giants' mainstays replicated their triumphs of 1888, and New York fans took a good deal of comfort in the experience and talent fielded by their club in 1889.

This does not mean that John B. Day had no worries getting his World's Championship team ready to defend its title, however. First of all, he lost the use of the Polo Grounds as the Giants' home ballpark. The Polo Grounds, located at 110th Street and Fifth Avenue, had been home to the Giants since 1883, but after the close of the 1888 season, real estate interests in New York City lobbied the city's board of aldermen to extend 111th Street from Fifth Avenue to Sixth Avenue, which would mean bisecting the Polo Grounds. Day fought the attempt to eliminate his ballpark. After a protracted political battle that reached the state capital in Albany he lost the struggle, and the Giants faced the 1889 season without a home.

When the season opened, Day, still scrambling to find real estate upon which to build a field, scheduled the Giants' home opening game in Oakland Park in Jersey City, New Jersey, and then used Erastus Wiman's St. George Park on Staten Island for the Giants' next twenty-five home games.[15] Although Giants' fans were required to take the ferry across the bay to reach the ballpark, it was a fairly easy commute. Among other things, the trip across the bay featured a glorious view of the Statue of Liberty, which President Grover Cleveland had dedicated on October 28, 1886. Even so, Day never seriously considered establishing his club's new home off Manhattan Island. He finally found suitable real estate for a new Polo Grounds on 155th Street, in the shadow of Coogan's Bluff overlooking the Harlem River, and immediately began construction. Contracts on the land were signed on June 22, and workmen immediately began raising the stands, building concession booths, and grading and sodding the field. Since ballparks in the 1880s were of wooden construction and were not overly large by modern standards, the work went quickly.[16] After he finally acquired the land, Day created a new ballpark, the third edition of the Polo Grounds, in only three weeks. His Giants inaugurated the park on July 8, 1889, when they played Pittsburgh before a capacity crowd.[17]

Day faced two other problems prior to the beginning of the 1889 season. One involved a salary dispute with Tim Keefe, who posed a special problem. The backbone of the Giants' pitching staff, Keefe won an astonishing

144 games for the Giants between 1885 and 1888, while losing only 64 for a .692 winning percentage. No one could deny his value to the Giants, but he was asking for more money at a time when owners were attempting to tighten salaries. Day and Keefe finally deadlocked, and the Giants began the season without Keefe on their roster. Some of the rancor between Day and Keefe may have been intensified because Keefe—who became John Montgomery Ward's brother-in-law later that summer when he married Helen Dauvray's sister Clara Helms—served as the secretary of the Brotherhood of Professional Base Ball Players.[18] Keefe's association with the players' organization certainly complicated the salary negotiations. The deadlock was finally broken, and Keefe, having got most of what he wanted, returned to the Giants in early May.[19]

Day also became involved in an ugly dispute with John Montgomery Ward. Ward's prominent role in the players' organization made him unpopular with NL owners, and Day realized that Ward's convenient location in New York City abetted the shortstop's efforts to organize his colleagues. In the years leading up to the crisis between players and owners, Ward took an active role as a spokesman for his peers in the major leagues. He wrote two influential articles depicting the dilemma faced by his colleagues and assailed the reserve clause, which bound players to their clubs. He condemned many of the owners' practices, which he saw as attempts to create and maintain a monopoly at the expense of labor.[20]

Although he was the spokesman for the Brotherhood, Ward managed to make himself unpopular with some of the Giants as well. Buck Ewing was also active in the players' association, but he clashed with Ward, who many claimed was aloof to his teammates, lived a lifestyle some of them resented, and antagonized some of the Giants by his manner and bearing. Tensions among the Giants surfaced in the summer of 1887, when Ward either resigned or was dismissed as team captain on July 12.[21]

Buck Ewing, the Giants' sturdy catcher, replaced Ward as team captain, and while the players presented an outward calm, internal affairs among the Giants were often cool. According to baseball gossip, Ewing, O'Rourke, and Keefe, even though he was courting Ward's sister-in-law, rarely spoke to Ward. After the championship season of 1888, Ward reputedly asked to be sold to Boston, and throughout the winter rumors abounded that Day would comply with Ward's request. News stories began to appear that Ward would be sold to either Boston or Washington.[22] Day ruled out a sale to Boston after the Beaneaters acquired Dan Brouthers, Hardy Richardson, Charlie Bennett, and Charlie Ganzel from the recently disbanded Detroit Wolverines. If the reinforced Beaneaters also acquired Ward, Day believed, the Boston club might prove too formidable for his Giants, so he began to negotiate with the Washington Statesmen. Rumors had it that Day asked twelve thousand dollars for Ward. The Washington club, apparently willing to meet Day's price, wanted Ward for his talents as a player, and the Statesmen, it was believed, would name him manager as well. In an effort to make the possible transaction with Washington palatable to Ward, Day stipulated that Ward would receive five thousand dollars of the sale price and a thousand dollar bonus if the Boston team won the 1889 pennant.[23] Washington was a hopelessly inept team, but its ownership seemed convinced that Ward's abilities could inspire the club to greater heights. Ward was only partly aware of all the machinations in New York as he traveled around the world, but his worries over his status with the Giants, the emergence of the Brush salary plan, and his stormy marriage to Helen Dauvray, from whom he eventually was divorced, prompted him to take leave of Spalding's World Tour when it reached Europe and to return to New York City earlier than originally planned. Once he was home, Ward met with Day and informed the owner he would not report to the Washington Statesmen. So, as opening day drew near, Day faced the possibility of beginning the season without Keefe, without Ward or a suitable replacement at shortstop, and without a permanent site for his Giants to play their home games. It was a turbulent winter for John Day.

In 1889 Charles H. Byrne's Brooklyn club—often referred to as the Trolley Dodgers, because the city was laced with trolley tracks, or as the Bridegrooms, because several Brooklyn players married while they were members of the team's roster—ended the St. Louis Browns' four-year domination of the American Association. Von der Ahe's Browns gave a good account of themselves in 1889, but Brooklyn won the pennant by a narrow two-game margin. Byrne became one of the more influential baseball executives during his tenure as president of the Brooklyn club. One historian correctly assessed Byrne; he was a man "compared by his friends to Napoleon and by his enemies to Satan."[24]

An aggressive and innovative businessman, Byrne quickly earned a leadership role among the moguls of major league baseball. Born in New York City in 1843, and educated at St. Francis Xavier College in New York, he pursued a varied career as a journalist, a railroad official, and a deputy sheriff for a time in Omaha, Nebraska, before he settled in New York City and launched a career that finally led him into major league baseball. After returning to New York City, Byrne formed a partnership with his brother-in-law, Joseph Doyle, who ran a gambling casino on Ann Street, and the two began to dabble in baseball. When funds ran short Doyle brought his casino partner, Ferdinand Abell, into the enterprise, and the troika of two gamblers and an innovative businessman proceeded to fulfill Byrne's ambitions.

In early January 1883 Byrne began to acquire players for his team and sought entry to the American Association. He located a piece of land for a ballpark on the site where General George Washington temporarily located his headquarters during the Battle of Long Island, at the outset of the Revolutionary War, and began construction of Washington Park as a home diamond for his team.[25] After he failed to gain entry to the AA, Byrne placed his team in the Interstate Association, a minor league. By late June 1883 the Brooklyn team was in fourth place, trailing the league-leading Merritt Club of Camden, New Jersey, by five and one-half games, and when the Merritt team disbanded on July 21, 1883, Byrne promptly purchased the contracts of several of Merritt's better players.[26]

The new players revitalized Byrne's club, and only one month later, his team had climbed into second place, only three games behind Harrisburg, Pennsylvania. By September 15, 1883, Brooklyn moved into first place by a narrow one-game margin over Harrisburg, clung to the lead, and finally won the Interstate Association's title. After finishing the regular season, Byrne's team played a final game at Washington Park against an all-star team representing the Long Island Amateur Association on October 5, 1883, before he disbanded the club for the winter.[27]

Always aware of the need for good public relations, Byrne's team handily defeated the amateurs while he turned a small profit from the affair, furthered his team's popularity with local ticket buyers, and kept a sharp eye out for talented players. All in all, his first year in baseball proved successful. One of the aspects of his franchise that was noticed by AA owners was that, when the New York Metropolitans crossed over to Brooklyn on May 14 to play an exhibition game with Byrne's new team, an estimated three thousand fans attended the contest even though the day was rainy and cool.[28] The AA leadership also recognized that Byrne's team played good baseball, and perhaps more important, that it was located in an area where the Association wished to place a franchise. These aspects, combined with Byrne's apparent agreement with the AA's marketing techniques, persuaded the leaders of the AA to admit Brooklyn to their association in 1884. In only one year, Byrne built a championship team and gained a major league franchise, each a fairly impressive accomplishment.

When Byrne's team entered the AA in 1884, it was not well prepared to compete at the major league level, however. Brooklyn's maiden AA season was the same year as the UA rose to challenge the existing major leagues—and as the UA furiously competed to sign players and as the AA expanded its number of franchises, expansion teams found only a small pool of marginal talent to stock their clubs. Byrne carried five of his Interstate Association players on his Brooklyn roster in 1884 and hurriedly signed additional players to his club. Among the five men who played on Byrne's minor league team in 1883, only William H. "Adonis" Terry, a right-handed pitcher, proved durable enough to survive the season and remain in the major leagues.[29] As a consequence, Brooklyn began its major league odyssey with only a handful of talented minor leaguers, and one talented pitcher; it is not surprising that the team did poorly in the 1884 pennant race.

Brooklyn finished ninth in the AA in 1884 with a record of forty wins and sixty-four losses, and over the next three years the Bridegrooms had only one winning season, in 1886, when they won seventy-six and lost sixty-one.[30] Byrne's club suffered through four seasons compiling a composite record of 229 wins against 258 losses for a .470 winning percentage. Brooklyn's fans, however, remained faithful to their team, and in 1887 Byrne dramatically reversed his club's fortunes. By 1887 Byrne had acquired third baseman George Pinkney and shortstop George J. "Germany" Smith to bolster his sometimes hapless club. And in 1888 his new players converted the Brooklyn club into a pennant contender. Pitchers Bob Caruthers and Dave Foutz along with catcher Doc Bushong were purchased from the St. Louis Browns; first baseman David Orr was acquired from New York in the AA; second baseman Hubert "Hub" Collins was obtained from Louisville late in the season; and outfielders Darby O'Brien, Thomas P. "Oyster" Burns, and John Stewart "Pop" Corkhill joined the Bridegrooms. Coupled with the existing nucleus of quality players on the Brooklyn roster, the new players energized the Bridegrooms, and in 1888 the club finished second with a record of eighty-eight wins and fifty-two losses.[31] Although Brooklyn finished six and one-half games behind the St. Louis Browns in 1888, the club's dramatic progress was not considered happenstance; Brooklyn became a good team that season, and baseball experts everywhere expected it would sorely challenge St. Louis in 1889.

Brooklyn opened the 1889 season with a roster nearly identical to that of the previous year. During the off-season, Byrne acquired Thomas Joseph Lovett, a pitcher, from Omaha in the Western Association where he had won thirty games while pitching 392 innings and compiling a 1.56 earned run average.[32] Lovett joined Caruthers and Adonis Terry on Brooklyn's pitching staff in 1889, and they accounted for seventy-nine of the club's ninety-three victories that season.[33] As is often the case with a championship team, the road to the pennant was not a smooth one.

Before the start of their seasons in the National League and the American Association, the Giants and the Bridegrooms played three preseason exhibition games in Washington Park in Brooklyn on April 6, 11, and 13, 1889. Day and Byrne saw the games as a means to earn some useful revenue while promoting interest in baseball in the metropolitan area, but somewhere in the back of each man's mind, they may also have seen the games as a precursor to the autumn championship series as well. The Giants won two of the three games in what proved to be an omen.[34] The games were well played and attracted good crowds of enthusiastic fans. The first game of the series, played on April 6, was particularly interesting. A good crowd of about ten thousand filed into Washington Park expecting to see a thrilling match between New York and Brooklyn, and to the surprise of most of the people in the ballpark, Spalding's World Tour contingent appeared in the grandstand just before game time. The steamship *Adriatic* carrying the Chicago White Stockings and the All Americas had arrived in New York Harbor early on the morning of April 6 and was out of quarantine by sunrise. Word of the tourists' arrival spread quickly about the city, and a group of the players' friends and admirers chartered the steamer *Laura M. Starin* and hastened out to Governor's Island to greet their heroes.[35] As the welcome party drew near, the players aboard the *Adriatic* recognized their friends and issued a loud cheer. Soon the players and their traveling companions were transferred to the *Laura M. Starin* and whisked to lower Manhattan to the Fifth Avenue Hotel where the celebration of the returning baseball show began.[36]

Greeted everywhere by adoring fans in New York City, the Spalding tourists then journeyed to Long Island in the afternoon to attend the Giants-Bridegrooms exhibition game, and when they appeared in Washington Park, they were roundly cheered by the assembled crowd. Byrne was delighted to see them, seated them in a special section of the crowded grandstand, and was chagrined when Ed "Cannonball" Crane, one of the returning heroes, promptly went down to the field and prepared to pitch for the Giants. Crane, although he was characteristically a little wild, pitched a one-hitter and led the Giants to an 11–3 victory over the Bridegrooms.[37] The afternoon, even from Byrne's perspective, was a success. The crowd obviously enjoyed the celebrities' presence in the park, and although Crane defeated Brooklyn, the fans relished the special occasion. Byrne and Day shared a nice profit from the day's proceedings, and one loss was not fatal to Brooklyn's hopes to win the series from the Giants. Everyone was in a buoyant mood that afternoon.

When the Bridegrooms finally began the regular season later in April, the club got off to a poor beginning by losing six of its first seven games. The St. Louis Browns, as usual divided by internal dissent and by salary quarrels with Von der Ahe, played well and by early May led the AA as they sought their fifth consecutive pennant. Brooklyn, owing to the club's poor start was mired in fifth place, five and one-half games behind St. Louis.[38] Caruthers was not pitching well, the team was not hitting well, and the infield seemed particularly porous. Byrne probably thought not much else could go wrong, but he would have been mistaken. On May 19, 1889, Washington Park was badly damaged by fire.[39] Now, not only was Byrne's team floundering, it was also homeless. Fortunately, the Bridegrooms were scheduled for an extended road trip in late May, and Byrne immediately went to work to replace his ballpark. He hired a contractor named D. E. Harris and began clearing the rubble from the site of old Washington Park.[40] Byrne was not a man to be easily daunted, and he announced that the new Washington Park would be in place when the Bridegrooms returned to Brooklyn for a crucial series with St. Louis on Decoration Day. Harris's construction crews, weather permitting, did not actually

The 1889 Brooklyn Bridegrooms posing along the left field foul line in their home ball park.

(Courtesy of Jay Sanford, Arvada, Colo.)

face an impossible task. The field, most of the outfield fences, and adjacent structures were unaffected by the fire, and Harris had only to replace the grandstand and the bleachers. Since the ballparks in the late nineteenth century were made of wood, the job was largely one of carrying off the ashes of the earlier structure and then unleashing an army of carpenters to erect new seating.

By Decoration Day, when the St. Louis Browns arrived in Brooklyn to play a four-game set, Brooklyn's record had improved, and the Bridegrooms were in second place trailing the Browns by only four games. Brooklynites experienced a memorable Decoration Day in 1889. In addition to the base-ball fever that gripped fans in the city, President Benjamin Harrison made an official visit to Brooklyn to celebrate Decoration Day. He spent the night at the home of Joseph F. Knapp prior to reviewing the Decoration Day parade of Civil War veterans. Thousands of residents lined the streets to view the fifteen thousand veterans, militia, musicians, and politicians who marched in the parade in honor of the men who fell in America's wars.[41]

Meanwhile, as the pageant inspired patriotic fervor among the parade's participants and onlookers, the Bridegrooms and the Browns prepared to play. A restored Washington Park greeted the Browns as they split a morning and afternoon doubleheader with the Bridegrooms before nearly nine thousand fans in the morning contest and twenty-two thousand in the afternoon.[42] Byrne and Von der Ahe shared impressive gate receipts from the doubleheader, and though the Browns proceeded to win the series from Brooklyn, Byrne was heartened by his club's play on the field, and by the fact that his restored ballpark attracted so many paying customers. The Bridegrooms continued to trail St. Louis through much of the remainder of the summer.

When Brooklyn invaded Sportsman's Park in St. Louis for a three-game series in early July the Browns held a three-game lead over Brooklyn, but now the Bridegrooms began their march to the pennant. On July 3, Bob Caruthers, once the stalwart of the Browns' pitching staff, defeated St. Louis 7–4, and the next day, the clubs split a morning and afternoon doubleheader.[43] Up to this point the Browns had been nearly unbeatable at home, but the Bridegrooms handily won two of the three games. From this point forward, the Browns fell upon lean days. A series of events beginning two months earlier contributed to their slow but steady decline.

On May 2, which was a Ladies Day event, the afternoon began innocently enough. Just before the contest, manager Comiskey suggested that Yank Robinson's uniform pants were too soiled, and that he should send out for a cleaner pair. Robinson agreed and dispatched a boy to his room across the street from the park to fetch clean trousers, but when the errand boy returned to the gate the attendant denied him entrance. According to *Sporting Life,*

> When the boy returned with the trousers on his arm Mr. Niehaus refused to admit him, remarking that he could not get in even if he had the pants on his legs as he had strict orders to let no one pass the gate without a ticket. To say that the second baseman of the Browns was angry and indignant when he learned of the action of Mr. Niehaus is a mild, genteel way of putting it. He was frothing at the mouth. Niehaus received a call from the ball player, and for a while listened to language that made his gray hair stand on ends. Robinson made no attempt to restrain or to protect the old man's feelings. When he finished the gate-keeper had a pretty fair idea of the second baseman's state of mind.[44]

With tears in his eyes the elderly gentleman appealed to Von der Ahe. Chris was outraged and rushed to the St. Louis bench to confront Robinson while fans were gathering nearby. They exchanged heated words, Von der Ahe fined Robinson, and Yank subsequently declared that he would not accompany the team to Kansas City for an upcoming series. Von der Ahe threatened to blacklist him, and after a good deal of tension and consequent bitterness, Yank was restored to the team. It was an unfortunate incident, and though it did not immediately derail the Browns' pennant drive, the nasty argument did nothing to improve team morale.

Later in the summer a series of rumors concerning possible collusion with gamblers swirled around the Browns. The suspicions centered on three players—Silver King, Yank Robinson, and Arlie Latham were often mentioned as possible offenders, but the rambunctious Latham drew most of the attention. In the nineteenth century, players and managers commonly bet on the outcomes of games, and few condemned the practice. Arlie Latham, however, played poorly on occasion and committed critical errors and caused his detractors to speculate that he might be capitalizing on his potential to control the outcome of a contest. He claimed a sore arm caused many of his throwing errors, but his critics, Von der Ahe and Comiskey among them, suspected something else.[45] Whatever the truth of the situation Latham was twice suspended in 1889, once for associating with a gambler and a second time for poor play.[46]

Throughout the summer the Browns went through a good deal of turmoil and yet managed to retain a tentative grip on their first-place standing. Finally, they began to falter, however, as Brooklyn shed the early season doldrums and began winning consistently. By Friday, September 18, with about a month remaining in the season, the Bridegrooms held a five-game lead over second-place St. Louis.[47] St. Louis, though wounded by the club's rancorous summer, did not collapse in September and challenged the Bridegrooms until the last moment. But Brooklyn finally prevailed by two games with a record of ninety-three wins and forty-four losses compared to the Browns' record ninety wins and forty-five losses.[48] The Browns were finally dethroned, and Von der Ahe's dynasty was ended. His Browns never won another pennant.

The 1889 National League season proved exciting. As did the Bridegrooms, the Giants began 1889 poorly. By the end of May, New York was in third place, four and one-half games behind league-leading Boston. Part of the Giants' wan beginning was because Tim Keefe did not join the team until about two weeks after the season began; another part of it was because the Boston Beaneaters were a powerful team that played good baseball all summer. Boston opened the 1889 season a greatly strengthened club. When newcomers Dan Brouthers, Hardy Richardson, Charlie Bennett, and Charles Ganzel were combined with King Kelly, Joe Quinn, Billy Nash, and Dick Johnston, Soden instantly created a potent and versatile club. Brouthers especially proved a valuable acquisition. Big Dan led the NL with a .373 batting average and finished second in runs batted in, hits, on base percentage, and slugging average.[49]

Other Beaneaters also excelled in 1889. King Kelly, in spite of his legendary nightlife, played 125 games mostly in the outfield and hit a respectable .294 while stealing sixty-eight bases. Hardy Richardson hit .304, and Charles

Ganzel proved to be the utility man for the club and played twenty-six games in the outfield, caught thirty-nine, and played seven games at first base, six at shortstop, and one at third base. Pitcher John Clarkson's performance was perhaps the most impressive of all of Boston players'. He had been acquired from the Chicago White Stockings in time for the 1888 season and had won thirty-three games. In 1889 he surpassed that performance, winning forty-nine games while losing only nineteen, and pitched a total of 620 innings, better than half the club's 1,166 innings played.[50] Hoss Radbourn, now in the final stages of his career, contributed another twenty wins to Boston's effort, but it was Clarkson's pitching that kept the Beaneaters in the pennant race.[51]

Throughout the summer Boston led the Giants by three or four games, but finally, in late September, New York took a narrow one-half game lead over the Beaneaters.[52] As the season neared its conclusion with the final series being played on October 3–5, the outcome of the pennant remained unsettled. New York and Boston were separated by a few percentage points. Boston finished its season on the road against fifth-place Pittsburgh, and the Giants, also on the road, finished against the Cleveland Spiders. As the Giants prepared to play the Spiders, rumors reached Cleveland that Arthur Soden, the Beaneaters' owner, was maneuvering to arrange a doubleheader with the Pittsburgh Alleghenys on the last day of the season. John Day credited the gossip and dispatched manager Jim Mutrie to Pittsburgh to monitor the situation. Should Soden, in the Giants' view, attempt to steal the pennant by altering the schedule, Day intended to arrange two games with Cleveland to counter Soden's ploy. Soden did not actually attempt to add a game to the schedule, which meant that the final games on October 5 were destined to decide the pennant. On October 5, John Clarkson, the Beaneaters' strongest pitcher, started the game for Boston and lost to Pud Galvin who pitched a masterful game for the Alleghenys. Meanwhile, in Cleveland, reliable Timothy Keefe defeated the Spiders, and New York won the pennant. According to *Sporting Life,* the 1889 NL pennant race

> was the closest struggle in the history of the League, the championship not being decided until the last game played. Another remarkable feature was that incidentally the positions of four clubs besides the leaders depended upon the last-day games. The New York team, despite a great deal of misfortune for full half the season, wins first place by steady, plucky uphill work. The high-priced Boston team, which led nearly all season, weakened slightly in the latter half of September, and this temporary halt lost it ground which it was never able to entirely recover and hold.[53]

The Giants celebrated their second pennant in high style in the Hollenden Hotel in Cleveland that evening and then boarded a train the next day to return to New York. The train was decorated with a banner proclaiming "We Are the People," and the fatigued but happy club prepared to celebrate its triumph with their fans at home.[54] When the Giants arrived in Jersey City, about seven hundred friends and admirers met them at the depot and escorted them to the ferryboat where the Giants and many of their exuberant fans crossed the Hudson River into the city.[55] The city's streets were thronged with people anxious to see the newly crowned NL champions. Everywhere the Giants ventured, singly or in groups, they were showered with adoration. Two weeks later, on Sunday evening, October 20, after the series with Brooklyn had begun, the ubiquitous Digby Bell and De Wolf Hopper staged a fete at the Broadway Theatre to celebrate the Giants' second consecutive pennant. A huge crowd filled every inch of the theater, and after several musical numbers, recitations, and speeches, the Giants were introduced to the adoring audience. When the team filed onto the stage, a banner declaring "We Are the People" was lowered so the audience could view it. The banner slipped from its moorings and nearly fell upon the players, but the spectators roared their approval anyway and the entire evening was a gigantic success. The celebration, among other things, raised four thousand dollars, which the Giants divided among themselves.[56]

Four days later, not to be outdone by the festivities in the city, fans in Brooklyn also honored their heroes with a parade, a public ceremony at City Hall, and a banquet, which attracted over three hundred of the Bridegrooms' admirers.[57] At this point the Bridegrooms led the Giants three games to two in the playoffs, and the banquet conducted at the Academy of Music in Brooklyn carried an extra measure of merriment as local dignitaries and special guests honored the Bridegrooms. October proved a heady time for baseball fans in New York City and in Brooklyn.

Amid all the excitement and bustle as prominent citizens in New York City and Brooklyn planned to honor their baseball heroes, the negotiations for the 1889 playoffs commenced. On Wednesday, October 16, Byrne and his partner Ferdinand Abell met with Day and Mutrie in New York City to arrange the World's Championship series, which the newspapers now regularly termed the World's Series. When the negotiations began, both parties were committed to the games' occurring only in New York City and Brooklyn, and for the first time since 1886, the World's Championship did not appear in areas outside the contestants' home municipalities. Day and Byrne agreed to a maximum of eleven games, but they stipulated that the series would end when one of the teams won six.[58] Game one was scheduled for the Polo Grounds on October 18, and game two for Washington Park in Brooklyn the following afternoon. Subsequent games were to alternate between New York City and Brooklyn through the first four games. After game four, the fifth game was to be played in Brooklyn, and games six and seven were scheduled for the Polo Grounds. In the event of rain, a canceled game was to be played at its originally scheduled site the next day or whenever the weather permitted before the teams returned to the Polo Grounds or Washington Park to continue the alternating cycle.

Byrne, Day, and their associates further resolved that each team should charge fifty cents admission to all games and that an additional twenty-five cents for seats in the grandstand was permissible. All gate receipts were to be evenly divided, but Day and Byrne agreed that the home team would be permitted to retain the extra income from the sales of grand-stand seats. To avoid any suspicions of inaccurate counts of tickets sold, Byrne and Day agreed that the visiting team would supply the ticket-takers at the gates and the grandstands so the visitors would be assured they had not been victimized.[59] Brooklyn chose Thomas Lynch as an umpire for the series, and the Giants chose John Gaffney, and each was offered one hundred dollars for his service.[60]

Two features in the arrangements for the 1889 games departed from recent experiences. First of all, Byrne and Day chose not to tour the country as their clubs competed for the World's Championship, which meant they minimized expenses and also rewarded the hometown cranks who had supported their teams well during the season. Major league baseball attracted 2,932,722 paid admissions in 1889, and New York and Brooklyn sold a combined 555,679 tickets that season, or 19 percent of the total.[61] Moreover, Day was not at all disposed to travel to Boston, play a game, and share the receipts with his nemesis Arthur Soden, and Byrne had no desire to enrich Von der Ahe or Spalding by traveling to St. Louis or Chicago. Second, the owners provided a mechanism whereby the title would be claimed as soon as one team won a majority of the games. In recent years, World's Championship games had been poorly attended when the teams continued to play once the title was decided. So, the Bride-grooms and the Giants agreed to play a geographically compact and, when compared to more recent World's Championships, potentially brief and more suspenseful series. What Byrne and Day could not realize was that they were participants in the first New York–Brooklyn series that was destined to reach legendary status only two or three generations later.

A large crowd of approximately nine thousand fans filled the Polo Grounds on October 18 to witness the first game of the 1889 World's Championship series. According to some estimates, nearly a third of the spectators were from Brooklyn, and the Bridegrooms' partisans were vocal and joyous when their heroes came onto the field about half past two in the afternoon to prepare for the upcoming contest. The weather was cool but fair, and the prospect of an all New York World's Series energized fans and players alike. Tim Keefe, the stalwart of the Giants' pitching staff, was scheduled to face Adonis Terry, Brooklyn's number two pitcher. As game time approached, umpire Tom Lynch did not appear on the diamond. He wanted more money for umpiring the series. Faced with the prospect of playing the game with only one umpire, Giant's manager Jim Mutrie consulted with Jim Mc-Gunnigle who managed the Bridegrooms, and after a brief discussion, they decided to invite Robert V. Ferguson, who had umpired in the NL and the AA in recent years, to replace the recalcitrant Lynch.[62]

At five minutes past three o'clock, the game began. New York elected to hit first, and Adonis Terry retired them in order. The redoubtable Timothy Keefe then took his place in the pitcher's box, and Brooklyn proceeded to hit him freely and scored five runs in the bottom of the first inning. The numerous Brooklyn fans in the Polo Grounds were delirious with joy. By the end of the sixth inning with the score 6–5, the Bridegrooms held on to a precarious one-run lead, and Giants' fans tensely waited for their club to take command of the contest. In the seventh inning, the Giants scored five runs and established a four-run lead over Brooklyn. The people seemed to assert themselves, but in the bottom of the inning, Brooklyn countered with two runs and narrowed New York's lead to two runs. As New York came to bat in the eighth inning, the sun was setting, and the likelihood that the game would run a full nine innings appeared doubtful. The Giants went down in order, but in the bottom of the inning, Brooklyn scored four runs and took a 12–10 lead. By now the fading light of the previous inning was turning to darkness, and the Bridegrooms began to stall. Although there was a rule against stalling, neither of the umpires attempted to halt Brooklyn's delaying tactic. Finally, the umpires called the game owing to darkness. It was probably already too dark to play, even without the stalling ploy, but the Bridegrooms earned the wrath of the New York fans, and in the eyes of the Giants' partisans, the umpires proved accessories in questionable tactics.[63] New York fans were livid over the conduct and outcome of the game. An account of the game declared:

> The umpiring, too, was, if anything but favorable to New York. Messrs. Gaffney and Ferguson, two American Association men, officiated. It was nine league players against eleven association men. Gaffney's work gave several dissatisfactions, but Ferguson's rulings greatly displeased the New York players and their friends. He is a life-long resident of Brooklyn. Everybody appeared to know it.[64]

Anticipating that Lynch might not appear for the second game, Ferguson was tentatively engaged to umpire in game two in Brooklyn. After the series' opener, Day, outraged by the umpires' apparent indifference to the Bridegrooms' tactics in game one, vehemently declared he would not put his Giants on the field in Washington Park if Ferguson was not dismissed from the umpiring corps. For the first time in two years, an umpiring controversy emerged during the World's Championship games. Day's anxieties were partially relieved on the evening of October 18 when Lynch and the owners reached a salary agreement that raised the umpires' compensation to a robust six hundred dollars for the series.[65] Lynch joined Gaffney in umpiring the second game of the series, which was played at Washington Park on Saturday, October 19.

Brooklyn fans' enthusiasm for the series did not disappoint their Bridegrooms. All season long the Bridegrooms played home games before large crowds and drew an average of 5,125 paid admissions per game. Game two far exceeded that norm. A throng of 16,172 attended the game.[66] Commenting on the attendance at the game, one newspaper observed:

> Washington Park, on Fifth Avenue, Brooklyn, where the game took place was a study for an artist. For nearly two hours before the game began the turnstiles at the gates kept clicking continuously, and the lovers of the game passed through them by the hundreds. In a short time all the seats were taken and standing room was at a premium. The spectators were forced to take to the field, where they formed a horseshoe of human heads around the playing field.[67]

The weather was fair, the crowd was excited, Washington Park was suitably adorned with flags, bunting, and banners, and the Bridegrooms were animated and anxious to extend their lead over the Giants. Unfortunately for the Bridegrooms and their fans, the Giants' Cannonball Crane pitched an excellent game. He characteristically began the game unable to spot his pitches as well as he wished, and the Bridegrooms scored single runs in the first and second innings, but after an erratic start, Crane settled down and pitched shutout baseball for the remaining seven innings. Bob Caruthers began the game for Brooklyn, and while the Giants did not hit him hard, they scored six runs in the first five innings and took a comfortable 6–2 lead. The Giants evened the series at one game apiece.[68]

The next day, the series paused to observe the NL ban on Sunday games. The Giants and their fans took advantage of the hiatus and staged the celebration of the Giants' pennant-winning season at the Broadway Theatre. Meanwhile, the Bridegrooms, rather than resting on the day off, played an exhibition game against Baltimore at Ridgewood Park. Although several of the Bridegrooms' regular players did not participate in the contest, Tom Lovett, one of Brooklyn's better pitchers, started the game and defeated the Baltimore Orioles 6–2 before three thousand spectators.[69]

Rain prevented game three from taking place in the Polo Grounds on Monday, and it was postponed until the next day. Although the diamond was still damp, the third game got under way without incident. Jim Mutrie surprised many Giants fans when he chose to send Mickey Welch to the pitcher's box rather than Tim Keefe. Keefe had been hit freely in game one, and playing the sort of hunch for which he was noted, Mutrie by-passed Keefe and cast his lot with Welch. Brooklyn countered with Mickey Hughes, who made his first appearance in the series. Welch pitched poorly and gave up eight runs in the first five innings and left the game with the Giants trailing Brooklyn 8–7 when he was replaced by Hank O'Day in the sixth inning. O'Day proved effective and held the Bridegrooms scoreless for the remainder of the contest. In the eighth inning, Brooklyn's Hughes was replaced by "Parisian Bob" Caruthers who proceeded to retire Tiernan, Ewing, and Ward in order. After eight innings the Bridegrooms held a slim 8–7 margin over the Giants. At this point the Bridegrooms, as they had done earlier in the series, began to stall as the evening dusk slowly turned to darkness. When they came to bat in the bottom of the eighth inning (although the game was in the Polo Grounds, the Bridegrooms won the coin toss and elected to hit last), Darby O'Brien refused to swing at O'-Day's pitches and finally garnered a base on balls. The next hitter, Hub Collins, took several pitches before he sacrificed O'Brien to second base, and Oyster Burns then took every pitch O'Day delivered and struck out. Finally, Dave Foutz grounded out and ended the inning. Meanwhile, the Brooklyn bench directed a steady stream of invective at umpire Gaffney demanding that the game be called owing to darkness. In the stands a Brooklyn partisan, Jim Cudworth, held lighted pieces of paper over his head so, he claimed, he could see the action on the diamond. Cudworth's none too subtle actions further provoked the Bridegrooms and their fans to hurl verbal abuse upon the umpires. When the Giants came to bat in the top of the ninth, Brooklyn fans howled for the game to be called while New York fans emphatically signaled their convictions that there was plenty of light. Caruthers got Roger Connor to ground out and then proceeded to walk the next two hitters. Gaffney was now the target of a steady stream of invective from the Brooklyn club, and after being subjected to the ongoing harangue by the Bridegrooms, he abruptly called the game because of darkness. An unsightly quarrel immediately erupted on the field. An outraged Buck Ewing rushed out to challenge Gaffney. Some of the Giants restrained Ewing, but Gaffney remained adamant and the game ended.[70] Brooklyn fans cheered while the Giants' faithful vented their anger in jeers and rowdy behavior. Game three proved less than an edifying experience to anyone who witnessed it.

Leading the Giants two games to one, the Bridegrooms returned to their home park for two games before rabid fans. Brooklyn's prospects appeared excellent. Cold weather now made an appearance in the series. Rain caused a postponement of the third game in the Polo Grounds, and when the series resumed on October 23, with a raw wind sweeping through Brooklyn, only 3,045 fans braved the cold, huddled in their seats.

Although it was frigid on the diamond, emotions ran high among the players. Quarrels over umpiring decisions, the Bridegrooms' stalling tactics in game three, and the natural rivalry existing between the clubs guaranteed that, although the playing conditions were miserable, the game itself would be hotly contested. And, as events proved, no one was disappointed. Cannonball Crane and Adonis Terry drew the starting assignments, and in many ways the contest mirrored events in game three. The Bridegrooms took an early lead and maintained it through five innings until the Giants tied the score, Brooklyn then regained the lead in the bottom of the sixth inning, a twenty-two-minute quarrel between the Giants and Gaffney delayed the game, and the evening gloom gathered as the contest stumbled toward an early end. Finally, the game was called owing to darkness after only six completed innings. The Bridegrooms triumphed 10–7 and took a two-game lead over the Giants. Outrage among the Giants peaked after the game. Buck Ewing declared, "And the umpires! I don't know what to make of them. In every game they have handicapped us, but it must be stopped. In the future Gaffney and Lynch will have to umpire the games strictly on their merit or I will know the reason why. It is an outrage the way we have been treated. Of course, the boys have not been playing sound ball, but if the umpiring had been just we should have won three games."[71] The Giants had won only one of the first four games, and the future looked bleak. After the game a reporter located De Wolf Hopper among the downcast Giants' fans and asked the actor for his opinion of the series. "The Giants are in the soup," Hopper declared. "It's a good thing their benefit is over, or this would hurt it. We are the people no more."[72] Even diehard partisans such as Hopper now doubted the Giants.

Ewing was not the only one disturbed by the umpires' decisions in the series. Owner John B. Day was visibly distressed as well. In an outburst of unguarded emotion earlier in the series, Day declared angrily that the umpires were either crooked or incompetent, and during the fourth game his fury intensified. As the game went badly for the Giants, Day concluded the umpiring was intolerable. He protested to Byrne who calmly agreed to meet with him after the game. Once the contest ended, Day balked and declared he was too upset to hold a conference with Byrne and the umpires any time soon. Byrne, who had the nerve of a pirate, informed Day that the meeting had to be now or not at all. The owners and the umpires met that evening and again the next morning. In heated sessions Day aired his complaints, and while the basic contents of the discussions were not released to the public, Day obtained at least one concession. Darkness had ended three of the first four games, and he and Byrne agreed that upcoming games in New York would begin at a quarter after two, and at half past two in Brooklyn, rather than at the originally scheduled three o'clock.[73] Whether Day intimidated Gaffney and Lynch cannot be determined now. The Giants began to play better baseball after game four, and quarrels with the umpires abated somewhat. Even so, the first games of the series were reminiscent of the bitter quarrelling that marred the Chicago–St. Louis games in 1885 and 1886.

Only 2,901 fans passed through Washington Park's turnstiles on Thursday, October 24, for game five of the series. A cold raw wind raked the park all afternoon, and many fans probably felt that the weather and the Bridegrooms' ongoing domination of the Giants made enduring the miserable conditions unattractive. Rather than send Keefe to the pitcher's box, Mutrie chose to start Cannonball Crane who had pitched game four, and Mutrie's hunch paid dividends. Crane faced the Bridegrooms' Caruthers, and Cannonball turned in his best performance of the series. He allowed Brooklyn only eight hits and three runs. Buck Ewing did not catch that afternoon, and his replacement, Willard Brown, made three hits, one of which was a home run, played flawlessly behind the plate, and had only one base stolen against him. Crane also homered, and the Giants breezed to an easy 11–3 victory. Although the temperature hovered around forty degrees throughout the game, the chilled fans were treated to a fine exhibition of baseball. The Giants and the Bridegrooms committed a total of only four errors, and the umpiring, for the first time in the series, did not provoke unsightly quarrels.[74] After game five the Bridegrooms led the Giants three games to two, but Brooklyn also had to face the fact that the next two games were scheduled for the Polo Grounds, and that the Giants, who so far in the series had not played well, appeared to be awakening as the World's Championship playoffs shifted to New York City.

When McGunnigle and Mutrie announced their starting pitchers for game six, the 2,556 fans who entered the Polo Grounds were surprised to learn that Hank O'Day, not Timothy Keefe, would represent the Giants. Since Tim had not appeared in the series since the opening game, he was well rested, but Mutrie did not call upon him to start game six. There were no reports that Keefe was injured, and no one speculated that he had somehow managed to earn Mutrie's wrath or that he was ill. Mutrie apparently was playing an instinctive feeling that O'Day and Crane were his best choices. As events proved, Mutrie's choice, whatever its origins, was a correct one. O'Day locked into a pitcher's duel with Adonis Terry and defeated him 2–1 in eleven innings. Brooklyn scored a run in the top of the second inning and led New York until the Giants tied the score in the bottom of the ninth when John Montgomery Ward provided the tying run. Ward, the darling of New York fans, further endeared himself to them. He singled and then stole second base and then stole third base. Part of his success in stealing arose from the fact the Bob Clark, the Bridegrooms' regular catcher, had sprained a leg muscle in the previous game and was replaced by Joe Visner.[75] Visner was a competent catcher, but he did not throw to the bases with Clark's authority, and when the opportunity presented itself, Ward ran the bases with daring and skill. Once he reached third, Ward then scored on a fielder's choice and tied the game.[76] Then, in the bottom of the eleventh, with two out, the Giants scored the winning run in what was the best game of the playoffs. Now the series was tied at three games apiece.

Game seven was also played in the Polo Grounds, this time in a drizzling rain before 3,312 spectators. Cannonball Crane again started for the Giants and faced Brooklyn's Tom Lovett, who made his single appearance in the series. Lovett gave up eight runs to the Giants in the second inning, and he subsequently was replaced by Bob Caruthers, but the damage was done. The Giants won the game by a score of 11–7. Crane also proved less than effective and walked several hitters. Finally, Mutrie decided that Crane was not on his game and replaced him with Keefe who finished the game for the Giants. This proved to be Tim Keefe's last appearance in the playoffs.[77] While the mystery of Keefe's slight role in the series continued, the Giants moved to a lead of four games to three over the Bridegrooms, and now De Wolf Hopper and his associates could once again chant "We are the People!"

Monday, October 28, dawned a cold cheerless day in Brooklyn, and 2,584 hardy fans entered Washington Park to witness the eighth game of the series. Adonis Terry started the game for Brooklyn, and Cannonball Crane again pitched for the Giants. Crane walked five hitters during the game and gave up five hits, but the Giants scored so frequently in the first four innings that Cannonball's less than sharp pitching mattered little. Dave Foutz relieved Terry, but it was too late for Brooklyn to recover from New York's hitting onslaught. By the end of the sixth inning, the Giants led the Bridegrooms 15–2, and Crane had no pressure upon him. John Montgomery Ward played his usual flawless shortstop, made three hits, and stole five bases in the game while leading the Giants to a 16–7 rout over Brooklyn.[78] From its beginning to its end, game eight was a dreary spectacle for Brooklyn's faithful boosters in Washington Park. As the cold air and the Giants' merciless attack numbed the Brooklyn fans, stunned and dispirited spectators gradually vacated the stands. Many of those who departed early must have entertained premonitions that disaster awaited the Bridegrooms when they returned to the Polo Grounds for the next day's game. The Giants needed only one victory to win the series.

Even though the Bridegrooms had not triumphed since the fourth game of the series, the ninth contest proved one of their better performances. The weather did not improve, however. The *Daily Tribune* reported that the "weather, as has been the case with most of the games, was cold, damp, and disagreeable, yet 3,067 people were present."[79] By now Brooklyn's pitching appeared to be in serious disarray. Caruthers recently had been ineffective, Dave Foutz was not equal to the challenges posed by the Giants, and Tom Lovett, who appeared in game seven, had been hit hard in his one assignment. More in desperation than anything else, manager McGunnigle chose to start Adonis Terry against the Giants. Terry had been taxed severely by the Giants the day before in Washington Park, and now with only a few hours' rest, he was again summoned to face New York. Mutrie again confounded New York fans and chose Hank O'Day as his starting pitcher and again bypassed Tim Keefe, who many fans assumed would take the pitching chores in the ninth game. Brooklyn tallied two runs in the top half of the first inning, and the Giants countered with one run in the bottom of the inning. The Giants tied the score in the sixth inning, scored a single run in the bottom of the eighth, and won the game by a score of 3–2. Hank O'Day was the hero of the game. He gave up two runs in the first inning and then came into his own and allowed the Bridegrooms only one hit after the second inning.[80] With their victory in game nine, the Giants repeated as world's champions, the only time a team won consecutive titles during the 1880s.

Baseball, pundits often declare, is a game of numbers. Among all sports, with the possible exception of track and field, baseball players and teams are measured and valued by the statistics they generate. Although concise statistics concerning baseball are more a penchant among modern fans than they were among cranks in the 1880s, an examination of runs, hits, errors, fielding averages, and earned run averages provides useful insights into the several World's Championship series. In the case of the 1889 World's Championship, such statistics tell the story of the Giants' success. After a feeble beginning in the first four games, the Giants asserted themselves against Brooklyn's inferior pitching and compiled a team batting average of .315 as compared to the Bridegrooms' .231. For the complete series, New York outscored the Bridegrooms seventy-three to fifty-two, stole ten more bases than Brooklyn, and narrowly edged Brooklyn with a fielding average of .931 to .925.[81] New York's pitchers compiled a 3.94 earned run average in the series whereas Brooklyn's staff finished the games with a 6.22 earned run average. Only in the category of bases on balls did the Brooklyn staff excel New York pitchers. Brooklyn walked thirty-one New York hitters; the Giants' pitchers walked fifty-one (Cannonball Crane alone walked thirty-two batters, but Brooklyn's hitters only managed a .206 batting average against him). From any perspective, the New York Giants decisively defeated the Bridegrooms.

Once the series was concluded, division of the spoils was the final event. When the teams assembled in their respective clubhouses immediately after the final games, spirits of jubilation, melancholy, and rancor were manifest among the players as they prepared to depart to their winter homes. Brooklyn players were downcast, the Giants were delighted. Many of the players realized that the Brotherhood would strike out on its own in 1890, and that they may have seen their last games with valued team-mates. Others were angry at ownership, eager to strike at baseball's cartel, and eager to begin their winter activities. The Bridegrooms presented their manager with an expensive gold watch and chain, and Dave Foutz made a short but graceful and heartfelt speech thanking McGunnigle for his fine work during the season and the series.[82] The Giants, on the other hand, voted not to share their proceeds with their manager, Jim Mutrie, and ad-ditionally denied him a portion of the income from the Broadway Theatre benefit organized by Hopper and Bell to celebrate New York's 1889 NL pennant.[83] Everyone, players and owners alike, knew that the Brotherhood of Base Ball Players soon would announce its plans to form a new major league, and they recognized that organized baseball faced an uncertain and turbulent future.

Even though bad weather had plagued the series, its financial outcome was positive. *Sporting Life* observed, "Had ordinary October weather fa-vored the series of eleven games between New York and Brooklyn, the se-ries in a financial sense would perhaps have been the greatest of the kind ever known to baseball, as the first two days, which were perfect, indi-cated."[84] Attendance for the series totaled 47,796 and gross receipts amounted to $20,067.01. Once Day and Byrne deducted expenses amounting to $7,902.86 from the receipts, they evenly divided $12,164.15 between them. The owners in turn then gave their players one-half of the profits to divide among themselves, and consequently, each Giant received $380.15 as his share, and the Bridegrooms each received $389.29.[85] Day and Byrne each pocketed a tidy profit from the series, and the players each earned shares equal to a sizable percentage of their annual salaries. Al-though financial returns were lucrative in spite of the weather, the season ended on a bittersweet note. Everyone understood that the upcoming win-ter and the following season were destined to be the most unusual since the National League was created in 1876.

CHAPTER EIGHT

Brooklyn and Louisville

The Year 1890

Change and confusion reigned supreme in major league baseball affairs in 1890. The Players' League was born during the winter of 1889–1890, and for the owners, players, and fans alike, the baseball scene the following summer was both intriguing and unsettling. Since the inception of the National League in 1876, the owners usually held the upper hand when dealing with their players, but this was dramatically altered when John Montgomery Ward and his cohorts in the Brotherhood of Professional Base Ball Players announced the birth of their new league after the 1889 season.

After more than four years of organizing, recruiting players into its fold, and futile negotiations with NL and AA owners, the Brotherhood decided to launch a revolt against the major leagues' management. From the Brotherhood's viewpoint the time had arrived to end the oppressive regulations that reduced them to abject subservience to the owners. On Monday, November 4, 1889, only days after the conclusion of the season and the World's Championship, delegates representing the Brotherhood met in the Fifth Avenue Hotel in New York City to assess the organization's relationship with the existing major leagues and to determine a course of action.[1] At 1:20 P.M., Ward called the Brotherhood's meeting to order, and the delegates took their first steps toward creating a new league. Routine matters such as reading the minutes and hearing reports consumed the first hour of the meeting. After the preliminary housekeeping chores were completed, Ward took the podium and addressed the delegates. He summarized the Brotherhood's unproductive efforts to meet with Spalding and other NL owners to obtain redress of its grievances. Ward's remarks carried an unmistakable tone:

> Brothers: Last June a committee was appointed by this organization to wait upon President A. G. Spalding, of the Chicago Club, and lay before him, as the representative of the League for consideration on any differences that might arise between the bodies. We had certain grievances. A request was made, couched in the most polite language, for the League to appoint a date

for an early meeting of the two organizations. The request was ignored, he, as the League's representative, not deeming it important enough to call a special meeting of the committee, although he was earnestly told that the players felt wronged and the least the League could do would be to meet with the Brotherhood and talk the matter over fairly and freely. It was clearly and comprehensively stated that the Brotherhood could not afford to wait until fall, and we said, "If you do not meet with us, we are going to get our rights one way or another."[2]

After Ward finished his remarks, the somber men who filled the room realized that the time for action finally was upon them. George Andrews, one of the delegates to the convention and unsurprised by the tenor of Ward's remarks, arose, gained recognition by the chair, and proposed that a five-man committee immediately be appointed to draft a statement to the public announcing the Brotherhood's determination to alter the balance of power in major league baseball. Andrews's motion, after being amended to guarantee Ward a place on the committee, was unanimously adopted by the assembled delegates. The newly appointed committee immediately began its work while the delegates recessed. When the meeting reconvened at 4:20 P.M., the statement, which condemned the practices of the past and announced the Brotherhood's determination to launch a new league, was reviewed and unanimously endorsed by the delegates. The manifesto concluded by declaring: "We believe it possible to conduct our National game upon lines that will not infringe upon individual and natural rights. We ask to be judged solely by our own work, and, believing that the game can be played more fairly and its business conducted more intelligently under a plan that excludes everything arbitrary and un-American, we look forward with confidence to the support of the public and the future of the National game."[3] Although the conference had just begun, the Brotherhood's purpose was unmistakable: It declared war upon the owners, the reserve clause, and blacklisting. An air of both exuberance and sadness filled the room once the declaration was adopted. Many players were elated. Others were somber as they contemplated the upheaval they soon would encounter. Nevertheless, the bridge had been burned, and they realized it was time to adopt rules to govern the new league they were about to midwife. The delegates passed a resolution thanking Ward and secretary Tim Keefe for their labors over the recent months and adjourned until Wednesday. At seven o'clock in the evening, the press was officially informed of the day's events, and the Brotherhood's revolt became a matter of public record.

The following afternoon, nearly thirty players met with financial backers in a saloon in Twenty-Seventh Street, and the group outlined an agenda for the organizational meeting scheduled for the next day,

Wednesday, November 6. Keefe later informed the press that the meeting featured a discussion of possible candidates for the new league's presidency, a review of the financial aspects affecting their plans, and a tentative agreement upon a constitution and bylaws to govern the new league. The delegates assembled the next morning in the Fifth Avenue Hotel and met throughout the day and well into the evening. They resolved a myriad of issues in their first day of formal debate, but as the hour grew late and the delegates became fatigued, they decided to adjourn until the next morning. By late evening of the next day, the basic work was completed, and the document governing the Players' National League of Base Ball Clubs was formally accepted by the delegates. It was an astonishing document. Prior to the Brotherhood's historic meetings in New York City, no organization had challenged the owners' grip on major league baseball in such a comprehensive fashion.

On December 16, the players and their financial supporters again assembled in the Fifth Avenue Hotel to implement the new constitution. The meeting lasted two days, during which the delegates systematically created the foundation for their challenge to the established major leagues through their newly formed "Players' League," as the press popularly styled the Players' National League of Base Ball Clubs (PL). One of the first items of business for the Brotherhood's December meeting called for the election of league officers. Colonel E. A. McAlpin, a wealthy New York City real estate investor and the leader of the faction that founded the PL club in the city, was elected as president. John Addison, a powerful Chicago contractor and a prime mover in the creation of the PL team in Chicago, was chosen as vice president. Frank H. Brunell, who, among other things, had served as a reporter for the *Chicago Tribune,* accepted the assignment as the league's secretary and treasurer.[4] In addition to the superstructure of executives, the PL was to be governed by a sixteen-man board of directors composed of two members (one player and one "contributor" or financial backer) from each of the eight clubs the league intended to organize. Each member was entitled to one vote in league affairs, and the league president and vice president were to be selected from among the board's membership. Any board member could be expelled by a two-thirds vote of the entire board, and the board of directors was granted broad powers to settle disputes arising among or between clubs or players. The PL proclaimed it would schedule seasons of one hundred forty games, would ban Sunday games, forbid the sale of alcohol in ballparks, abolish the reserve clause and blacklist, and require players to sign three-year contracts. After fulfilling a three-year commitment players were free agents, and they expected to seek new contracts on whatever terms they found acceptable or could obtain. In view of the standard practices and contracts of the NL and the AA, the PL's policies appeared truly revolutionary in content.[5]

Annual dues for membership in the PL were set at fifteen hundred dollars for each club. Each club was to be governed by an eight-man board composed of four players and four contributors who supplied the financial backing to launch the team. The contributors were entitled to the first ten thousand dollars in profits. Profits beyond that up to twenty thousand dollars were to be divided among the club's players, and any profits in excess of twenty thousand were destined to be split equally between the team's contributors and players.[6] In addition, the Players' League eventually agreed to establish a twenty-thousand-dollar prize fund that would be divided among the clubs at season's end. At a meeting in March 1890, the leadership ruled that the fund would be divided in a manner whereby the first-place club would receive $6,250; the second, $4,800; the third, $3,500; the fourth, $2,500; the fifth, $1,750; the sixth, $800; the seventh, $400; and the last place team, nothing.[7] Profit-sharing and incentives abounded in the PL's philosophy of labor-management relations. By the end of 1889, the details of most of the PL's organization were well reported in the newspapers, and many readers made surprising discoveries as they followed the new league's maturation.

Accustomed to the authoritarian policies of the NL and AA, the PL's approach to baseball business affairs surely appeared visionary to dedicated cranks who superficially observed the Brotherhood's deliberations. A closer examination, however, revealed that the brothers often emulated their NL and AA mentors. Tim Keefe, for example, served as the Brotherhood's secretary and rendered valuable services to the organization. Yet he, as well as many of his brothers, also saw more than a fulfillment of an idealistic goal in the players' revolt. Most of Keefe's peers expected to earn good salaries, share in profits and prize money, and at the end of their three-year terms with original PL clubs, earn bonanzas as they negotiated new contracts. Keefe shared in these expectations, but he went further than most of his colleagues. He sought to emulate A. G. Spalding who earned tidy profits supplying the NL with official baseballs. Keefe successfully lobbied for the contract to supply the PL with baseballs and other paraphernalia.[8] So, while the players might have been spending a good deal of time fulminating against the reserve clause, the despotic policies of major league owners, and their rights as free men, they also sought to fulfill more mundane and immediately rewarding objectives.

The American Association was profoundly affected by the Brotherhood's revolt, but it was the National League that appeared the new league's primary opponent. Gossip concerning where the Brotherhood would locate its franchises in 1890 centered on the fact that NL towns would be the PL's primary targets. Such speculations soon proved essentially accurate. Six of the Players' League's eight teams (New York, Boston, Chicago, Philadelphia, Pittsburgh, and Cleveland) were situated in cities that featured NL teams in 1889. Conversely, the AA, other than losing players, was not as immediately threatened.

Shortly after the PL's November meetings, the NL launched its counter-attack. The NL suspended the salary classification plan, eliminated its struggling franchises in Indianapolis and Washington, D.C., and appointed a war committee composed of John B. Day, John Rogers, and A. G. Spalding, who served as chair.[9] Recognizing that the upcoming season was destined to be a battle for survival, the NL admitted the Brooklyn Bridegrooms and the Cincinnati Reds, two of the AA's prize franchises, to membership in order to replace the dying Indianapolis and Washington clubs, in effect declaring war on the American Association.[10]

When Byrne's Brooklyn Bridegrooms entered the National League, the abrupt transfer of one the American Association's premiere franchises to the NL shocked the baseball world. Byrne was a ruthless businessman, and he reasoned that the already fragile AA might not survive a war for the fans' dollars and that his best strategy was to cast in his lot with the older and better established NL. Brooklyn did not escape a challenge by the Players' League, which placed a club in Brooklyn in 1890, and all the NL teams except the Cincinnati Reds had cross-town PL rivals.

Another interesting facet to the Brooklyn story in 1890 arose when the AA hastily added a replacement team to offset the Bridegrooms' defection, and the city of Brooklyn boasted three major league teams at the beginning of the 1890 season. In addition to declaring war on the American Association, the National League issued its own broadside answering the players' manifesto. The NL's counterblast, signed by Day, Rogers, and Spalding, reviewed baseball's dreadful state of affairs during the reign of the National Association, portrayed the League as the savior of professional baseball, justified the controversial reserve clause, and roundly condemned the players for their misrepresentations of the owners' policies, which contributed to the stabilization of the major and minor leagues.[11] The League's actions and words left no doubt that it saw itself locked in a death struggle with the emerging league, and, parenthetically, that it also recognized an opportunity to crush the long-despised American Association into the bargain.

Meanwhile, as the National League girded for war with the Players' League, the AA leadership attempted to cope with the problems posed by the baseball war to the younger of the established major leagues. The defections of the Brooklyn and Cincinnati teams to the NL were devastating blows. In addition Kansas City and Baltimore resigned membership in the AA. (The AA managed to revive the Baltimore franchise before the 1890 season commenced, but it floundered hopelessly and played only thirty-four games before it collapsed.) With four of its franchises abandoning the Association, the AA entered desperate straits late in 1890. Owners of the

Clarence Duval, the mascot.
The photograph was taken
during the 1888–1889 World
Tour. (Courtesy of Jay Sanford,
Arvada, Colo.)

remaining clubs, Von der Ahe excepted, were stunned and frightened by the grim prospects of the emerging war between the NL and the PL. Unlike his counterparts in the AA, Chris seemed unconcerned about the crucial threat posed by the PL in 1890. With the imminent departures of Brooklyn and Cincinnati from the AA, Von der Ahe believed the Browns, even though they soon faced massive defections by his longtime stars, could be rebuilt to capitalize on the crisis faced by baseball in 1890, if he could re-tain Comiskey's loyalty. One reporter wrote, "Von der Ahe is in a state of mind bordering on paresis over the probable withdrawal of Comiskey from the ranks of the Browns."[12]

The remaining AA owners were not so optimistic, and on December 6, 1889, several of them, or their designated representatives, held a special meeting in Columbus, Ohio. Allen Thurman, legal counsel for the AA and an active participant in the management of the Columbus team, hosted a daylong meeting in his office, and after a torturous series of discussions, the AA's representatives authorized Thurman to draft a proposal for an amalgamation with the PL. Nothing came of this effort. Tim Keefe was subsequently quoted as saying, "All the talk of consolidating the two organizations is being done by the American Association not the Brotherhood. You can put it down to that."[13] One thing, however, was apparent. The AA was wounded, confused, and vulnerable. As subsequent events proved, the winter of 1889–1890 was the beginning of the end for the American Association.

By early spring in 1890, the impact of the surge of players to the PL became painfully apparent to NL and AA management. Premiere players flooded into the PL, and the NL was especially wounded by massive defections of star players to the upstart league. Danny Richardson, Art Whitney, Jim O'Rourke, George Gore, Buck Ewing, Mike Slattery, Tim Keefe, Cannonball Crane, and Hank O'Day abandoned John B. Day's New York Giants and signed contracts with the New York club in the PL.[14] John Montgomery Ward also left the Giants, but he joined the PL's new club in Brooklyn where he managed and played shortstop for the Brooklyn Wonders.[15] Other teams were similarly decimated as players joined the Brotherhood's effort to make war on both major leagues. Dan Brouthers, Hardy Richardson, King Kelly, and Charles Ganzel abandoned Boston; St. Louis lost Charles Comiskey, Yank Robinson, Arlie Latham, Tip O'Neill, Silver King, and Nat Hudson.

At least one mascot also defected to the PL. Clarence Duval, the longtime favorite with Chicago White Stockings fans, was enticed to affiliate with the Chicago Pirates (PL). The Pirates were composed of several former White Stockings (Fred Pfeffer, Ned Williamson, Hugh Duffy, Duke Farrell, and Mark Baldwin), and several of Von der Ahe's Browns (Comiskey, Latham, Silver King, Tip O'Neill, and Jack Boyle). Duval felt some affinity for several of the White Stockings who had joined the Pirates' roster, so the diminutive and talented mascot joined his friends as they cast their lots with the PL. Fifty-three of the fifty-nine players on the top four clubs in the PL were experienced major league players who had abandoned their contracts and joined the Brotherhood's league.[16] Only a few established stars, Cap Anson being perhaps the most notable among them, resisted the temptation to bail.[17] When the PL finally opened its season in 1890, a little over 100 of the 123 men on the rosters of the Brotherhood's eight new teams had prior major league experience, most of them in the NL.[18]

A few teams, especially the Brooklyn Bridegrooms, survived relatively unscathed by the exodus. Brooklyn's Foutz, Collins, Pinkney, Burns, Lovett, Terry, O'Brien, and Caruthers chose to stay on their championship club and compete in the NL. Other AA and NL clubs were not so fortunate, and

The Brooklyn Bridegrooms in 1890.
(National Baseball Hall of Fame Library, Cooperstown, N.Y.)

once-powerful franchises fell upon barren days. The New York Giants, the defending World's Champions, sank to sixth place in the NL standings in 1890, one notch below the Boston club that had challenged them for the 1889 pennant. Some clubs, most notably Louisville, profited from the dislocations brought on by the players' revolt. The Louisville club was one of the original AA teams, but it had never prospered. From 1882 through 1889, the club never finished higher than third place and finished six times in fourth place or lower. Overall, the Louisville team, variously known as the Eclipse or as the Colonels, compiled a record of 432 wins and 510 losses in its first eight seasons in the AA.[19] In 1889 the Colonels finished a pathetic last in the AA with a record of 27 wins and 111 losses. Then, when the Brotherhood revolt altered baseball's equations in the existing major leagues, the Louisville team emerged as winner of the AA pennant. Louisville's journey from a dismal last place in 1889 to the pennant in 1890 truly was one of baseball's most amazing reversals of fortune. Obviously, from the Colonels' perspective, the players' war was a godsend, even though Louisville fans may not have completely shared the club's sentiments since one of their favorite players, Louis Rogers "Pete" Browning, bolted to the Players' League.

Even though the players' revolt turned the baseball world upside down during the winter of 1889–1890, many fans remained constant in their admiration of baseball's premiere figures. Great stars such as King Kelly, Charles Comiskey, Cap Anson, John Montgomery Ward, and others retained their celebrity status, and sensible fans made allowances for their rhetoric and conduct during the opening phase of the great baseball war of 1890. No one was more roundly praised or bitterly condemned than Ward, who was seen (correctly) as the principal architect of the Players' League.

In retrospect, it is difficult to comprehend the impact the revolt had on Ward's life. Throughout 1889 and 1890 he had endured a difficult situation. He administered much of the Brotherhood's campaign against the NL and the AA, managed the Brooklyn club and played shortstop, and unsuccessfully tried to save his marriage with Helen Dauvray. Ward was one of the great stars of major league baseball in the 1880s, and his role in creating the PL, combined with his transition from player to player-manager, added luster to his reputation as a renaissance man. He engendered real animosity among the embattled NL and AA club owners, but he also fortified the affection showered upon him by his many constant fans. One example of the hero worship he enjoyed occurred in early 1890 when the actress Sydney Cowell published a fairy tale in *The Cosmopolitan: A Monthly Illustrated Magazine* that allegorically lauded Ward and his many talents.

Miss Cowell was a prominent member of the New York stage community who, along with De Wolf Hopper, Digby Bell, and Helen Dauvray, adored the pre-1890 Giants. Like them she often spent her weekday afternoons at the Polo Grounds enjoying the Giants' successes during the championship seasons of 1888 and 1889.[20] Ward, even before he became romantically involved with Helen Dauvray, was an habitué of the theater, and not only was he admired by many of the city's famous actors and actresses, he also socialized with them. Miss Cowell, who never was romantically linked to Ward, intensely admired the debonair shortstop, and she elevated hero worship to a new height when she published "The Enchanted Baseball: A Fairy Story of Modern Times."

In her fairy tale Miss Cowell related the story of the adventures of Algernon De Witt Caramel who is portrayed as the champion shortstop of the New York Giants:

> Algernon De Witt Caramel was a highly accomplished young gentleman. He conversed fluently in all modern languages, and mastered Greek, Latin, and Hebrew with utmost ease. His voice was an exquisite tenor, and his paintings far excelled those of any living artist. In appearance, he was a veritable Adonis. He was, moreover, a graceful dancer, a fearless swimmer, a daring equestrian, a brilliant conversationalist, and was acknowledged to be, by all odds, the best dressed man in town.[21]

Miss Cowell took a few liberties to embellish her story, but Ward undeniably was an attractive and popular figure in her social environment. Ward was supposedly fluent in two or three languages, and he certainly was a man about town known for his good companionship, handsome features, and polished manners. In her fairy tale, she subsequently posed the question: "Who has not heard of Algernon De Witt Caramel, the Champion Short-Stop of America?"[22]

The fairy tale opens in the Polo Grounds as the Giants prepare to play their arch rivals, the Brooklyn Bridegrooms. Caramel, exercising on the field before the adoring eyes of his fiancée Miss Violet Veronica Van Sittart (a thinly disguised reference to Helen Dauvray) and his thousands of fans, is innocently unaware of the evil designs of the Bridegrooms' evil Rudolf Von Hostetter. Von Hostetter once competed for Miss Van Sittart's affections until she met Caramel. Since then, Miss Cowell informs her readers, the Brooklyn player (who was created only for the fairy tale and directly compares to no one on the 1889 Bridegrooms' roster) carefully plots revenge against Caramel. Later, at a critical juncture in the clash between the Giants and the Bridegrooms, while the gallant Timotheus (Tim Keefe) is pitching to Von Hostetter, the Brooklyn player surreptitiously replaces the game ball with a magic baseball he purchased from a magician in New York City. Von Hostetter drives Timotheus's next pitch to Caramel who is swept across the Atlantic Ocean to Europe as he pursues the baseball. Caramel soon finds himself before the gates of a remote, imposing castle, and undaunted he enters the magical kingdom of Prince Otto Von Blitzenburg. There, aided by a fairy named Iolanthe, the enchanted Caramel narrowly escapes the spell cast on him by Von Blitzenburg's daughter, the beautiful but evil Aldegonda. Caramel returns to the Polo Grounds as Von Hostetter passes third base on his way to score the potentially game-tying run (Caramel's journey to and from Von Blitzenburg's evil realm occurs during the seconds it takes Von Hostetter to circle the bases); the champion shortstop of America throws the ball to his catcher, Duck Owing (Buck Ewing), Hostetter is retired at home plate, and the Giants triumph. After this fateful adventure in which virtue prevails over evil, Caramel and the lovely Violet Veronica Van Sittart live happily ever after. Miss Cowell's tale is not an especially good one, but it illustrates how Ward, adored by his fans in the 1880s, became an important figure in popular culture. Along with men such as King Kelly, who was wildly revered by his Irish American contemporaries, Ward achieved a level of acceptance enjoyed by only a few players in any era of baseball history. The bitter strife raised by the players' revolt took its toll on Ward's personal life, but his fame and popularity flourished among his admirers.

When the major league season finally got under way in mid-April, baseball fans faced a bewildering scene. Not since 1884, when the UA challenged the NL and the AA, had so many teams and so many players demanded the cranks' attention. In 1884 three major leagues fielded a total of thirty-three teams. In mid-April 1890, the NL, PL, and the AA opened their respective seasons with only slightly fewer teams than the high-water mark set six years earlier. The National League featured clubs in Boston, New York, Philadelphia, Brooklyn (lately of the AA), Pittsburgh, Cincinnati (also lately of the AA), Cleveland, and Chicago. The American Association opened the season with franchises located in Louisville, St. Louis, and Philadelphia (holdovers from 1889), replacement clubs in Brooklyn and Baltimore, and new franchises in Toledo, Ohio, Rochester, New York, Columbus, Ohio, and Syracuse, New York. If all this was not enough to disconcert the most dedicated fans, there was also the Players' League to factor into the equation. The Brotherhood's league offered its style of baseball in Boston, New York, Brooklyn, Philadelphia, Pittsburgh, Cleveland, Chicago, and Buffalo, New York. Not only did the fans have to learn the new geography of the major leagues, they also found their old favorites no longer in their familiar places in the box scores and had to identify new faces, as many unknown players appeared on the rosters of new or depleted teams. In 1889 the sixteen NL and AA clubs had carried at least 344 players on their rosters.[23] As many of the established major leaguers migrated to the PL, and as their clubs struggled to replace them while the stricken AA expanded from eight to nine teams for 1890, owners scoured the country for men to fill their rosters. Aging players in the minor leagues, promising young players, and talented semi-pro players soon found opportunities in the peculiar circumstances brought on by the Brotherhood's revolt. In 1890, the twenty-five teams in the National League, the American Association, and the Players' League listed a total of 553 men on their rosters.[24] In a single winter, at least 209 men who otherwise would have spent more time in the minor leagues before coming to the major leagues, or would have played out their days in obscurity, or would have retired after careers in professional baseball, found unexpected, premature, or final opportunities to be major leaguers. Some major league clubs experienced impressive changes in their rosters as they sought competent players and thereby provided brief opportunities to marginal or faded players during the 1890 season. The Pittsburgh Alleghenys in the NL and the Philadelphia club in the AA were two of the more extreme examples. The Alleghenys amassed a dismal record of 23 wins and 113 losses while employing forty-six different players on the club's roster, and Philadelphia, which won 54 and lost 78 games, used forty-four assorted players. Keeping informed perspectives on the new teams, the new league, and the many new faces in all three major leagues certainly challenged the dedicated crank—and confounded the casual baseball fan.

The Brooklyn Bridegrooms, after abandoning the American Association, opened the 1890 season in the National League. Unlike many of their counterparts in other major league cities, Brooklyn fans did not have to adjust to major alterations in their club's personnel. Familiar faces and old heroes abounded on the Bridegrooms' roster, and once the Brooklyn cranks adapted to the NL style of baseball, the transition was complete. Louisville was another matter. Although the club remained in the AA, it underwent massive changes during the winter of 1889–1890. After a disastrous season in 1889, Lawrence S. Parsons, the Louisville owner, probably would have overhauled the Colonels' roster, but the advent of the PL nearly stripped his club of what little talent it possessed. Infielders Guy Hecker and Dan Shannon departed the club during the winter; Hecker signed with the Pittsburgh NL club, and Shannon joined the Philadelphia PL franchise. In addition, Louisville lost other players to the PL; catcher and utility-man Harry Francis "Farmer" Vaughn and pitcher John Ewing went to the New York club, and outfielder Pete Browning became a member of the Cleveland team.[25] As a result Louisville fans, fairly expecting to see changes in the club's roster after the calamitous 1889 campaign, were nearly overwhelmed with new faces when the 1890 season opened.

If there was a bright side to Parsons's sometimes frenzied labors to refashion the Colonels, it was that William Van Winkle "Chicken" Wolf resisted the temptation to join the PL and elected to remain with Louisville. Chicken, who allegedly earned his nickname by gorging on stewed chicken prior to a game in which he committed several errors, was a hard-hitting outfielder who joined the Colonels in 1882 when the American Association was born. Known for his ever-expanding waistline, Wolf often showed flashes of brilliance on the field and was one of the few players to compete in the AA throughout its existence. When the AA finally died after the 1891 season, Chicken became the AA record holder in several categories. He played the most games (1,195), collected the most hits (1,438), most doubles (214), triples (109), and total bases (1,921).[26] Throughout most of his career Wolf played in the shadow of Pete Browning, who joined the Colonels in 1882, as did Wolf. During his nine years with Louisville, the colorful Browning won two AA batting championships while recording a composite .344 batting average.[27]

Browning was a great hitter, a terrible fielder, quite eccentric, and always interesting on and off the field. When he jumped to the PL in 1890 he won the new league's batting championship when he posted a .373 average. In addition to his significant accomplishments as a batsman, Pete had another long-lasting impact on baseball. Early in the 1884 season, he broke his favorite bat, and a staunch Colonels fan, John A. "Bud" Hillerich, offered to turn out a custom-made replacement. Browning was quite satisfied with the bat provided by Hillerich and ended the season with a .341 batting average. Reports of Hillerich's skill soon spread beyond the Colonels, and soon his woodworking shop was flooded with orders for new bats. The deluge of requests led to the creation of Hillerich and Bradsby Company, which became world famous for producing a custom-made bat—the Louisville Slugger—for major leaguers and retailing those models to baseball players everywhere.

After Browning departed for the PL, Chicken emerged as the Louisville fans' favorite, and he responded by hitting a league-leading .363 in 1890. In addition to Wolf, the Colonels also retained four other position players who were ready to contribute to the club's efforts. Shortstop Phil Tomney, third baseman Harry Raymond, catcher Jack Ryan, and outfielder William B. "Farmer" Weaver were not assigned to a PL club, and having no other choice each remained with the Colonels. While none of the four was more than an average major leaguer in talent, each probably was superior to any replacements Parsons could have recruited as he filled the vacancies on his club's roster. Parsons also retained two seasoned pitchers, Scott Stratton and Phillip Sydney "Red" Ehret, who (like Tomney, Raymond, Ryan, and Weaver) had joined the Colonels in 1888 or 1889. In 1889 Stratton and Ehret combined to win sixteen games, about two-thirds of the club's victories, and lost a combined fifty-nine, better than half of the Colonels' losses.[28] Neither distinguished himself against major league hitting, but each had experience, and against weakened or new teams Parsons counted on them to be the heart of his pitching staff. As dismal as the situation appeared Parsons retained, as the nucleus of his club, one legitimate major leaguer in Chicken Wolf, four mediocre but veteran position players, and two experienced but undistinguished pitchers.

Parsons filled the remaining gaps in his club with three rookies. He signed Harry Taylor to play first base, Tim Shinnick to play second, and Charles Hamburg to fill in the outfield. Taylor had spent the previous three seasons with Elmira in the New York State League; Shinnick played second base for Auburn also in the New York State League in 1889; and Charles "Charlie" Hamburg, born and bred in Louisville, had spent six years in the minor leagues in such places as Bridgeport, Connecticut, Columbus, Georgia, and Buffalo, New York, before becoming a Colonel in 1890.[29] None of the three was to have a long career in the major leagues. Taylor lasted four years, Shinnick two years, and Hamburg only one. They were prime examples of how the Brotherhood's revolt opened doors to players with only marginal talent. Nevertheless, Taylor, Shinnick, and Hamburg were briefly major leaguers, enjoyed a momentary fulfillment of their dreams, and unlike many baseball stars of their era, played for a pennant-winning club.[30] Louisville also opened the season with a new manager, John Curtis Chapman, and perhaps he proved one of the greatest assets of the jerry-built club.

Chapman was a sound baseball man. After a brief career in the National

Association and a seventeen-game career in the National League in 1876, Chapman turned to managing. He was the manager of the Louisville Grays in 1877 when four of his players were accused of hippodroming. A subsequent investigation, in which Chapman was found blameless, resulted in the lifetime banishment of Jim Devlin, George Hall, Al Nichols, and Bill Craver for their connivance with gamblers.[31] After his unhappy experience in Louisville, Chapman successfully managed other clubs and finally returned to Louisville to lead the Colonels in 1890. He was an excellent tactician, patient with young players, a stoic and genial man. Chapman's appointment as manager was the perfect choice for the young and essentially untried club.

When the season opened, the eight position players on the Colonels' roster boasted a total of nineteen years of major league experience, with an average of under three years per player. Actually, the situation was worse than it appeared. Wolf had eight seasons under his belt as the 1890 campaign began, which meant that the seven regulars, Wolf aside, had only eleven years of experience among them. Even worse, three of the lightly experienced seven players were untried rookies. Conventional baseball wisdom holds that experience is essential to winning seasons, and if this maxim were true, the Colonels' fans reasoned, then the 1890 edition of the Colonels was doomed. But 1890 was not a season for conventional wisdom to prevail, and the Colonels, as events proved, were anything but doomed. According to historian David Nemec, Jack Chapman did not share the pessimism surrounding the 1890 version of the Louisville Colonels: "Chapman's achievement with Louisville in 1890, when he piloted the club from the worst to first, appears to have stunned everyone but him. He seemed to know from almost the outset of the season that he was going to win."[32]

In addition to a new manager and several new players, the Colonels also had a new nickname when the 1890 season opened. About nine o'clock in the evening of March 27, a tornado, popularly termed a "cyclone," devastated Louisville. First reports set the death toll at nearly 150 people, but as workers cleared the rubble while local officials reestablished order and assessed the city's losses, the figure was revised downward to slightly less than one hundred.[33] In addition to the physical damage it inflicted on Louisville, the tornado left a pronounced psychological scar on the community. As the city recovered from the storm during the fateful spring of 1890, the local press and fans adopted the name "Cyclones" for their ravaged and hastily rebuilt team. The new name seemed appropriate for the Louisville club caught up in the whirlwind of events beyond its control. Most of the sporting press accepted the new name, and more often than not, accounts of Louisville's doings in the AA referred to the Cyclones, not the Colonels.

The 1889 Louisville Colonels. Chicken Wolf is located to the extreme right in the back row.

(Courtesy of Jay Sanford, Arvada, Colo.)

Opening day, April 18, was a rainy one in Louisville, and the game with the St. Louis Browns had to be postponed. To some, this probably seemed an omen and a justification for calling the club the Cyclones, but Chapman and his players were unaffected when the club began its historic campaign the following afternoon.[34] Louisville lost its opening game on April 19 to St. Louis by a score of 11–8. The Cyclones took an early lead and held it until the eighth inning when several errors coupled with timely hitting by St. Louis allowed the Browns to score seven runs, which decided the contest. Weary Louisville fans must have had visions of seasons past as their young players faltered late in the contest, but the youngsters rebounded and won the next three games from St. Louis. The Browns were supposed to be the team to beat in the American Association, and the Cyclones acquitted themselves well against Von der Ahe's club. Perhaps some of Louisville's more optimistic or farsighted fans viewed the opening series as an augury of events yet to come.[35]

By June 6, 1890, to the amazement of the baseball world, the Cyclones ranked third in the American Association standings behind Philadelphia and Rochester, New York, with a record of 19–16. Considering that

Louisville won only twenty-seven games all season in 1889, the club's performance seemed barely short of miraculous.[36] At the season's outset, the Philadelphia Athletics played good baseball and established a slim lead over their competitors, maintaining their tenuous occupancy of first place until early July, but when the Athletics arrived in Louisville for a crucial series beginning on July 9, the Cyclones asserted themselves. Louisville won all four games of the series, took a narrow lead on the Athletics, and served notice to all that the Cyclones were a serious threat to win the AA pennant in 1890.[37]

Several factors explained the Cyclones' surge to first place. Foremost among them, Chicken Wolf enjoyed the best season of his career. Chicken finished his eleven-year career in 1892 with a respectable lifetime batting average of .290. Only once, other than in 1890 when he hit .363, did Wolf hit .300, and that was in 1884 when he hit an even .300.[38] Throughout his career he was a reliable if unspectacular hitter, but in 1890, with many young and inexperienced pitchers toiling in the AA, Chicken feasted on what often amounted to minor league pitching.[39] Following Wolf's example, others of the Cyclones also hit well. Harry Taylor hit .306 and Charlie Hamburg .272, while veterans Phil Tomney and Farmer Weaver hit .277 and .289.[40] Pitching staffs in the American Association, as well as in the National League, were badly diluted in 1890, and good hitters such as Wolf and mediocre hitters such as Taylor, Hamburg, Tomney, and Weaver did well in the new environment.

Conversely, mediocre pitchers also enjoyed improved records against clubs with rosters populated by players past their prime or with men who probably should have been in the minor leagues. Red Ehret and Scott Stratton, each in his third year in the major leagues, combined to win fifty-nine games for the Cyclones in 1890. Prior to 1890, Ehret's career record was thirteen wins and thirty-one losses, and Stratton's was thirteen and thirty.[41] In 1890 Ehret won twenty-five games and Stratton thirty-four. Neither subsequently came close to replicating their achievements of 1890. Ehret finished his eleven-year career with a lifetime record of 139 wins and 167 losses, and in eight seasons in the major leagues Stratton compiled an overall record of 97 wins and 114 losses.[42] Ehret recorded one-fourth of his career wins in 1890, and Stratton one-third. Both pitchers, at best, were average in talent, but in the topsy-turvy atmosphere of 1890 they responded impressively against the competition they encountered.

Finally, Chapman's leadership proved invaluable. Steady, patient, and innovative, Chapman encouraged or cajoled amazing performances out of his younger, inexperienced players. In July 1890, as the Louisville club surged into first place, a sportswriter observed: "Too much credit can not be given to Manager Chapman for the successes of the Cyclones."[43] Although the sentence is perhaps reminiscent of Orator Jim O'Rourke's convoluted style, the writer makes a good point. Chapman's performance and personality were vital to his team's startling successes. After the crucial series with the Philadelphia Athletics in July, leaders in the AA viewed Louisville with greater interest, and although Von der Ahe and his peers may initially have been surprised, they soon had to reconcile themselves to the specter of the new Cyclones.

Philadelphia went into a rapid decline after the Cyclones swept the four-game series from them in early July, and they finally finished the season in eighth place. By season's end the Columbus, Ohio, Buckeyes, trailing Louisville by ten games, finished second, and Von der Ahe's Browns finished third. The *Louisville Courier-Journal* probably best expressed the sentiments of baseball fans everywhere when it stated: "The playing of the club this year has been the wonder of the base ball world. With a team that appeared ridiculously weak on paper, with hardly a star among them, and with a record of having lost 111 games the past season, Manager Chapman took the nine in hand and has brought them up from the tail end to the front. There is nothing like it in base ball history."[44] For everyone associated with the Cyclones, the 1890 season proved an extraordinary occurrence.

Byrne's Brooklyn Bridegrooms opened the 1890 season with greater expectations than did the Louisville club. Brooklyn's status was unique. The club was the reigning American Association champion, which now found itself in the National League. The Bridegrooms, moreover, remained relatively untouched by the massive defections experienced by the other NL clubs during the winter of 1889–1890. Baseball experts expected the Brooklyn club to be a serious contender for the NL pennant. In 1889 the New York Giants and the Boston Beaneaters had waged an exciting struggle for the NL crown, but in 1890 each club opened the season minus key players. New York had lost nearly all of its starting lineup, and so too had Boston. The Chicago White Stockings were in dismal condition in 1890. Although Cap Anson elected to remain, Spalding's White Stockings, like New York and Boston, were decimated by defections to the Players' League. With the exception of 1887 (when the now-defunct Detroit Wolverines had won the NL pennant), New York, Boston, and Chicago had dominated the league. Now, in 1890, most of the men who had led these clubs had cast their fortunes with the PL, and Brooklyn entered a vastly altered NL.

The Bridegrooms opened the season inauspiciously. They saw their first action in Boston against the newly rejuvenated Boston Beaneaters and lost three out of four games.[45] The Bridegrooms rebounded from this disappointing beginning, and by the end of May they had established themselves in second place behind the Philadelphia Phillies, only one game out of first. As was the case in the AA where the Philadelphia Athletics established an early lead in the race, Philadelphia's NL club got off to a good start and then withered late in the summer. Throughout most of the summer the NL pennant race featured five teams in contention—Brooklyn, Philadelphia, Chicago, Boston, and Cincinnati (also a newcomer to the NL in 1890). By early September the Bridegrooms had established themselves in first place and proceeded to win.[46]

Brooklyn's veterans acquitted themselves well in their maiden experience in the NL. They led the NL in runs scored with 884, in stolen bases with 349, and in slugging average with .369.[47] Although the Bridegrooms' hitters did not win the club batting title in 1890, they finished second in that category only five percentage points behind the Philadelphia Phillies' league-leading .269. George Pinkney led the club with a .309 batting average, and other than shortstop Germany Smith, who hit a meager .191, the Bridegrooms' regulars performed creditably with the bat. Defensive play was one of Brooklyn's keys to success. The club finished the season with a .940 fielding average and tied with Chicago in that category for first place, but perhaps more important, the Bridegrooms committed only 320 errors, the fewest of any club in the NL.[48] Brooklyn's great strength proved to lie in its pitching staff. While starting pitchers Tom Lovett, Adonis Terry, and Bob Caruthers did not lead the league in earned run averages, they recorded seventy-nine of the club's eighty-six victories.[49] Steady if not robust hitting, good defense, speed on the bases and in the field, and strong pitching were the Bridegrooms' trademarks during the 1890 pennant race. The Bridegrooms' manager, Bill McGunnigle, also made the transition to the NL with comparative ease, and as in 1889, he proved again that he was a fine tactician and a resourceful leader. Byrne could not have asked for more of his club in 1890. Although many of Byrne's former colleagues in the AA doubted his ethics when he abandoned them at a critical juncture in 1889, they had to admit that, from a purely business point of view, the Bridegrooms vindicated his decision to lead his club into the NL. It was a unique experience for the Bridegrooms. They earned the distinction of being the only club to win pennants in rival major leagues in consecutive seasons.

As the season moved toward its conclusion in 1890, rumors abounded that a postseason playoff might not occur, or if one took place, it would be a series between the AA and PL. No one ever suspected that the NL and the Brotherhood's league would challenge each other to a postseason series; there was too much bad blood between them. But some fans speculated that the AA's leaders—who now eyed the NL suspiciously after the League readily adopted Brooklyn and Cincinnati prior to the 1890 season—might retaliate by meeting the PL in a new version of the World's Championship. As rumors mounted that the Louisville Cyclones (AA) might challenge the Boston Reds (PL) to a postseason series, Lawrence Parsons, the Cyclones' owner, felt obliged to scotch them. In a public statement issued only a week before regular season play ended, he declared:

Playing the Brotherhood is out of the question for the simple reason that we are parties to the national agreement [the document which, in part, governed the relationship between the NL and the AA]. The American Association entered into the national agreement in good faith, and has never yet broken it, all reports to the contrary notwithstanding. To play the Boston club would of itself act as an expulsion from the protection of the national agreement and it would be the utmost folly when base-ball is in its present precarious condition to render ourselves liable to expulsion for the sake of eight or ten games with any club.[50]

Parsons's statement went on to indict the PL for its raids on his club, and on others in the AA, and indicated that he resented the Brotherhood's motives and tactics. He, nevertheless, was free to challenge Boston if he wished. No formal agreement governed postseason playoffs. Owners of pennant-winning clubs were free to arrange championship games. Parsons apparently viewed a playoff with the Boston Reds as being disloyal to his colleagues in the NL and the AA, and he would have no part of such self-serving foolishness.

Even though Parsons unequivocally stated his mind, he and Byrne, Brooklyn's owner, procrastinated in renewing the World's Championship series. By October 11, only four or five days before the playoffs usually began, nothing had been done to arrange a series between Louisville and Brooklyn. Quoting a report out of Louisville, the *Sporting Life* informed its readers that "Very little yet has been done about the World's Championship series."[51] The report, which appeared in the October 11 issue of the *Sporting Life,* was accurate at the point the journal went to press, but unbeknownst to the editors (or too late for them to alter their statement), Byrne arrived in Louisville that evening to meet with Parsons and Chapman to discuss the possibility of an 1890 edition of the World's Championship games. On October 12, the representatives met in the Louisville Hotel and quickly negotiated an accord for another World's Series. Byrne and Parsons apparently first considered a series that would resurrect the touring format employed in earlier playoffs by scheduling games in Louisville, Brooklyn, Boston, New York, Philadelphia, and Chicago, but they soon discarded that notion. Later, the *Sporting News* observed that, "on account of the lateness of the season and the lack of interest in the several cities mentioned resulting from the baseball war, it was decided to play only in Louisville and Brooklyn."[52] Consequently, Byrne and Parsons opted for a nine-game format featuring four games in Louisville, four in Brooklyn, and a ninth game, if necessary, in a mutually agreeable site. The owners stipulated that the series would terminate once a team won a majority of the games. Tickets to all games were priced at fifty cents each with an additional twenty-five cents for grandstand seating (for games in

Eclipse Park, the pricing system permitted Louisville to charge an extra ten cents for each seat in the Pavilion).[53] Brooklyn chose Wesley Curry as its umpire, and Louisville selected John McQuaid. Thursday, October 16, was designated as opening day for the series, only four days after the meeting between Byrne and Parsons, who issued no statement on how the proceeds from the series were to be divided. The press implied the owners would divide the gains equally.[54]

Reactions to the announcement concerning the playoffs were mixed. Most newspapers reported the upcoming event in the usual manner, but *Sporting Life* proved mildly critical of the presumption that the games were the World's Championship and headlined its report by labeling them "Inter-League Games." Richter's paper took the position that any series between the National League and the American Association fell short of deciding the "World's Championship" and editorialized that the upcoming games were "nothing more than the relative superiority of the League and Association, since the equally strong, if not stronger competitor—the Boston Players' League club—is excluded from competition, which, to establish a world's championship, must be open to all."[55] Not only had fans witnessed a frustrating, divisive, and bloody civil war in major league baseball, but now, Richter declared, cranks also were to be denied a true decision as to which club was the world's reigning champion. Baseball truly was in a dreadful state of affairs late in 1890, and interest in the World's Championship series reached its nadir among fans.

Heavy rain fell in the Louisville area on October 16, and the opening game was postponed until the next afternoon. Better weather greeted the series on October 17, and a fine crowd, about fifty-six hundred, filled Eclipse Park. As was the custom of the time, Parsons sold standing-room tickets to fans who stood along the diamond's foul lines and next to the outfield fences behind the outfielders. World's Championship baseball in Louisville was a gala event, and many ladies were evident among the spectators. Eclipse Park was the place to be seen on October 17. Although the fans were excited and expectant, they quickly were disappointed when the Bridegrooms scored three runs in the first inning and promptly established a lead over Louisville and Scott Stratton, the Cyclones' best pitcher. From this point forward, things only got worse for the Cyclones. Brooklyn scored three more runs in the fifth inning, and an additional three in the eighth. Bolstered by Adonis Terry's two-hitter, the Bridegrooms handily defeated Louisville by a score of 9–0.[56] Considering the inexperience among the Louisville players who in several cases were barely accustomed to being major leaguers, many of Louisville's cranks may not have been too surprised that the team appeared a bit unnerved during the game. Louisville committed six costly errors in the contest and caused *Sporting News* to observe that the Cyclones "were taken with stage fright when the game started, and did not have a chance to recover themselves, so vigorously did the visitors push their advantage."[57] Game one was an inauspicious beginning for Louisville.

A disappointing crowd of 2,860 gathered at Eclipse Park for game two. Rather than calling upon Red Ehret to pitch the second game, Chapman surprised many Louisville fans and chose Ed Daily to pitch for the Cyclones. Daily had begun the season with the AA's new Brooklyn club, and when it faltered he found employment with the Giants in the NL where he won two games before finally joining the Cyclones.[58] Daily quickly won six games for the Cyclones and posted a sparkling 1.94 earned run average and impressed Chapman in the process.[59]

In game two, as events proved, Chapman again demonstrated uncanny insight. Daily faced Brooklyn's Tom Lovett, who had pitched the first game for Brooklyn, and the two men locked into a duel in which each acquitted himself well. Louisville scored one run in the first inning and led the Bridegrooms for the first time in the series. Their lead was short-lived. Brooklyn gained the lead in the fourth inning, and Lovett again proved stingy with hits and runs through the next four innings. Finally, Lovett appeared to weaken in the ninth inning, and the Colonels staged a brief but futile rally. With only one out, the Cyclones scored one run and put two men on base, but Lovett asserted himself, retired the next two hitters, and ended Louisville's threat. The Bridegrooms won by a score of 5–3. It was a good game, but Louisville fell behind two games to none.

Bad weather returned for the third game. Only 1,146 fans braved the cold weather to witness the contest, and at best, it proved an unpleasant experience for players and fans alike.[60] After seven innings Brooklyn trailed Louisville by a score of 6–4. The Bridegrooms scored three runs and established a one-run lead over the Cyclones. Louisville countered with one run in the inning, and at the end of eight, the score was tied at 7–7. By the end of the eighth, the ballpark was enveloped in darkness, a cold wind swept the area, umpires Curry and McQuaid decided to end the contest and declared the game tied. Red Ehret, the Cyclones' stalwart pitcher, did not appear in the game. On Tuesday, October 21, a day that had been originally planned as an open date, game four took place in Louisville. Red Ehret finally made his debut in the series and led the Cyclones to a 5–4 victory over the Bridegrooms. The cold weather and Louisville's poor performance in the series accounted for the fact that only slightly over one thousand fans attended the game.[61] Even though the Louisville fans had their first opportunity to host a World's Championship, their patronage at the ticket window proved disappointing. The four games in Louisville attracted about twelve thousand to Eclipse Park. Any hopes for significant financial success from ticket sales now depended on the enthusiasm of the fans in Brooklyn.

Not long after midnight, on the morning of October 22, the Cyclones and the Bridegrooms departed Louisville destined for Jersey City, New Jersey, by way of the Louisville and Nashville Railroad. The train—decorated with the obligatory flags, banners, and bunting advertising the series to anyone who might be near the railway in the middle of the night—made good time and arrived in Jersey City a little after eight o'clock in the morning. After the clubs ferried across the Hudson River, the Cyclones went immediately to the Grand Central Hotel in New York City, and the Bridegrooms dispersed to their homes.[62] Cold damp weather followed them to Brooklyn and delayed the resumption of the series for an additional two days. Biting winds and cold rain dominated the New York City area while players idled away the weather-induced hiatus, and fans lost interest in the playoffs. Finally, on Saturday, October 25, in less than ideal weather, the series resumed play. One sportswriter observed, "No one supposed that ball playing was possible on any field after the two days' storm which raged during the week, but the Brooklyn club managed to get their field in order in time yesterday to announce the first game of the home series of contests with Louisville."[63] In its account of the fifth game *Sporting News* reported, the "grounds were in a sad state, and the addition of plenty of sawdust did not improve their condition very much. There were a little over a thousand spectators and the chilly atmosphere and high winds made them as uncomfortable as possible." Despite the deplorable weather conditions, the Bridegrooms and the Cyclones managed to play nine innings. Brooklyn scored two runs in the bottom of the first inning, and coasted to an easy 7–2 victory.[64] Brooklyn now led the Cyclones three games to one. When Byrne and Parsons sat down to their dinners that evening, they must have entertained gloomy thoughts. After five games the playoffs averaged about two thousand attendance per contest, and the weather, which had plagued nearly the entire series, showed no signs of improving. Fans who attended the games were docile, seeming more curious than enthusiastic. Part of the fans' mild-mannered conduct was attributable to the foul weather, but Byrne and Parsons also must have sensed an air of indifference among the spectators. Byrne had a standard for comparison. The previous year's playoffs with the Giants had been an emotional and raucous affair, and this year's playoff often resembled a wake. Nevertheless, the owners felt they had to press on and complete the series.

As was the custom, the clubs did not play on Sunday, and over the weekend the weather steadily deteriorated. By Monday, October 27, the weather was truly disagreeable. Rain did not prove a problem, but the entire metropolitan area was swept by strong, bitterly cold winds. When it came time to play game six in Washington Park, only six hundred hardy baseball fans appeared to buy tickets. The *New York Daily Tribune* informed its readers that game six was played "under even more unfavorable circumstances than the game of Saturday. The weather was bitterly cold in the Gowanus Swamp, and a cutting wind fairly froze the blood of both players and spectators. The crowd was small; it was a wonder there was anyone there at all."[65] Not only did the frozen six hundred fans endure punishing conditions, they saw their Bridegrooms fall to Louisville by a score of 9–8 in nine innings. Considering the environment in which the game was played, those who endured the frigid wind and stayed throughout the nine innings were treated to a well-played contest. Two games remained on the schedule, and Brooklyn's lead over the Cyclones had dwindled to a count of three games to two.

Before they left Washington Park on the evening of October 27, managers Chapman and McGunnigle, Byrne, and Parsons met and decided to terminate the series after next day's game:

> The agreement between Managers Chapman and McGunnigle was reached on Monday night after each realized the fact that between the cold weather and the public apathy in regard to professional ball playing there was no longer any profit in the series; in fact, a further continuance of the games would prove costly to both, as neither team had realized expenses since Saturday's game. It was therefore arranged to end the series no matter which team won, the understanding being that the two clubs should finish the series next April before the championship season of 1891 began.[66]

So, when the seventh and last game began on October 28, the players knew they were ending the season on an unexpected note.

In the short history of the World's Championships, the situation they faced was unprecedented. The 1885 series between the White Stockings and the Browns ended in a controversy with Chicago claiming a tied series and St. Louis claiming the championship, but neither seriously contemplated a formal agreement to settle the dispute the following year. By no stretch of the imagination could one claim the 1885 series halted because the teams failed to make expenses. Tempestuous weather, indifference to the series partly brought on by the baseball war, and the absence of marquee players, all conspired to render the 1890 games financially disastrous to both clubs.

When the players, coaches, and club officials assembled at Washington Park on a cold, blustery afternoon for the seventh and final game, they nearly outnumbered the estimated three hundred shivering onlookers who courageously attended the contest. Red Ehret started for Louisville and pitched a masterful game. He allowed the Bridegrooms only four hits, walked four, and gave up only two earned runs while leading Louisville to a 6–2 victory.[67] It was, however, a miserable afternoon for baseball, and the *Daily Tribune* informed its readers that when "the ball struck a player's hand, it sounded like a pistol shot."[68] The players comported themselves admirably in the game, and considering the condition of the field, the icy wind, and the small crowd, they played good baseball. Brooklyn and Louisville committed only five errors in the ball game, and they completed nine innings in an hour and one-half. With that, the World's Championship, which stood tied at three games apiece, came to a conclusion. Perhaps it was fitting that no one won the title outright. By late October, baseball fans everywhere had become accustomed to unusual events in major league baseball, and to many cranks, a tied and stalled World's Championship series probably seemed an appropriate capstone to a frustrating season of major league baseball.

From any viewpoint, the 1890 World's Championship games ranked the poorest of any played. Attendance totaled about fourteen thousand for the seven games. Some of the games played in St. Louis in 1886 and 1887 drew nearly that many fans to a single contest. Under normal circumstances Brooklyn was a good baseball town. In the second game of the 1889 series against the Giants, a throng of 16,172 fans crowded into Washington Park. In the 1890 playoffs a total of slightly less than 2,000 fans attended the three games in Washington Park. Cold weather certainly had a lot to do with the poor attendance, but Chapman and McGunnigle also understood the realities of 1890. Fans were not enthusiastic about the series. Most of their favorite players were in the Players' League. The Cyclones failed to excite baseball fans outside Louisville, and even in Louisville, where the series enjoyed two days of fairly decent baseball weather, attendance proved disappointing. Consequently, Byrne and Parsons did not make a profit, and the players got nothing. Baseball clubs were awash with red ink in 1890, and the World's Championship receipts mirrored the trend. In the midst of the series, *Sporting News* rendered its opinion: "The World's Championship (?) series thus far has been a gigantic failure."[69]

As harsh as the judgment may have seemed to Byrne and Parsons, it was apt. An inconclusive series between a renegade former AA club and an AA club virtually unknown to baseball fans nationwide certainly failed to enhance the World's Championship in 1890. Inclement weather set aside, the fans, even the insatiable Brooklyn fans who historically demonstrated their love of the Bridegrooms, lost interest in baseball's autumn games and shunned the cold, windswept ballparks. Perhaps the series' most distinctive hallmark was its spirit of harmony. Not a single serious quarrel with the umpires occurred, no charges of hippodroming surfaced, neither Byrne nor Parsons uttered public statements that created a public furor. The 1890 World's Championship was less than exciting, but it was orderly. It also was the last of the World's Championships between the National League and the American Association.

Conclusion

Other than the 1990s, no decade in the history of major league baseball proved as turbulent and controversial as the 1880s. Only six major leagues have appeared in organized baseball since the owners took control of the game in 1876, and the 1880s gave birth to half of them. The decade produced the American Association, the Union Association, and the Players' League and witnessed the deaths of the last two. Both sought to rival the dominant National League and the struggling American Association, and both died after only a single season. Few were surprised that the Union Association perished once the 1884 season concluded; it was poorly organized, inadequately financed, and staffed with second-rate clubs at the outset.

The Players' League, on the other hand, was stocked with talented players and proved popular with the baseball fans during the summer of 1890. Even so, it faced financial losses it could not withstand in its war against the other two major leagues. Soon after the season ended, National League and Players' League leaders held a "harmony conference" in New York City to seek a rapprochement in order to stem the financial hemorrhaging caused by the titanic 1890 struggle among the leagues.[1] Players were excluded from the conference. In effect, the financial backers of several of the players' franchises sold out to the League. Benjamin Rader aptly described the Players' demise:

> When Spalding called for a peace meeting at his Fifth Avenue Hotel suite in New York in October 1890, he refused to negotiate with Ward or any of the players. While the Brotherhood men seethed, in the words of Spalding "the monied men met with the monied men." By a combination of complex stratagems that included buying out PL backers and allowing them to invest in NL clubs, Spalding brought down the PL. As a sop to the rebel players, he allowed them to return to their original NL and AA teams without penalties.[2]

Spalding was delighted with the results of the National League's war with the Brotherhood. His tactics were the sort that robber barons of the late nineteenth century employed in other fields, and by 1891, even though the AA survived the great 1890 baseball war, the NL again emerged as unchallenged master of major league baseball.

Events of the 1880s also led to the demise of the American Association after the 1891 season. Already stricken before the players' revolt, the association was severely damaged during the summer of 1890 as the three major leagues competed for the patronage of the baseball fans. Once the Players' League was buried, the other two leagues launched a second war as they competed to sign players seeking contracts. The AA, ill-prepared to contend with the NL, struggled through the 1891 season.[3]

When the 1891 season ended, baseball fans waited to see if the NL and the AA would continue the World's Championship series. The Boston Reds (AA) led by Dan Brouthers and Hugh Duffy easily won the Association's pennant over the St. Louis Browns, while the Boston Beaneaters (NL), led by pitchers John Clarkson and Kid Nichols who won a combined sixty-three games for the Beaneaters, captured the League's crown by three and one-half games over the Chicago White Stockings. Baseball fans anticipated a unique series in 1891. For the first time a World's Championship offered the prospect of two teams from the same city competing for the title, but it was not to be. On October 9, 1891, the Boston Reds issued a challenge to the Boston Beaneaters, and the Beaneaters rejected it. When queried about the impasse between the two Boston clubs, Nick Young, NL president, sustained the Beaneaters' position and declared that the League's champion was justified in refusing to play the Reds. Young asserted that the NL's arrangement with the AA had been voided during the recent baseball wars, and that the NL was fully justified in ignoring the challenge offered by the Boston Reds.[4]

In reality, the National League leadership sensed the American Association was on the verge of collapse. Now, they realized, was the time to destroy the Association. When they held the annual meeting in November 1891, NL leaders clearly indicated their willingness to expand the League to twelve teams in 1892. The upshot of this tactic was to entice four of the stronger AA teams to affiliate with the NL and, by so doing, end the AA as a major league.[5] After a good deal of posturing by nearly everyone associated with major league baseball, a deal was struck.

The National League admitted four of the American Association's franchises (St. Louis, Baltimore, Washington, and Louisville) into the League and allegedly paid $135,000 for the rights to the remaining five AA clubs, which were then allowed to die.[6] Thus when the 1892 season began, the Players' League was dead, the American Association was also, and the National League (now a twelve- rather than an eight-team circuit, giving rise to the term *Big League,* which remained synonymous with major league baseball) dominated major league baseball until the modern-day American

League was born in 1901. The 1880s proved a fertile birthing-time for major leagues, and a potent contributor to the cemeteries in which the National League buried its rivals.

Not only did the 1880s produce and dispatch major leagues, it was also an era in which the National League owners and their counterparts in the doomed American Association managed to assert firm control over their players. The reserve clause was maintained; salary restrictions were ultimately enforced when rival leagues faltered; the Brotherhood of Professional Base Ball Players was routed; and Albert Goodwill Spalding and his peers achieved their goals of limiting competition and reducing players to subservience. As testimony of the owners' successes, several generations of major league baseball players labored well into the twentieth century under the terms Spalding and his cohorts fashioned during the baseball wars of the 1880s. Although he did not live to see the NL emerge as the sole major league during the 1890s, William Ambrose Hulbert certainly would have approved of the NL's triumphant navigation of the 1880s.

Judged by modern standards, the seven World's Championships of the 1880s were none too successful. One (1890) ended in a tie, one (1885) was indecisive, and three (1884, 1885, and 1890) attracted only 29,500 spectators to seventeen games for an average of 1,735 per game, well below the norm for major league teams in the thick of pennant races in the 1880s. Four series (1886, 1887, 1888, 1889) were a bit more successful and more complex than the other three World's Championships. They enjoyed a total attendance of 170,900 patrons, or about 85 percent of all the tickets sold during the seven championship series. Owing to the number of games (forty) comprising these four series, the attendance averaged only slightly above 4,200 per contest. The 1886 series between St. Louis and Chicago was the highlight of the World's Championships. Von der Ahe and Spalding earned a good deal of money from the six-game series, which attracted an estimated 42,500 spectators. St. Louis's games with Detroit in 1887 and with New York in 1888 also yielded profits for the clubs' owners, but these championships entailed substantial travel as games were played in several cities. Travel expenses coupled with the Browns' poor showing against the Wolverines in 1887 and the Giants in 1888 lessened the 1887 and 1888 series' net financial returns to Von der Ahe, Stearns, and Day. The World's Championship of 1889, the first between New York and Brooklyn clubs, drew 49,600 fans to nine games (an average of 5,511 per contest) and earned John Day and Charles Byrne tidy profits. The 1890 series between Louisville and Brooklyn barely earned enough to cover expenses. As a consequence, owners only occasionally scratched a profit out of the interleague championships.

One factor was certainly obvious during the history of the World's Championships of the 1880s: The owners failed to establish a standardized, successful format for the playoffs. The first, between the New York Metropolitans and the Providence Grays, proved too restricted as it occurred on three successive days in New York City. Its extreme opposite, the fifteen-game playoff between the Detroit Wolverines and the St. Louis Browns in ten cities in 1887, was too open-ended. Once the Wolverines won the Dauvray Cup, the remaining games, except for the homecoming game in Detroit, attracted meager attendance. The best approach to maximizing attendance and profits proved to be the style followed in the St. Louis–Chicago games in 1886 or New York–Brooklyn series in 1889 when all games were played on the clubs' home fields before their adoring and excited fans. The 1886 series averaged better than seven thousand paid admissions per game, and the Giants and the Bridegrooms attracted more than 5,500 fans per contest in 1889. Extended road trips employing what amounted to exhibition formats usually did not enthuse fans in neutral cities. The playoffs drew a good deal of attention from the press, but the fans in neutral cities rarely showed up at the ticket windows.

Bad weather often influenced the World's Championships in the 1880s and undoubtedly affected ticket sales. Late afternoon contests were frequently suspended owing to failing light as October presaged the coming of winter. Nineteen of the seven championships' fifty-seven contests failed to play nine innings, and shortened games probably convinced patrons that the contests were really not the sort of baseball they wished to witness. In spite of all the publicity and ballyhoo, many fans, and especially those in communities not directly tied to the contestants, probably viewed the World's Championships as a curiosity and ignored them. On at least two occasions, suspicious cranks circulated rumors that the players were hippodroming to inflate gate receipts. While no credible evidence emerged to substantiate allegations that players colluded to lengthen playoffs, such rumors undoubtedly discouraged attendance and tarnished the affected championships. Nasty quarrels between owners frequently marred the World's Championships, lessening fans' enthusiasm for what should have been major league baseball's premiere event. In the competing clubs' hometowns, if the title was still in the balance, fans usually turned out in numbers great enough to fund the teams' expenses and to generate respectable profits for the owners. But, even in St. Louis and Brooklyn, a decided series or inclement weather conditions often lessened attendance and eroded or destroyed profits. Fans clearly did not accept the World's Championship with the enthusiasm with which their children and grandchildren embraced the World Series of the twentieth century.

Another factor that limited the success of the World's Championships was the evident rancor between owners and players. Throughout the decade, the moguls of baseball steadily endeavored to enforce the reserve clause, to employ the blacklist, to restrict salaries, and to subjugate their players. In desperation the players formed a brotherhood of baseball players to defend themselves against predatory management. Although the Brotherhood's actions were amply justified, many of baseball's patrons, already shocked by the unrest in organized and unorganized labor in the United States during the 1880s, were probably alienated during the bitter quarrel between the owners and the players, and much like modern baseball fans, annoyed by the evident lack of concern about their interests, fans in the 1880s frequently were irked by the constant bickering. The St. Louis Browns, who participated in four of the series, had a particularly venomous relationship with their owner, Christian Von der Ahe; and the Chicago White Stockings regularly clashed with Albert Goodwill Spalding and his tory manager, Cap Anson. If baseball was America's sport, many fans apparently viewed the game as being infected with un-American traits common with their suspicions that the American labor movement in general was powered by foreign ideologies. Whereas cranks usually proved willing to support their local heroes during the regular season, they often refused to patronize grasping owners and sulking players from other cities in postseason play.

Failure to create an incentive for the players often led to poorly or indifferently played games. Owners such as Von der Ahe and Spalding (with an exception in 1886) usually refused to share with their players whatever income their clubs generated in the World's Championships. Frederick Kimball Stearns and his partners granted their triumphant Wolverines only token compensation for their marvelous accomplishments in 1887. In some of the moderately profitable experiences in the playoffs, the Giants and the Bridegrooms were virtually ignored financially by their owners. Most owners simply viewed the World's Championships as a part of the players' contract duties and with these rather cavalier attitudes alienated their players, who understandably wanted substantial financial rewards for postseason games. The players' resentment often manifested itself through lackluster play and rowdy behavior. Some of the players distrusted teammates who, they believed, were too cozy with management, and championship clubs were often divided into factions that openly disliked each other. Championship games often were conducted in a poisoned atmosphere, and potential ticket buyers were repelled.

Although the series in the 1880s were styled the World's Championships, the games were not inclusive. In their determination to crush competition, the National League and the American Association ignored the Union Association in 1884 and the Players' League in 1890. In the case of the Union Association, the league was poorly organized, and few observers were distressed when it was not invited into the playoffs; but in the case of the Players' League, many of baseball's experts, newspaper editors, and reporters clearly believed it was a superior league, stocked with accomplished players, and that its champion ought to have been included in the World's Championship games. In the eyes of many devotees of major league baseball, the exclusion of rivals tainted the concept of World's Championships in 1884 and 1890. Such games managed to wring a few more dollars from baseball-hungry fans, but rational observers certainly understood that the World's Champions emerged from leagues bent on destroying competitors and quelling players' discontents, not on deciding the World's Championship through inclusive and sportsmanlike means.

The National League undeniably dominated the playoffs with the American Association. Of the five championships settled on the diamond, the NL won four. In total games (ties excepted), the NL won 60 percent of its contests with the AA. Some of the NL champions administered sound thrashings (in 1884, 1887, 1888, and 1889) to their AA rivals in the World's Championships. Such victories reinforced the widely held perception among NL owners, players, and loyal fans that the AA, perhaps excepting the St. Louis Browns, was largely comprised of sophisticated minor league clubs. Even in the case of the Browns, they were easily defeated by the Wolverines in 1887 and by the Giants in 1888. Few knowledgeable cranks argued that the AA was superior to the NL, and many would have maintained it was not even the other's equal. The World's Championship series did, indeed, appear to verify the AA's inferior status. Debates on the relative merits of the NL and the AA ended in 1892 when the NL conquered its rival.

After the demise of the American Association during the winter of 1891–1892, the National League attempted to perpetuate the concept of postseason championship games. In 1892 the League developed the idea of a split season to produce teams to compete in a championship series. In 1892 the Boston Beaneaters (the first-half winners with a record of 52–22) defeated the Cleveland Spiders (the second-half winners with a record of 53–22) in the first of the NL intramural championship series.[7] The NL did not sponsor a championship series in 1893, but in 1894, at the urging of William C. Temple, a Pittsburgh businessman and former president of the Pittsburgh Pirates, the National League revived the idea of championship games and adopted a new format in which the first place team met the second place club in a postseason series. Temple donated a handsome silver cup to commemorate the intramural spectacle, and for each of the next four years, the NL featured a season-ending "World Series." The Temple Cup series did not capture the imagination of baseball fans, and after the 1897 series between Boston and Baltimore, the Temple Cup playoffs died.[8]

For the next five years, major league baseball did not pretend to conduct a championship series. When the American League (AL) arose in 1901 to challenge the NL, it met the same sort of hostility as the AA encountered in the 1880s. The NL leadership attempted to downplay the AL's claim as a legitimate rival, as it had done with the AA in the early 1880s. After two years, in January 1903, the NL and the AL representatives gathered in Cincinnati, Ohio, and concluded a peace treaty.[9] Once the leagues made peace, baseball fans again anticipated a championship series between them. Championship baseball was reborn in 1903 when the Boston Pilgrims (AL) defeated the Pittsburgh Pirates (NL) five games to three in a best of nine series. The 1903 series was reminiscent of those in the 1880s. Once the season concluded, the clubs arranged the championship games, set ticket prices, and discharged all the series' details as they saw fit.

Then, in 1904, the NL and the AA did not conduct a championship series. John T. Brush's New York Giants won the NL pennant in 1904, and he and his manager, John J. McGraw, refused to play the AL's Boston club. Both Brush, who purchased John B. Day's controlling interest in the Giants in 1903, and McGraw had clashed with the AL president, Byron Bancroft "Ban" Johnson, and their hatred of Johnson motivated their decisions regarding a possible series in 1904. Personal animosities coupled with complete freedom to accept or reject a challenge enabled Brush and McGraw to do as they pleased. But, even though they acted within their rights, they encountered intense criticism for vetoing the 1904 championship. Brush was so stung by his critics he promptly drafted a plan to institutionalize an annual series between the NL and the AL. His plan, which made no reference to the World's Championships of the 1880s, was presented to the NL owners during their annual conference early in 1905. It was quickly accepted and forwarded to the AL owners who were simultaneously conducting their annual meeting in New York City. The AL owners promptly approved the proposal without a dissenting vote.[10]

The new plan was a complete departure from the World's Championships of the 1880s, the National League's attempts to stage intramural championships in the 1890s, and the 1903 World Series. Prior to 1905, the pennant winners made all the arrangements for a series, but the new agreement drastically altered this concept. Brush's plan, which continued the practice of referring to the postseason games as the World's Championship, called for a best of seven series that would be arranged by baseball's National Commission, created by the National Agreement of 1903. The National Commission, a three-man body that automatically included the presidents of the NL and AL, possessed enormous powers in settling disputes, issuing directives, and governing baseball under the guidelines granted it by major league baseball's owners. Brush's plan outlined the basic ingredients of a championship series. In addition to mandating a best of seven series (the opening site of a series was to be chosen by lot, all games were to be played in the teams' home ballparks, and a seventh game, if necessary, was to be conducted at a location selected by the National Commission), the Brush proposal attended major concerns relating to future championship matches. In all, 10 percent of the gross receipts were to be reserved to the National Commission to defray administrative costs; the players were to share in 40 percent of the remaining 90 percent of gross receipts from the first four games; and the owners were granted the remainder of gross receipts for all games. Each club was obligated to pay its own expenses and to post a forfeit bond prior to the series.

Selections of umpires and their compensation were to be governed by the National Commission, which, in addition, was empowered to settle all disputes arising from championship games. As a result of the 1905 agreement between the two major leagues, upcoming championship games were destined to be tightly controlled by a central authority constituted by the several owners in both leagues. Pennant-winning teams were obligated to meet in a season-ending playoff.

Beginning in 1905, postseason series between league champions no longer varied as they had in the past. Instead, baseball's magnates turned to a specific format to conduct future championships. Owners of pennant-winning clubs no longer dictated schedules, game locations, ticket prices, compensation to players, or umpire selections and their salaries. The National Commission, with the example of the 1880s to guide them, handled the myriad administrative details surrounding postseason championship play. Major league baseball finally rejected the laissez-faire style of the World's Championships of the 1880s. Nevertheless, the National Commission and all of baseball were mindful of the experiences of the 1880s, and those distant and now nearly forgotten championship series between the National League and the American Association helped establish the groundwork for the modern-day World Series.

Appendix

World's Championship Series, 1884–1890

Year	Teams[a]	Games	Total Attendance[b]
1884	Providence (NL) and New York (AA) (Providence 3–0)	3	4,000
1885	Chicago (NL) and St. Louis (AA)[c] (Ended in a 3–3–1 tie)	7	13,000
1886	St. Louis (AA) and Chicago (NL) (St. Louis 4–2)	6	42,500
1887	Detroit (NL) and St. Louis (AA) (Detroit 10–5)	15	32,800
1888	New York (NL) and St. Louis (AA) (New York 6–4)	10	46,000
1889	New York (NL) and Brooklyn (AA) (New York 6–3)	9	49,600
1890	Brooklyn (NL) and Louisville (AA)[d] (Ended in a 3–3–1 tie)	7	12,500
Totals		57	200,400
Average attendance per game			3,515

[a] Parentheses indicate champion and number of games won.
[b] Attendance based on newspaper estimates and turnstile counts.
[c] A bitterly contested series.
[d] A poorly attended series plagued by harsh weather.

Notes

Introduction

1. George B. Kirsch, "Baseball in the Civil War," *Civil War Times* 14 (May 1998): 30–39.

2. David L. Spotts, *Campaigning with Custer and the Nineteenth Kansas Volunteer Cavalry on the Washita Campaign, 1868–1869,* ed. E. A. Brininstool (New York: Argonaut Press, 1965), 111–12.

3. W. S. Nye, *Carbine and Lance: The Story of Old Fort Sill* (Norman: University of Oklahoma Press, 1943), 88.

4. Spotts, *Campaigning with Custer,* 111–12, 115. On July 4, 1885, Company A of the Thirteenth Infantry was stationed on the Mexican border participating in the Geronimo campaign. Company A's baseball team challenged a group of local cowboys to a game and wagered as a prize two barrels of Milwaukee beer, a choice beverage for lovers of quality American beer. The soldiers won the game, but they generously shared the beer with the cowboys and the spectators who gathered to watch the contest. Don Rickey Jr., *Forty Miles a Day on Beans and Hay* (Norman: University of Oklahoma Press, 1963), 205. At remote Fort Larned on the Pawnee Fork of the Arkansas River in Kansas, soldiers stationed there after the Civil War played baseball to relieve their boredom while waiting to escort wagon traffic on the Santa Fe Trail or to participate in an occasional skirmish with marauding Indians. See Leo E. Oliva, *Fort Larned: Guardian of the Santa Fe Trail* (Topeka: Kansas State Historical Society, 1997), 81.

5. *New York World,* 7 August 1883, 4. See also John Rickards Betts, "Sporting Journalism in Nineteenth-Century America," *American Quarterly* 5 (spring 1953): 53; and Donald J. Mrozek, *Sport and American Mentality, 1880–1910* (Knoxville: University of Tennessee Press, 1983), xiv.

6. Robert Knight Barney and Frank Dallier, "I'd Rather Be a Lamp Post in Chicago than a Millionaire in Any Other City: William A. Hulbert, Civic Pride, and the Birth of the National League," *Nine* 2 (fall 1993): 46–48; Albert G. Spalding, *America's National Game* (Lincoln: University of Nebraska Press, 1992), 210–14.

7. *Constitution and Playing Rules of the National League of Professional Base Ball Clubs, 1876* (Philadelphia: Reach and Johnston, 1876), 6.

8. Dean A. Sullivan, ed., *Early Innings: A Documentary History of Baseball, 1825–1908* (Lincoln: University of Nebraska Press, 1995), 92–96; Peter Levine, *A. G. Spalding and the Rise of Baseball: The Promise of American Sport* (New York: Oxford University Press, 1985), 23–24. Spalding later was certain that the crusade to cleanse baseball was both holy and overdue: "Base-ball could not be said to have been put on a permanent and honest basis, independent of the gambling influence until the organization of the National League in 1876." A. G. Spalding, "Base-Ball," *Cosmopolitan* 7 (October 1889): 606. See also David Stevens, *Baseball's Radical for All Seasons: A Biography of John Montgomery Ward* (Lanham, Md.: Scarecrow Press, 1998), 9; Alfred H. Spink, *The National Game* (St. Louis: National Game Publishing, 1910), 11.

9. Benjamin G. Rader, *Baseball: A History of America's Game* (Urbana: University of Illinois Press, 1992), 40–41; Charles C. Alexander, *Our Game: An American Baseball History* (New York: Henry Holt, 1991), 37.

10. David Nemec, *The Beer and Whiskey League: The Illustrated History of the American Association—Baseball's Renegade Major League* (New York: Lyons and Burford, 1994), 20–24; Sullivan, *Early Innings,* 119–21; Harold Seymour, *Baseball: The Early Years* (New York: Oxford University Press, 1960), 78–80.

11. Rader, *Baseball,* 54; Robert F. Burk, *Never Just a Game: Players, Owners, and American Baseball to 1920* (Chapel Hill: University of North Carolina Press, 1994), 72–73; *New York Times,* 18 February 1883, 8; *New York Daily Tribune,* 18 February 1883, 10.

12. James D. Hardy Jr., *The New York Giants Base Ball Club: The Growth of a Team and a Sport, 1870 to 1900* (Jefferson, N.C.: McFarland, 1996), 83.

1—The 1880s

1. Department of the Interior, Census Office, Report on the Population of the United States at the Eleventh Census, 1890 (Washington, D.C.: U.S. GPO, 1895), pt. 1, lvi.

2. Ibid.; Department of the Interior, Census Office, Statistics of the Population of the United States at the Tenth Census (Washington, D.C.: U.S. GPO, 1883), xxxix, 536.

3. Department of the Interior, Eleventh Census, pt. 1, xi.

4. Ibid., xi, lxv.

5. Howard P. Chudacoff and Judith E. Smith, *The Evolution of American Urban Society* (Englewood Cliffs, N.J.: Prentice-Hall, 1994), 115.

6. House of Representatives, Exec. Doc. no. 406, 51st Cong., 2d sess., Statistical Abstract of the United States, 1890 (Washington, D.C.: GPO, 1891), 209.

7. Gunther Barth, *City People: The Rise of Modern City Culture in Nineteenth Century America* (New York: Oxford University Press, 1980), 15.

8. Dale A. Somers, "The Leisure Revolution: Recreation in the American City, 1820–1920," *Journal of Popular Culture* 5 (summer 1971): 126.

9. Peter Levine, *Ellis Island to Ebbets Field: Sport and the American Jewish Experience* (New York: Oxford University Press, 1992), 88; John M. Murrin and James M. Rosenheim, "America at Play: The National Pastime versus College Football, 1860–1914," *Princeton Alumni Weekly,* 6 October 1975, 14.

10. Department of Commerce, Bureau of the Census, *Historical Statistics of the United States, Colonial Times to 1970* (Washington, D.C.: U.S. GPO, 1975), pt. 1, 134, 165.

11. Chudacoff and Smith, *The Evolution of American Urban Society,* 78.

12. Jane Addams, *Twenty Years at Hull House* (New York: Macmillan, 1911), 80–81. Also see Jane Addams, *The Spirit of Youth and the City Streets* (Urbana: University of Illinois Press, 1972), 4–5; Barth, *City People,* 8–10.

13. Ann Cook, Marilyn Gittell, and Herb Mack, *City Life, 1865–1900: Views of Urban America* (New York: Praeger, 1973), 136.

14. Department of the Interior, Eleventh Census, pt. 1, 681. As early as 1883 the revolution in street transportation was apparent. In 1883 the recently elected leader of the National Street Railway Association, Moody Merrill, on the occasion

of his elevation to the association's governing board delivered a speech to his colleagues in which he informed them that North American cities in Canada and the United States boasted nearly three thousand miles of track, employed thirty-five thousand workers, and depended upon one hundred thousand horses to draw streetcars. He estimated that the street railways annually transported 1,212,400,000 passengers. *New York Daily Tribune,* 13 December 1883, 3.

15. Seymour, *Baseball,* 203. See also John Rickards Betts, "The Technological Revolution and the Rise of Sport, 1850–1900," *Mississippi Valley Historical Review* 40 (September 1953): 247; Steven A. Riess, *Sport in Industrial America, 1850–1920* (Wheeling, Ill.: Harlan Davidson, 1995), 33–36.

16. John M. Thomas, "Frank DeHass Robison," and "Matthew Stanley Robison," in *Baseball's First Stars,* ed. Frederick Ivor-Campbell, Robert L. Tiemann, and Mark Rucker (Cleveland, Ohio: Society for American Baseball Research, 1996), 142.

17. Department of Interior, Census Office, Report on Transportation Business in the United States at the Eleventh Census, 1890, part 1—Transportation by Land (Washington, D.C.: GPO, 1895), 53.

18. Betts, "Technological Revolution," 235.

19. U.S. Department of Commerce, *Historical Statistics,* pt. 2, 786. For an early example of telegraphed reports of baseball games, see *New York Clipper,* 30 June 1884, 234. Telegraphing sports news also had its dangers. Criminals soon learned that tapping telegraph wires allowed them to forward bogus information so their confederates could victimize bookmakers. *New York Clipper,* 21 July 1883, 282.

20. Betts, "Sporting Journalism," 42–43, 49. When Joseph Pulitzer purchased the *New York World* in 1883, he set out to create what was probably the first sports section in an American newspaper designed for daily circulation. At first the *World* emphasized racing, yachting, pedestrian events, football, and billiards, but baseball soon became a staple as well. Pulitzer's success caused others to follow suit, and by the 1890s, sports sections were common in most daily newspapers. Ibid., 53; William Henry Nugent, "The Sports Section," *American Mercury* 16 (March 1929): 330–36. Sports reporters in the 1880s usually referred to spectators as "cranks." According to Gunther Barth, the term *fan* originated as a shortened version of the English expression for *fancy,* meaning those who fancied dogfights and boxing matches as entertainment. The term *fan* migrated across the Atlantic and eventually replaced the term *crank.* Barth, *City People,* 152.

21. Bruce Catton, "The Great American Game," *American Heritage* 10 (April 1959): 18.

22. David Pietrusza, *Lights On! The Wild Century-Long Saga of Night Baseball* (Lanham, Md.: Scarecrow Press, 1997), 4–26; Oscar Eddleton, "Under the Lights," *Baseball Research Journal* (1980): 37–38; Larry G. Bowman, "'I Think It Is Pretty Ritzy, Myself': Kansas Minor League Teams and Night Baseball," *Kansas History* (winter 1995–1996): 252; Sheila E. Schroeder, "When Technology and Culture Collide: The Advent of Night Baseball," *Nine* 3 (fall 1994): 85–86; Larry Bowman, "Night Baseball Comes to the Texas League," *Nine* 5 (spring 1997): 210.

23. Philip J. Lowry, *Green Cathedrals: The Ultimate Celebration of All 271 Major League and Negro League Ballparks Past and Present* (New York: Addison-Wesley, 1992), 127–28. There were no minimum distances for outfield fences in the 1880s. In 1892 the NL ruled that any ball hit over a fence less than 235 feet from home

plate was a ground rule double. David Nemec, *The Rules of Baseball* (New York: Lyons and Burford, 1994), 3.

24. Lowry, *Green Cathedrals,* 108, 115, 226, 242.

25. Ibid., 215, 205, 188.

26. *Sporting Life,* 27 August, 24 September 1884, 7, 3.

27. *National Police Gazette,* 18 October 1884, 13; John Thorn and Peter Palmer, eds., *Total Baseball: The Ultimate Encyclopedia of Baseball* (New York: Harper-Collins, 1993), 1902; Marshall D. Wright, *Nineteenth Century Baseball: Year-by-Year Statistics for the Major League Teams, 1871 through 1900* (Jefferson, N.C.: McFarland, 1996), 140–44.

28. Nemec, *Rules,* x, 4–7; Rick Wolff, editorial director, *The Baseball Encyclopedia,* 8th ed. (New York: Macmillan, 1990), 2777.

29. Wolff, *Baseball Encyclopedia,* 2777; *New York Clipper,* 1 December 1883, 609.

30. *New York Clipper,* 22 December 1883, 672.

31. Wolff, *Baseball Encyclopedia,* 2777; Bill James, *The Bill James Historical Baseball Abstract* (New York: Villard Books, 1988), 22; Mark S. Foster, "Playing by the Rules: The Evolution of Baseball in the Nineteenth Century," *Colorado Heritage* (spring 1995): 47–49.

32. Nemec, *Rules,* 10, 44–47.

33. Wolff, *Baseball Encyclopedia,* 1883, 1962, 2140.

34. Nemec, *Rules,* 38; James, *Baseball Abstract,* 22; Frederick Ivor-Campbell, "Charles Radbourn(e), Jr.," and John J. O'Malley, "Timothy John Keefe," in *Baseball's First Stars,* 131–32, 83–84; Robert L. Tiemann, "Charles Frederick King," in *Nineteenth Century Stars,* ed. Robert L. Tiemann and Mark Rucker (Manhattan, Ks.: Ag Press, 1989), 72; David L. Holst, "Charles G. Radbourne: The Greatest Pitcher of the Nineteenth Century," *Illinois Historical Journal* 81 (winter 1988): 255–68.

35. Nemec, *Rules,* 16–17; numbered uniforms did not become mandatory until 1931 (ibid., 20).

36. The official rosters of the fourteen teams participating in the playoffs series between 1884 and 1890 listed a total of one hundred seventy players, or an average of twelve per team. Wolff, *Baseball Encyclopedia,* 81, 88, 90, 92, 94, 96, 99, 101, 103, 105, 107, 109, 111; Donald D. Jones, *Former Major League Teams: An Encyclopedia* (Jefferson, N.C.: McFarland, 1995), 68–70, 81–94, 96–98, 115–16, 125, 128–29, 136–39.

37. *Sporting News,* 24 May 1886, 4; *New York Clipper,* 24 March 1883, 5.

38. Nemec, *Rules,* 26, 141–42. Some of baseball's most distinguished patrons in the 1880s were annoyed by the noisy coaches. One such was Helen Dauvray, a noted actress and the wife of Giants' star John Montgomery Ward. She wrote a letter to Nicholas Young, the NL president, bemoaning the trend in baseball toward the base coaches' verbal abuse of opposing players. In her letter Miss Dauvray observed that good coaching was essential for a team's success on the field, but she found the sort of coaching designed to "rattle" the opposition "annoying to the spectators and [it] lowers the tone of the game." Helen Dauvray to Nicholas F. Young, June 12, 1887. *Sporting Life,* 22 June 1887, 1. Young politely replied to Miss Dauvray's letter and agreed with her that some of the coaches did indeed go too far in their enthusiasm for their tasks. Ibid. See also John Richard Husman, "Walter Arlington Latham," in *Nineteenth Century Stars,* 76; *Sporting News,* 18 June 1887, 1.

39. Larry Bowman, "Moses Fleetwood Walker," in Peter Levine, ed., *Baseball History: An Annual of Original Baseball Research* (Westport, Conn.: Meckler Books, 1989), 66; David W. Zang, *Fleet Walker's Divided Heart: The Life of Baseball's First Black Major Leaguer* (Lincoln: University of Nebraska Press, 1995), 45. For a brief account of the evolution of sports equipment in the late nineteenth century, see Riess, *Sport in Industrial America,* 37–42. For examples of baseball equipment advertised in sporting journals during the 1880s, see *Sporting News,* 19 May, 2 June 1888, 5, 8; 4, 13 April 1889, 6, 6. Also see Richard E. Noble, "Saving Face: The Genesis of the Catcher's Mask," *Baseball History* (fall 1987): 46–49.

40. *New York Clipper,* 23 March, 12 December 1883, 5, 609. St. Louis (AA) and Chicago (NL) were notorious as "kickers." Much of their reputation for challenging umpires was earned by the Browns' Arlie Latham and the White Stockings' Cap Anson, both volatile men and dedicated umpire-baiters. *Sporting News,* 24 May 1886, 4. Umpires were rarely assaulted by fans in the ballparks, but once on the streets they were vulnerable to abuse. In 1886 a gang of street thugs attacked an umpire in Brooklyn after a game, and according to one account, it was "a gang of hoodlums that infest the corner of Nassau and Adams Streets and who make Kennedy's gin mill their headquarters." *Sporting News,* 31 May 1886, 5. In 1884 a notorious altercation between a player and an umpire occurred in Buffalo, New York. John Montgomery Ward of the New York Gothams (NL) encountered John Gaffney, an NL umpire, in the rotunda of the Genessee House in Buffalo, and the player and the umpire physically clashed. Earlier in the afternoon Gaffney had called a game because of growing darkness, and even though Ward's team won the game, he criticized Gaffney's judgment and general umpiring abilities. Gaffney responded that Ward was not much of a player, whereupon Ward struck Gaffney and opened a nasty cut above the umpire's left eye. *New York Times,* 28 September 1884, 2. For an interesting interpretation of the urban fans' attitudes toward umpires, see Barth, *City People,* 173–74. Many historians have argued that attitudes toward umpires showed that crowds in the 1880s were often mainly composed of working-class Americans, who did not espouse the Victorian ideal of gentlemanly comportment in the face of adversity. A minor poet of the 1880s clearly expresses this viewpoint:

> Mother, may I slug the umpire
> May I slug him right away?
> So he cannot be here, mother,
> When the clubs begin to play?
> Let me clasp his throat, dear mother,
> In a dear, delightful grip
> And with one hand and with the other
> Bat him several in the lip.
> Let me climb his frame, dear mother,
> While the happy people shout;
> I'll not kill him, dearest mother,
> I will only knock him out.
> Let me mop the ground up, mother,
> With his person, dearest, do;
> If the ground can stand it, mother
> I don't see why you can't too . . .

(reproduced in Murrin and Rosenheim, "America at Play," 15). See also Larry Gerlach, "On Umpires: Historical Perspectives, Contemporary Observations," *Nine* 7 (fall 1998): 16–19.

41. Quoted in Barbara C. Schaaf, *Mr. Dooley's Chicago* (Garden City, N.Y.: Anchor Press/Doubleday, 1977), 164. Mr. Martin Dooley was a fictional creation, a philosopher-bartender through whom Finely Peter Dunne, his creator and a prominent journalist in the late nineteenth century and early twentieth century, dispensed wit and wisdom to his readers. Charles Fanning, *Finley Peter Dunne and Mr. Dooley: The Chicago Years* (Lexington: University of Kentucky Press, 1978), ix.

42. Nemec, *Rules*, 170–74; *New York Daily Tribune*, 8 December 1882, 5; James M. Kahn, *The Umpire Story* (New York: G. P. Putnam's Sons, 1953), 233. By 1888 baseball experts were freely predicting that the two-umpire system soon would become the norm for major league baseball. *Sporting News*, 26 May 1888, 1. Owners resisted the change on the grounds of increased expense; and many players opposed the idea of a second umpire, who could survey the action and limit their options to cut corners and create obstacles to play.

43. "Big League Superstitions," *Literary Digest* 48 (May 1914): 1151–54.

44. *Chicago Tribune*, 6 April 1890, 36.

45. Benedict de Spinoza, *A Theological-Political Treatise and a Political Treatise*, trans. R. H. M. Elwes (New York: Dover, 1951), 3.

46. Gustav Jahoda, *The Psychology of Superstition* (London: Penguin, 1969), 69.

47. *Chicago Tribune*, 6 April 1890, 36. Not all mascots were African American. Fred Boldt, described as a freckle-faced street urchin from Chicago, attached himself to the New York Giants during the 1888 season and dutifully played the role of talisman. Many of the Giants put a good deal of faith in the efficacy of his ministrations. Tim Keefe, for one, was rather unenthusiastic about Boldt's role with the team, but several of the Giants supported Boldt, bought him new clothing, had him barbered and bathed, and tended his daily needs so the mascot could promote the team's fortunes on the diamond. *Sporting News*, 28 July 1888, 3; Hardy, *New York Giants Base Ball Club*, 80.

48. C. J. S. Thompson, *The Hand of Destiny: The Folk-Lore and Superstition of Everyday Life* (Detroit: Singing Tree, 1970), 67.

49. Ibid.; Gertrude Jobes, ed., *The Dictionary of Mythology, Folklore, and Symbols* (New York: Scarecrow Press, 1961–1962), 1:205–6.

50. Walter Addison Jayne, *The Healing Gods of Ancient Civilization* (New York: University Books, 1962), 32.

51. Maria L. Leach, *Dictionary of Folklore, Mythology, and Legend* (New York: Funk and Wagnalls, 1949), 1:502.

52. *Hoodoo*, as defined by Maria Leach, is a "category of magic in the beliefs found among Negroes in the southern United States. The derivation of the word may come from the Haitian *Vodun*, that in turn comes from the identical Dhomean word that means deity. The meaning found in customary American speech, whereby hoodoo signifies bad luck, is an extension of Negro usage." Ibid.

53. *Sporting News*, 30 July, 9 August 1889, 6, 5. Clarence Duval is the classic example of a mascot in the late nineteenth century. He joined the Chicago White Stockings in 1888 as their mascot and abandoned the team later that summer to join a vaudeville troupe, which upset Cap Anson. Later that year when the White

Stockings went on a world tour, to demonstrate baseball overseas with the hand-picked All Americas team, Duval (with A. G. Spalding's blessing) rejoined the White Stockings. Duval served as the mascot for the world tour, which left the United States in autumn 1888 and returned in spring 1889. During the tour Duval drew a good deal of attention from the press and, as a result, became the model for many mascots and set the norm for fans' expectations of how mascots should function. See Harry Clay Palmer, *Athletic Sports in America, England, and Australia* (Philadelphia: Hubbard Brothers, 1889), 168; "The Great Trip," *Sporting Life,* 17 April 1889, 6. Not much is known about Duval prior to his arrival as the White Stocking's mascot, nor is much known about his subsequent life. In July 1892 he was hit by a train in Bloomington, Illinois. *Chicago Tribune,* 24 July 1892, 7. The Chicago paper reported that he died of his injuries, but a Bloomington newspaper subsequently reported that he recovered. *Daily Pantagraph,* 14 July 1892, 7. Whatever his ultimate fate, Duval remains an enigmatic figure on the fringe of major league baseball.

54. Bowman, "Moses Fleetwood Walker," 65–67; Zang, *Fleet Walker's Divided Heart,* 31, 45, 52.

55. In the 1898 Kansas State League, Bert Jones played for Atchinson and Bert Wakefield played for Salina. In 1899 Bill Galloway participated in twenty games for Woodstock in the Canadian League, but after the departure of these black players from white baseball, Jim Crow reigned supreme until 1947. Phil Dixon and Patrick J. Hannigan, *The Negro Baseball Leagues: A Photographic History* (Mattituck, N.Y.: Ameron, 1992), 80; Mark Ribowsky, *A Complete History of the Negro Leagues, 1884 to 1955* (New York: A Birch Lane Press Book, 1995), 45, 47.

2—Interleague Play

1. Department of the Interior, Tenth Census, 536. In the census of 1880, when the NL was formed, New York City boasted a population of over one million; Philadelphia over eight hundred thousand; Chicago in excess of five hundred thousand; Boston and St. Louis each better than three hundred thousand; and Cincinnati a little over two hundred thousand. Louisville's population was approximately one hundred thousand in the late 1870s, and Hartford's census numbered less than fifty thousand. In 1876 the average population for an NL franchise site was about four hundred thousand. At the outset of the 1876 season, it seemed that Louisville and Hartford were likely candidates for an early grave, but each survived two seasons before leaving the NL. Thorn and Palmer, *Total Baseball,* 1887–88. The NL Constitution clearly intended to locate its teams in major urban centers, but if a city with less than the requisite population count applied for membership, it could be admitted by a unanimous vote of current team owners or their delegated agents. *Constitution and Playing Rules,* 7.

2. Seymour, *Baseball,* 86.

3. Ibid., 91; Alexander, *Our Game,* 33–34.

4. Seymour, *Baseball,* 92; Nemec, *Beer and Whiskey League,* 15–17.

5. Hulbert died of heart failure on April 10, 1882, but he had realized that Cincinnati would probably not return to the NL. The rival AA appeared just as his life was ending, and he witnessed the Cincinnati team's role as one of the creators of the association. William E. Akin, "William A. Hulbert," in *Nineteenth Century Stars,* 65.

6. Thorn and Palmer, *Total Baseball*, 1887–92.

7. In 1883 the AA placed a team in New York City to challenge the NL Gothams, and in 1885 it also located a team in Brooklyn in an effort to dominate professional baseball in the metropolitan area. In 1888 it added franchises in Kansas City and Cleveland, where NL teams had earlier functioned and failed. In the wake of the war with the Players' League in 1890, the AA invaded NL territory in Boston, which had been exclusively a League town up to that time. In return the National League opened a rival franchise in Cincinnati, which along with St. Louis had been one of the AA bulwarks. Thorn and Palmer, *Total Baseball*, 1883, 1885, 1907, 1913–14.

8. Spalding, *America's National Game*, 241.

9. Several American Association decisions alarmed its rivals. When AA owners met in Pittsburgh in October 1881 and composed the new charter, they departed from standard NL practices in several areas other than just permitting Sunday games, the sale of alcoholic beverages where local law condoned such commerce, and lower ticket prices. The AA also declared that a ballplayer released by his club was due one half-month's pay rather than the standard ten days' pay provided by the NL. Rather than follow the NL practice of declaring the team with most wins the league's champion, the AA also ruled that its champion would be determined by the team with the highest winning percentage. And finally, the AA took an ambiguous stance on the reserve rule, deciding not to implement it until a later date, if at all; ultimately the AA did adopt the reserve rule, but to nervous NL owners it appeared the AA intended to raid their teams for players. The AA also did not adopt the NL rule that required cities to have a population of at least seventy thousand before becoming an AA member. In the past the NL had occasionally waived the population minimum; the AA saw no need to go through the somewhat embarrassing process of circumventing a rule that simply proved inconvenient. Nemec, *Beer and Whiskey League*, 22–24.

10. Indeed, the Troy and Worcester teams resigned their NL membership after they successfully, albeit painfully, completed their entire schedules. *New York Daily Tribune*, 6 December 1882, 2; *New York Times*, 8 December 1882, 8.

11. *New York Times*, 8 December 1882, 2; *New York Clipper*, 7 October 1882, 467. Worcester finished the season, but just barely. When it came time to disband the team at season's end, the club's treasury contained only $650 and owed the players $1,450 in salary. The stockholders tried to raise enough money to meet payroll but failed. The players divided the $650 among themselves. For names of the various major league teams such as the Ruby Legs, see Wolff, *Baseball Encyclopedia*, 60–61.

12. *New York Times*, 30 October 1882, 8.

13. *New York Clipper*, 14, 21, 28 October 1882, 485, 499, 517.

14. *New York Times*, 30 October 1882, 8; *New York Clipper*, 4 November 1882, 531.

15. Frank V. Phelps, "Oliver Perry Caylor," in *Baseball's First Stars*, 25; Nemec, *Beer and Whiskey League*, 36.

16. Thorn and Palmer, *Total Baseball*, 1893; Wolff, *Baseball Encyclopedia*, 74, 2034; William McMahon, "James McCormick," in *Nineteenth Century Stars*, 85.

17. Thorn and Palmer, *Total Baseball*, 1894.

18. Joseph M. Overfield, "William Henry White," in *Nineteenth Century Stars*, 137; Wolff, *Baseball Encyclopedia*, 74, 2291. After his playing career ended, White

studied ophthalmology in Corning, New York, and finally settled in Buffalo, New York, where he founded the Buffalo Optical Company. His company thrived, and he became an important figure in Buffalo and among opticians across the nation.

19. Thorn and Palmer, *Total Baseball,* 1894. Readers should recall that statistics such as earned run averages, runs batted in, and similar calculations are an invention of a later era in baseball, but they are useful to understand the various teams' accomplishments in the 1880s.

20. *New York Clipper,* 7 October 1882, 467.

21. Nemec, *Beer and Whiskey League,* 36. The Reds handily won the second game (5–2). *New York Clipper,* 14 October 1882, 485.

22. *Cincinnati Commercial,* 6 October 1882, quoted from John C. Tattersall, *The Early World Series, 1884–1890* (Havertown, Pa.: Privately printed, 1976), 89.

23. Ibid.; *New York Clipper,* 14 October 1882, 483.

24. *New York Times,* 11 December 1882, 8.

25. Ibid., 14 December 1882, 3; *New York Daily Tribune,* 15 December 1882, 5.

26. Nemec, *Beer and Whiskey League,* 45–46; Seymour, *Baseball,* 145–46; Spink, *The National Game,* 14; Spalding, *America's National Game,* 244–46.

27. *New York Daily Tribune,* 18 February 1883, 10.

28. Ibid.

29. Spalding, *America's National Game,* 247; Sullivan, *Early Innings,* 130.

30. *New York Clipper,* 14 April 1883, 50.

31. Ibid. Readers should recall that the Giants ballpark, the Polo Grounds, went through a long evolutionary process. By the time Carl Hubbell and Willie Mays enthralled New York baseball fans, they were playing in the fifth edition of the Polo Grounds.

32. Ibid., 5 May 1883, 101.

33. Ibid., 14, 21, 28 April, 5 May 1883, 50, 66, 69, 82–83, 98, 101.

34. Ibid., 5 May 1883, 98.

35. Ibid., 12 May 1883, 114.

36. Adrian Cook, *The Armies of the Street: The New York City Draft Riots of 1863* (Lexington: University Press of Kentucky, 1974), 208–9. See also Barth, *City People,* 186–90. Barth discusses the homogenizing and tranquilizing effect baseball exercised by baseball on urban dwellers.

37. Steven Riess, *City Games: The Evolution of American Urban Society and the Rise of Sports* (Urbana: University of Illinois Press, 1989), 67–68.

38. Benjamin G. Rader, *American Sports: From the Age of Folk Games to the Age of Spectators* (Englewood Cliffs, N.J.: Prentice-Hall, 1983), 121–22. Specs Toporcer, whose boyhood and playing days came well after the 1880s, recalled that the practice of late afternoon games continued into his era. See Lawrence Ritter, *The Glory of Their Times: The Story of the Early Days of Baseball Told by the Men Who Played It* (New York: William Morrow, 1984), 261.

39. *New York Clipper,* 6 October 1883, 468.

40. Wright, *Nineteenth Century Baseball,* 85–86, 91–92; *New York Clipper,* 6 October 1883, 468, 474.

41. *New York Clipper,* 11 November 1883, 543.

42. Ibid., 13 October 1883, 489.

43. Ibid., 20 October 1883, 506–7; 27 October 1883, 522, 525; 3 November 1883, 541.

3—The Beginning

1. Ralph Horton, "Henry Van Noye Lucas," in *Nineteenth Century Stars,* 81. Lucas was born to wealth. His father had made a fortune as one of the founders of the Missouri Pacific Railroad and later continued to advance the family's fortunes.

2. *New York Clipper,* 9 September 1883, 399.

3. Ibid., 22 September 1883, 435; Alexander, *Our Game,* 38; Spalding, *America's National Game,* 242–43; Jerry B. Orenstein, "The Union Association of 1884: A Glorious Failure," *Baseball Research Journal* 19 (1990): 3–6.

4. Alexander, *Our Game,* 38. When the Washington team faltered in early August, Richmond, Virginia, joined the AA as its replacement. *New York Clipper,* 16 August 1884, 346. W. C. Seddon led a group known as the Virginia Association, which voted to issue ten thousand dollars of capital stock and enter the Richmond team into the AA. The new club was known as the Virginians and played home games in Virginia Base-Ball Park in Richmond. Lowry, *Green Cathedrals,* 223.

5. Department of the Interior, Eleventh Census, pt. 1, lxviii.

6. Wright, *Nineteenth Century Baseball,* 111, 208.

7. Ibid., 116–23; Thorn and Palmer, *Total Baseball,* 1899.

8. Wright, *Nineteenth Century Baseball,* 115; *New York Clipper,* 20 August 1884, 377.

9. *New York Clipper,* 11 November 1884, 522.

10. Wright, *Nineteenth Century Baseball,* 100; Lowry, *Green Cathedrals,* 127; Dennis Goldstein, "Edward Nagle Williamson," in *Nineteenth Century Stars,* 139.

11. Thorn and Palmer, *Total Baseball,* 1723.

12. David L. Holst, "Charles G. Radbourne: The Greatest Pitcher of the Nineteenth Century," *Illinois Historical Journal* 81 (winter 1998): 255–68. (In his article Holst chose to spell Radbourn's name with an "e." Spellings of Hoss's surname varied; newspapers rendered it "Radbourne" and "Radbourn," whereas modern-day historians favor the latter. Thorn and Palmer, *Total Baseball,* 1723.) Jack E. Harshman, "The Radbourn and Sweeney Saga," *Baseball Historical Research Journal* 19 (1990): 7–10; Andrew Kull, "Baseball's Greatest Pitcher," *American Heritage* (April–May 1985): 103–8; Frederick Ivor-Campbell, "Charles W. Sweeney," in *Nineteenth Century Stars,* 123. For an account of the Bancroft-Sweeney quarrel, see *Sporting Life,* 30 July 1884, 3.

13. *Sporting Life,* 30 September 1884, 5.

14. *Sporting Life,* 11 November 1883, 2; Bowman, "Moses Fleetwood Walker," 64–65; Zang, *Fleet Walker's Divided Heart,* 35–39; *Toledo Daily Blade,* 23 July 1884; William A. Brewer, "Barehanded Catcher," *Negro Digest* 9 (1951): 84–87; Ocania Chalk, *Pioneers of Black Sport* (New York: Dodd, Mead, 1975), 6–11.

15. Wright, *Nineteenth Century Baseball,* 109.

16. *Sporting Life,* 22 July 1884, 7.

17. Division of Vital Statistics, Columbus, Ohio, Certificate of Death, File Number 270001, Moses Fleetwood Walker. *Cleveland (Ohio) Gazette,* 17 May 1924. Walker was admitted to Cleveland's City Hospital and died of lumbar pneumonia only six hours later. Bowman, "Moses Fleetwood Walker," 72.

18. Wright, *Nineteenth Century Baseball,* 99; Thorn and Palmer, *Total Baseball,* 1897.

19. *Sporting Life,* 27 August 1884, 7.

20. Ibid., 24 September 1884, 3. For all practical purposes the Grays' successes at the home ticket window in 1884 were a repeat of the previous year. In 1883 the Grays finished third in the League. When the Grays' treasurer issued his annual report for 1883, he announced that Providence drew 61,341 paid admissions to their home games, an average of slightly more than 1,000 per contest. The games with Boston averaged 2,103 per game, but attendance for Philadelphia and Buffalo games averaged 763 and 549 respectively. *New York Clipper,* 9 February 1884, 797. Although 1884 proved a championship year for the Grays, the Providence fans did not flock to the ballpark. Poor attendance contributed to the demise of the Grays only a little over a year after their great 1884 season.

21. Wright, *Nineteenth Century Baseball,* 106; Nemec, *Beer and Whiskey League,* 73.

22. *New York Clipper,* 30 August 1884, 378.

23. *Sporting Life,* 13 August 1884, 3.

24. John J. McGraw, *My Thirty Years in Baseball* (Lincoln: University of Nebraska Press, 1995), 157.

25. *Sporting Life,* 13 August 1884, 3; *National Police Gazette* 45 (October 18, 1884): 13.

26. *Sporting Life,* 24 September 1884, 3.

27. *New York Clipper,* 23 August 1884, 362.

28. *Sporting Life,* 24 September 1884, 3.

29. *New York Times,* 8 October 1884, 6.

30. Ibid., 18 October 1884, 2.

31. Tattersall, *Early World Series,* 1; *Sporting Life,* 22 October 1884, 6; *New York Times,* 23 October 1884, 5.

32. *Sporting Life,* 22 October 1884, 6. The NL allowed pitchers to use any motion they preferred while delivering to the plate, but the AA required that they employ a throwing motion that did not rise above the level of the shoulder.

33. Lynch's remark quoted in Nemec, *Beer and Whiskey League,* 62. See also Lowry, *Green Cathedrals,* 190; John J. O'Malley, "John H. Lynch," in *Baseball's First Stars,* 98. As the park was under construction, one account of the location declared, "at present the site is ash heaps and rubbish." *New York Clipper,* 1 March 1884, 848 (see also 2 February 1884, 783).

34. Lowry, *Green Cathedrals,* 188.

35. *Providence Daily Journal,* 13 October 1884, 10.

36. *New York Times,* 23 October 1884, 5; *New York Clipper,* 11 November 1884, 524.

37. Edwin G. Burrows and Mike Wallace, *Gotham: A History of New York City to 1898* (New York: Oxford University Press, 1999), 1042–44, 1050, 1074.

38. Burrows and Wallace, *Gotham,* 1133–35.

39. *New York Clipper,* 11 November 1884, 523.

40. Ibid.; Tattersall, *Early World Series,* 2; *Providence Daily Journal,* 24 October 1884, 1.

41. *New York Times,* 23 October 1884, 5.

42. *Sporting Life,* 29 October 1884, 3; *New York Daily Tribune,* 24 October 1884, 10; Jerry Lansche, *The Forgotten Championships: Postseason Baseball, 1882–1981* (Jefferson, N.C.: McFarland, 1989), 7–8; *New York Clipper,* 1 November 1884, 523.

43. *New York Times,* 24 October 1884, 10.

44. *Sporting Life,* 29 October 1884, 3; *New York Clipper,* 1 November 1884, 523; Lansche, *Forgotten Championships,* 8.

45. *New York Times,* 25 October 1884, 10. See also Sullivan, *Early Innings,* 138; *Providence Daily Journal,* 27 October 1884, 9.

46. Mutrie's choice of Becannon fostered no comment in the New York press. John "Jack" Lynch did not appear in the 1884 playoff games even though he won thirty-seven games during the season. None of the papers made an issue of his absence and none mentioned injuries barring him from action. Five days after the playoff ended, Lynch boarded the steamship *City of Richmond* in New York City and departed for an extended tour of major European cities. *New York Clipper,* 11 November 1884, 540. When he returned from Europe at the end of November, the paper noted his arrival. *New York Clipper,* 6 December 1884, 604. Neither mention of Lynch's recreational activities alluded to his failure to appear in the championship series with Providence.

47. Most of the newspaper accounts misspelled his name as Foster. Forster, according to the *New York Clipper,* was "late of the Allegheny Club." *New York Clipper,* 1 November 1884, 523. This was in fact Thomas Forster, a member of the Mets' roster in 1885 and 1886. The newspapers' misspelling persists in subsequent accounts of the 1884 world's championship.

48. *New York Times,* 26 October 1884, 14. Accounts of the statistics of baseball games vary greatly. Reporters scored the games themselves and computed their box scores from their personal score cards. In the last game, for example, the *New York Times* report listed ten errors by the Mets while the *New York Clipper's* charged only two errors against the Mets. *New York Clipper,* 1 November 1884, 523. The same can be said of all other aspects of box scores. The final score of the third game varied in newspaper accounts. The *New York Herald* reported the final score as 11–2, and the *New York Clipper* correctly reported the final score as 12–2. See Tattersall, *Early World Series,* 3; *New York Clipper,* 1 November 1884, 523. Such disparities are the bane of modern statisticians.

4—Chicago and St. Louis

1. William E. McMahon, "Albert Goodwill Spalding," in *Baseball's First Stars,* 154.

2. For an excellent, succinct account of Spalding's early life and character, see Levine, *Spalding,* 3–11.

3. McMahon, "Albert Goodwill Spalding." Thorn and Palmer in *Total Baseball,* 1778, list Spalding's total of wins at 253. Whatever the actual number, Spalding enjoyed some remarkable years. He won more than fifty in two seasons and more than forty in two more.

4. Marty Appel, *Slide, Kelly, Slide: The Wild Life and Times of Mike "King" Kelly, Baseball's First Superstar* (Lanham, Md.: Scarecrow Press, 1996), 102–9; Norman L. Macht, "Michael Joseph Kelly," in *Baseball's First Stars,* 90; Levine, *Spalding,* 40.

5. See J. Thomas Hetrick, *Chris Von der Ahe and the St. Louis Browns* (Lanham, Md.: Scarecrow Press, 1999), 3–5.

6. G. W. Axelson, *Commy: The Life Story of Charles A. Comiskey* (Chicago: Reilly and Lee, 1919), 59. See also Richard Egenriether, "Chris Von der Ahe: Baseball's Pioneering Huckster," *Baseball Research Journal* 18 (1989): 27, and a later ver-

sion of this article, Richard Egenriether, "Chris Von der Ahe: Baseball's Pioneering Huckster," *Nine* 7 (1999): 14–19.

7. Hetrick, *Von der Ahe*, 22.

8. *St. Louis Post-Dispatch*, 17 April, 11 May 1898, 1, 5; *Sporting Life*, 23 April 1898, 5.

9. Obituary cited from *St. Louis Post-Dispatch*, 6 June 1913, 4. See also Spink, *The National Game*, 52.

10. David Haward Bain, *Empire Express: Building the First Transcontinental Railroad* (New York: Viking, 1999), 43; Donald L. Miller, *City of the Century: The Epic of Chicago and the Making of America* (New York: Simon and Schuster, 1996), 99.

11. Miller, *City of the Century*, 48–49.

12. Department of the Interior, Eleventh Census, pt. 1, lxviii.

13. Thorn and Palmer, *Total Baseball*, 1896–97; Wright, *Nineteenth Century Baseball*, 133.

14. The exact origin of the title the "Freshest Man on Earth" is a bit clouded. Latham apparently used the term before it was immortalized in 1888 when he joined a troupe performing "Fashion" at Hueck's Opera House in Cincinnati after the World's Championship series. Latham appeared in the first act and sang a song, "I am the Freshest Man on Earth," that apparently had recently been written for him. As he prepared to sing his part the usher, accompanied by substantial and knowing applause from the audience, brought forward to the stage a stand of flowers formed in the shape of a diamond. The flowers, a gift from the Cincinnati Reds, were intended to commemorate the occasion. *Sporting News*, 24 November 1888, 3. See also Husman, "Walter Arlington Latham."

15. *New York Clipper*, 15 September 1883, 421 (quotation); Thorn and Palmer, *Total Baseball*, 1903, 1905. 1907.

16. Husman, "Walter Arlington Latham." Latham often played pranks on his teammates, but on at least one occasion he was the victim. He usually carried a bottle of good liquor to the ballpark, and one afternoon one of his fellow Browns emptied his bottle, filled it with turpentine, and placed it where he was certain to take a sip. Latham later picked up the bottle, took a swig, and without any noticeable reaction declared, "There seems to be more body to that liquor than usual." *Sporting News*, 10 May 1886, 5.

17. Robert L. Tiemann, "Charles Albert Comiskey," in *Baseball's First Stars*, 36–37; Hetrick, *Von der Ahe*, 36.

18. Wright, *Nineteenth Century Baseball*, 126–30; Thorn and Palmer, *Total Baseball*, 1900.

19. Thorn and Palmer, *Total Baseball*, 1900.

20. *Sporting Life*, 7 October 1885, 1; Levine, *Spalding*, 35; Lansche, *Forgotten Championships*, 9–13; Larry G. Bowman, "Christian Von der Ahe, the St. Louis Browns, and the World's Championship Playoffs, 1885–1888," *Missouri Historical Review* 91 (July 1997): 390; Tattersall, *Early World Series*, 5.

21. *Chicago Tribune*, 15 October 1885, 1; *St. Louis Post-Dispatch*, 15 October 1885, 1; Lansche, *Forgotten Championships*, 9; Tattersall, *Early World Series*, 6 (quotation).

22. Two examples suffice to demonstrate his attitude toward African Americans and Asians. The White Stockings had a mascot named Clarence Duval, in 1888–1889 during their world exhibition tour, and Anson in his book referred to

Duval as "coon" and as a "chocolate covered coon." He proclaimed his concern over the "Yellow Peril" and the dangers of Asian immigration to the United States in his account of his baseball career. What is dismaying about Anson's views is that they were not too removed, if at all, from those of a great many Americans. Adrian C. Anson, *A Ball Player's Career* (Chicago: Era Publishing, 1900), 196, 220–21. See also William E. McMahon and Robert Tiemann, "Adrian Constantine Anson," in *Baseball's First Stars*, 3–4.

23. *Chicago Tribune,* 16 October 1885, 4.

24. Sunday's appearance in the series immediately raised the question of his foot speed compared to that of Arlie Latham of the Browns. Two weeks after the series was concluded, Sunday and Latham staged a one-hundred-yard footrace at St. Louis's Union Grounds on November 8, 1885, before a good-sized crowd, who paid admission to see the race, cheer the runners, and (some of them) place bets on the outcome. Sunday beat Latham by three and one-half yards in an announced time of 10.25 seconds. *New York Clipper,* 11 November 1885, 554. Another source reported that Sunday and Latham repaired to the Lindell Hotel where they divided the gate receipts, about three hundred dollars, and denied that Latham "tossed" the race. *Sporting Life,* 2 December 1885, 1. Betting on the race was heavy, and according to rumor Von der Ahe lost twenty dollars to Cap Anson. *Sporting Life,* 25 November 1885, 3.

25. Thorn and Palmer, *Total Baseball,* 1265.

26. *New York Times,* 18 October 1885, 3; *Sporting Life,* 21 October 1885, 1; Sullivan, *Early Innings,* 139–40. A maximum of two thousand dollars meant that many players faced salary cuts of as much as 50 percent.

27. *Sporting Life,* 1 November 1885, 1.

28. Burk, *Never Just a Game,* 96; Stevens, *Baseball's Radical,* 42; Hardy, *New York Giants Base Ball Club,* 15. For an excellent account of Ward's involvement in the Brotherhood movement, see Bryan Di Salvatore, *A Clever Base-Ballist: The Life and Times of John Montgomery Ward* (New York: Pantheon Books, 1999), 175–77.

29. *Sporting Life,* 17 November 1886, 1.

30. James Neal Primm, *Lion of the Valley: St. Louis, Missouri* (Boulder, Colo.: Pruett, 1981), 393–94.

31. *Chicago Daily News,* 16 October 1885, 1.

32. *St. Louis Post-Dispatch,* 16 October 1885, 1.

33. *Sporting Life,* 28 October 1885, 4.

34. Ibid.

35. *Chicago Tribune,* 17 October 1885, 2.

36. Ibid., 18 October 1885, 11.

37. *Chicago Tribune,* 17, 26 October 1885, 2, 2; *Chicago Daily News,* 24 October 1885, 4. Chicago later tried to sign Holliday to a contract but failed. Bug eventually enjoyed a ten-year career with Cincinnati. Thorn and Palmer, *Total Baseball,* 930–31.

38. *Chicago Daily; News,* 17 October 1885, 6. Writers in St. Louis expressed similar sentiments; see *St. Louis Post-Dispatch,* 17 October 1885, 11.

39. Wright, *Nineteenth Century Baseball,* 129–30. The Browns eventually swept the three-game series with the Maroons. Lansche, *Forgotten Championships,* 80–81. The Maroons and the Browns met each other again in 1886 in a six-game series,

which the Browns won five games to one. *Sporting News,* 18, 25, 30 October, 6 November 1886, 2, 7, 4, 1.

40. *Sporting Life,* 4 November 1885, 2; *Chicago Tribune,* 23 October 1885, 2.

41. *St. Louis Post-Dispatch,* 26 October 1885, 4. *Sporting Life* agreed, and informed its readers, "Before Saturday's game, however, it was mutually agreed to throw out the forfeited game, leaving the clubs even at two games each, and that Saturday's game decide the series." *Sporting Life,* 4 November 1885, 2. See also Tattersall, *Early World Series,* 9.

42. Lansche, *Forgotten Championships,* 13.

43. *New York Times,* 25 October 1885, 7; *Sporting Life,* 4 November 1885, 2.

44. *Chicago Tribune,* 26 October 1885, 2; *Sporting News,* 11 November 1885, 3.

45. *Sporting Life,* 11, 25 November, 16 December 1885, 3, 1, 2.

46. Ibid., 16 December 1885, 1; *St. Louis Post-Dispatch,* 9 December 1885, 7. Most newspapers were more concerned with reporting the death of railroad tycoon William H. Vanderbilt, and with the quarrel within the American Association as it prepared to expel the New York team. One writer asserts that an owners' committee declared the series tied, but there is no evidence that such action was taken. See Lansche, *Forgotten Championships,* 13. Spalding does not mention the controversy in *America's National Game.* Spink's *The National Game* likewise says nothing of an adjudicated series.

47. *Sporting News,* 11 November 1885, 3; Levine, *Spalding,* 35.

48. *Sporting Life,* 2 December 1885, 1. Accounts do not discuss what the players gained from the championship games. One report speculated the players each received "just $48." Ibid., 25 November 1885, 3. The monetary figure of forty-eight dollars is about what each player would have received if his owner's original five hundred dollars for the championship purse was divided evenly among the players on the roster. There is, however, no official evidence that either owner gave his part of the purse to the players.

49. Wright, *Nineteenth Century Baseball,* 133, 147; Thorn and Palmer, *Total Baseball,* 1122. In 262 times at bat, pitcher Bob Caruthers hit .334, but among the everyday players, O'Neill led his teammates by a substantial margin.

50. Wolff, *Baseball Encyclopedia,* 1305. Baseball's rules in 1886 counted a base on balls as a hit, and if the walks Tip earned during the season are factored into his average, it reaches the stratosphere. The rules were amended the following year, and bases on balls no longer counted as hits or official times at bat. Also see Robert L. Tiemann and William E. Akin, "James Edward O'Neill," in *Nineteenth Century Stars,* 99.

51. The Browns' colors remained the same, white trimmed in brown, but for the 1886 season their uniforms were of "best imported English cricket flannel." C. and W. McClean's of St. Louis imported the cloth and designed and manufactured the Browns' new uniforms. *Sporting News,* 10 May 1886, 5.

52. *Sporting News,* 17 March 1886, 2. Prior to the team's departure for Arkansas, Spalding gathered the White Stockings in his sporting goods store on Madison Street in Chicago and had them raise their hands and solemnly swear they would abstain from alcohol all season. He also announced he was withholding $250 of Kelly's and pitcher Jim McCormick's pay as an incentive for them to maintain their pledges of abstinence. Kelly's salary in 1886 was two thousand dollars.

Spalding's edict carried a potential 12 percent loss for Kelly, and it contributed to the tension between the two men in 1886. Spalding eventually paid the $250 to Kelly as a bonus for winning the pennant. Spalding's dictatorial, paternalistic, and puritanical habits particularly galled men with Kelly's temperament. Appel, *Slide, Kelly, Slide,* 84, 99.

53. Ralph Horton, "The Big Four Come to Detroit," *National Pastime* 19 (1998): 34–37.

54. Larry G. Bowman, "Detroit's First World Champions," *Michigan History* 81 (September/October 1997): 42; Alexander, *Our Game,* 43; Burk, *Never Just a Game,* 87.

55. Thorn and Palmer, *Total Baseball,* 1902.

56. Wolff, *Baseball Encyclopedia,* 1902–3.

57. *Sporting News,* 7 June 1886, 5.

58. Ibid., 18 October 1886, 2; *Sporting Life,* 13 October 1886, 1, 3.

59. *Sporting News,* 4 October 1886, 1.

60. Ibid.

61. Ibid., 9 October 1886, 1.

62. Kahn, *Umpire Story,* 238–39.

63. Richard A. Puff and Robert L. Tiemann, "Joseph Quest," in *Nineteenth Century Stars,* 104.

64. *St. Louis Post-Dispatch,* 7 October 1886, 8; *Chicago Tribune,* 19 October 1886, 2; *Sporting News,* 11 October 1886, 1.

65. *St. Louis Post-Dispatch,* 18 October 1886, 1. The St. Louis correspondent set the crowd at three thousand, whereas *Sporting News* later reported five thousand attending the game. *Sporting News,* 25 October 1886, 2. Willie Hahn was a Caucasian lad who caught Anson's eye and became the team's mascot in 1886. Anson wrote of Hahn, "The first time I ever saw him he came to the grounds arrayed in a miniature Chicago uniform, and so cunning was he that we at once adopted him as our 'mascot' giving him the freedom of the grounds, and he was always on hand when the club was at home, being quite a feature, and one that pleased the lady patrons immensely." Anson, *A Ball Player's Career,* 135.

66. Lansche, *Forgotten Championships,* 15; Tattersall, *Early World Series,* 13.

67. *Chicago Tribune,* 19 October 1886, 2.

68. Wright, *Nineteenth Century Baseball,* 147.

69. *Chicago Daily News,* 16, 18 October 1886, 1, 1; *Chicago Tribune,* 20 October 1886, 2; *Sporting News,* 25 October 1886, 2; *St. Louis Post-Dispatch,* 21 October 1886, 8.

70. *Chicago Daily News,* 20 October 1886, 1; *St. Louis Post-Dispatch,* 20 October 1886, 1.

71. As usual the newspaper estimates of attendance varied. The *Post-Dispatch* reported an attendance of ten thousand, and the *Daily News* reporter saw twelve thousand cranks in the stands. *St. Louis Post-Dispatch,* 21 October 1886, 2; *Chicago Daily News,* 21 October 1886, 1.

72. *St. Louis Post-Dispatch,* 21 October 1886, 2.

73. Ibid.; *Sporting News,* 25 October 1886, 2; Tattersall, *Early World Series,* 18; Lansche, *Forgotten Championships,* 16.

74. *St. Louis Post-Dispatch,* 22 October 1886, 1.

75. Ibid., 23 October 1886, 8; *Chicago Daily News,* 22 October 1886, 1; *Chicago Tribune,* 23 October 1886, 6; *New York Clipper,* 30 October 1886, 521.

76. *St. Louis Post-Dispatch,* 23 October 1886, 8.

77. *Chicago Tribune,* 22 October 1886, 2.

78. Ibid., 21 October 1886, 2.

79. Ibid., 24 October 1886, 10.

80. Lansche, *Forgotten Championships,* 15–16; Tattersall, *Early World Series,* 22.

81. Robert L. Tiemann and L. Robert Davids, "Robert Lee Caruthers," in *Nineteenth Century Stars,* 26; Tattersall, *Early World Series,* 22.

82. *Chicago Daily News,* 23 October 1886, 1; *Chicago Tribune,* 24 October 1886, 10; *St. Louis Post-Dispatch,* 25 October 1886, 5.

83. Ibid.; *New York Clipper,* 30 October 1886, 521; Hetrick, *Von der Ahe,* 64.

84. *St. Louis Post-Dispatch,* 25 October 1886, 5.

85. Robert L. Tiemann, "Curt Welch," in *Nineteenth Century Stars,* 132.

86. Alexander, *Our Game,* 42; Levine, *Spalding,* 36.

87. *Sporting News,* 30 October 1886, 3.

88. Appel, *Slide, Kelly, Slide,* 104–5.

89. Anson, *A Ball Player's Career,* 137.

90. *Sporting News,* 30 October 1886, 3.

91. Ibid. Also see *St. Louis Post-Dispatch,* 25 October 1886, 5.

92. *Sporting News,* 30 October 1886, 3.

5—The Browns and the Wolverines

1. Alexander, *Our Game,* 33.

2. Department of the Interior, Eleventh Census, pt. 1, xi.

3. Thorn and Palmer, *Total Baseball,* 110; Wright, *Nineteenth Century Baseball,* 68; Burk, *Never Just a Game,* 57, 59, 69; Sullivan, *Early Innings,* 119–21.

4. Thorn and Palmer, *Total Baseball,* 1897; Wright, *Nineteenth Century Baseball,* 102–3.

5. Ralph Horton, "Henry Van Noye Lucas," in *Nineteenth Century Stars,* 81.

6. Joseph M. Overfield, "Dennis Joseph Brouthers," in *Baseball's First Stars,* 11–13; Joseph M. Overfield, "Hardy Richardson," "John Rowe," and "Deacon White," in *Nineteenth Century Stars,* 107–9, 110–11, 135–36; Thorn and Palmer, *Total Baseball,* 707, 1174, 1192, 1325.

7. *Sporting Life,* 23 September 1885, 3; Bowman, "Detroit's First World Champions," 42.

8. *Sporting Life,* 23 September 1885, 1.

9. Ibid.; Burk, *Never Just a Game,* 87.

10. Dennis Goldstein and Richard A. Puff, "Frederick C. Dunlap," in *Nineteenth Century Stars,* 40.

11. Wright, *Nineteenth Century Baseball,* 70, 77, 89, 103, 128, 140, 154. Calculations of runs per game are based on the statistics presented in this source.

12. Thorn and Palmer, *Total Baseball,* 1374, 1515; Robert L. Tiemann, "Charles H. Getzien," in *Nineteenth Century Stars,* 50. Tiemann points out that sportswriters routinely misspelled Getzien's surname rendering it "Getzein." Also

see *Nineteenth Century Baseball,* 140, 154.

13. F. Clever Bald, *Michigan in Four Centuries* (New York: Harper Brothers, 1954), 298.

14. David Quentin Voigt, *American Baseball: From Gentlemen's Sport to the Commissioner System* (University Park: Pennsylvania State University Press, 1983), 1:112.

15. Robert L. Tiemann, "Charles Frederick King (Silver)," in *Nineteenth Century Stars,* 72; Hetrick, *Von der Ahe,* 65–67. King remained on the Browns' roster through the 1889 season, and during those four years he won a total of 112 games. He left the Browns in 1890 to join the Pittsburgh franchise in the newly formed Players' League (PL), and when that player-instituted rebellion failed, he did not return to the Browns.

16. Wright, *Nineteenth Century Baseball,* 161.

17. *Sporting News,* 29 January 1887, 6.

18. Prior to becoming a renowned infielder John Montgomery Ward was a pitcher, and he disapproved of many of the changes that altered the pitchers' style. For a helpful insight into how the change affected pitchers, see Di Salvatore, *A Clever Base-Ballist,* 125–29.

19. Nemec, *Rules,* 193.

20. Wright, *Nineteenth Century Baseball,* 158, 165. When O'Neill's batting average is factored without the bases on balls, he amassed an impressive .435. Thorn and Palmer, *Total Baseball,* 1122; Wolff, *Baseball Encyclopedia,* 1305.

21. Thorn and Palmer, *Total Baseball,* 1902–5.

22. Wright, *Nineteenth Century Baseball,* 161; *Sporting News,* 1 October, 4 June 1887, 3, 1; Hetrick, *Von der Ahe,* 68.

23. *Sporting News,* 1 October 1887, 3; Wright, *Nineteenth Century Baseball,* 154–55.

24. Thorn and Palmer, *Total Baseball,* 1281; Wright, *Nineteenth Century Baseball,* 154; Norman L. Macht, "Samuel Luther Thompson," in *Baseball's First Stars,* 165.

25. *Sporting News,* 27 August 1887, 1.

26. Ibid.; *Sporting News,* 1 October 1887, 1; Lansche, *Forgotten Championships,* 20; Hetrick, *Von der Ahe,* 77.

27. Some of the Browns' and Wolverines' rivals were a bit amused by the fines agreement. The *Boston Herald* observed, "In the world's championship series, any and all fines imposed on the players are to be sustained and devoted to some charitable institution in St. Louis and Detroit. The greatest charitable institution in Detroit is the Detroit League Club." Cited in *Sporting News,* 22 October 1887, 5.

28. Tattersall, *Early World Series,* 24. Stearns and Von der Ahe first met in Detroit to arrange the details of the upcoming series. Game sites were among the many details they considered. They never varied from the fifteen-game format, but the sites of the games changed as the agreement between the owners evolved. Louisville, Kentucky, for example, was among the sites Stearns and Von der Ahe originally selected, but by the time the games began, Louisville was no longer on the itinerary. *St. Louis Post-Dispatch,* 23, 26 September, 10 October 1887, 8, 5, 5; *Sporting News,* 1 October 1887, 1. Stearns and Von der Ahe also encountered other difficulties while selecting game sites. John B. Day originally demanded that Stearns

and Von der Ahe agree to pay him one-third of the gross receipts for the use of his Polo Grounds. Day eventually agreed to rent his park for a lesser, straight fee, but for a few days, it appeared unlikely that the Polo Grounds would be available for a championship game. *Sporting News,* 24 September 1887, 1.

    29. Appel, *Slide, Kelly, Slide,* 101.

    30. Larry L. Gerlach, "John H. Gaffney," in *Baseball's First Stars,* 64. According to Gerlach, who declares him the "King of the Umpires," Gaffney also was a careful student of the game and frequently recommended changes in rules to improve it.

    31. *Detroit Evening News,* 5 October 1887, 1; *St. Louis Post-Dispatch,* 10 October 1887, 5, 1 (quotation); Tattersall, *Early World Series,* 25.

    32. *Detroit Free Press,* 24 October 1887, 5 (quotation); *Sporting News,* 2 November 1887, 4.

    33. *St. Louis Post-Dispatch,* 2 October 1887, 8.

    34. Ibid., 26 September 1887, 10.

    35. *Detroit Evening News,* 19 October 1887, 1.

    36. *St. Louis Post-Dispatch,* 2 October 1887, 10.

    37. Robert L. Tiemann and L. Robert Davis, "Robert Lee Caruthers," and Frank V. Phelps, "Albert John Bushong," in *Nineteenth Century Stars,* 26, 23.

    38. Hetrick, *Von der Ahe,* 75.

    39. *Detroit Free Press,* 9 October 1887, 6; *Detroit Evening News,* 10 October 1887, 1.

    40. *St. Louis Post-Dispatch,* 10 October 1887, 5; *Sporting Life,* 19 October 1887, 2.

    41. *Detroit Free Press,* 11 October 1887, 2; *St. Louis Post-Dispatch,* 10 October 1887, 5.

    42. *St. Louis Post-Dispatch,* 10 October 1887, 1; Tattersall, *Early World Series,* 25; Lansche, *Forgotten Championships,* 19; *Detroit Free Press,* 11 October 1887, 2 (quotation).

    43. Attendance for the playoff remained encouraging. After a week's games, the *New York Clipper* observed, "The receipts for the first week's games of the World Championship series were enough to pay the expenses, not a rainy day, after the opening games, marring financial success of the games." *New York Clipper,* 22 October 1887, 510.

    44. *St. Louis Post-Dispatch,* 22 October 1887, 1.

    45. Ibid., 11 October 1887, 5.

    46. Ibid., 12 October 1887, 1; *Detroit Free Press,* 13 October 1887, 2.

    47. *Detroit Free Press,* 13 October 1887, 2.

    48. Ibid.; Tattersall, *Early World Series,* 26; Bowman, "Detroit's First World Champions," 44.

    49. *St Louis Post-Dispatch,* 18 October 1887, 8. See also *Detroit Evening News,* 14 October 1887, 1; Bowman, "Christian Von der Ahe," 400; and Hetrick, *Von der Ahe,* 76.

    50. *St. Louis Post-Dispatch,* 12 October 1887, 1.

    51. Tattersall, *Early World Series,* 27; Lansche, *Forgotten Championships,* 21; *St. Louis Post-Dispatch,* 14 October 1887, 8.

    52. *Detroit Free Press,* 14 October 1887, 2.

    53. *St. Louis Post-Dispatch,* 14 October 1887, 1; *Sporting News,* 22 October 1887, 2.

54. *Detroit Free Press,* 15 October 1887, 2. Peter Conway was a mediocre member of the Wolverines pitching staff. In 1887 he pitched 146 innings, winning 8 and losing 9. Bill Watkins, whose Wolverines held a lead on the Browns three games to one, apparently decided to rest his stronger pitchers Getzien, Baldwin, Stump Weidman, and Larry Twitchell. Watkins's strategy paid dividends. After losing to the Browns in Brooklyn, the Wolverines then won the next four games and took a commanding 7–2 lead and needed only one win in the next five games to claim the championship.

55. *St. Louis Post-Dispatch,* 15 October 1887, 1.

56. *Detroit Free Press,* 16 October 1887, 6; *Sporting News,* 22 October 1887, 2; Tattersall, *Early World Series,* 29.

57. Lansche, *Forgotten Championships,* 21–22; Hetrick, *Von der Ahe,* 76.

58. Although St. Louis and Detroit did not play on Sunday, October 16, Von der Ahe scheduled a game with the Browns' AA rival, Brooklyn, before departing for Philadelphia. It was an exhibition game designed only to fatten Von der Ahe's purse. Instead of resting his players, he put them on the diamond in a meaningless game that they then lost 10–3. The only concession Von der Ahe made to the continuing playoff was to rest Silver King, Bob Caruthers, and Dave Foutz, the Browns' pitching stalwarts. Nat Hudson pitched the Sunday game in Brooklyn. During the regular season, Hudson pitched only sixty-seven of the nearly twelve hundred innings the Browns played and amassed a record of four wins and four losses. A day's rest probably would have benefited the Browns, but Von der Ahe did not hesitate to wring extra innings from his players. *New York Daily Tribune,* 17 October 1887, 3; Wright, *Nineteenth Century Baseball,* 161.

59. Larry Bowman, "Baseball's Intriguing Couple: Helen Dauvray and John Montgomery Ward," *National Pastime* 17 (1998): 70–71.

60. Larry G. Bowman, "The Helen Dauvray Cup," *National Pastime* 17 (1997): 74; Di Salvatore, *A Clever Base-Ballist,* 210–14.

61. Two of the medals are on display in the Baseball Hall of Fame Museum. Bowman, "The Dauvray Cup," 76. After the AA collapsed in 1891, the Dauvray Cup was awarded to the winner of the NL pennant. In 1893 the Boston team won a third title and claimed permanent possession of the cup. *Kansas City Star,* 8 October 1893, 3; *New York Daily Tribune,* 9 October 1893, 10; *Boston Daily Globe,* 7 October 1893, 5. The cup's whereabouts is currently unknown. Should the Helen Dauvray Cup ever reappear and be placed on sale at a sports memorabilia auction, its value would vastly exceed the five hundred dollars Helen Dauvray spent to commission it.

62. *Detroit Free Press,* 18 October 1887, 2.

63. Lansche, *Forgotten Championships,* 22; Tattersall, *Early World Series,* 29–31.

64. Lowry, *Green Cathedrals,* 107. A larger and more hospitable South End Grounds II opened in 1888 and served as home to Boston's NL Beaneaters until 1894. Ibid., 108.

65. *St. Louis Post-Dispatch,* 18 October 1887, 1.

66. *Detroit Free Press,* 20 October 1887, 2; Lansche, *Forgotten Championships,* 22–23; Tattersall, *Early World Series,* 34.

67. *St. Louis Post-Dispatch,* 20 October 1887, 8.

68. Tattersall, *Early World Series,* 35–37; *St. Louis Post-Dispatch,* 21, 22 October 1887, 8, 8; *Detroit Free Press,* 22 October 1887, 2.

69. Melvin Holli and Peter d'A. Jones, *Biographical Dictionary of American Mayors* (Westport, Conn.: Greenwood Press, 1981), 61–62.

70. Bowman, "Detroit's First World Champions," 40.

71. *Detroit Sunday News,* 23 October 1887, 2.

72. *St. Louis Post-Dispatch,* 22 October 1887, 1 (quotation); *Detroit Free Press,* 23 October 1887, 5 (quotation); *St. Louis Post-Dispatch,* 23 October 1887, 1.

73. Tattersall, *Early World Series,* 37; *Detroit Free Press,* 22 October 1887, 2. Not only did Brouthers's ankle give him physical pain, it also gave him mental anguish. He was a sturdy man who felt he did not deserve a share of the playoff money. Dan offered to turn his portion of the prize money over to his teammates, but the offer was declined. Overfield, "Dennis Joseph Brouthers," 12.

74. *Sporting News,* 22 October 1887, 4.

75. *Detroit Free Press,* 25 October 1887, 2; Bowman, "Detroit's First World Champions," 40.

76. *Detroit Evening News,* 24 October 1887, 1.

77. *Sporting Life,* 2 November 1887, 4.

78. *St. Louis Post-Dispatch,* 24 October 1887, 1; *Detroit Free Press,* 25 October 1887, 2.

79. *Detroit Free Press,* 1 November 1887, 7.

80. Ibid., 26 October 1887, 2.

81. *St. Louis Post-Dispatch,* 27 October 1887, 8; Tattersall, *Early World Series,* 38.

82. *Sporting News,* 29 October 1887, 2.

83. *New York Clipper,* 11 November 1887, 559.

84. Tattersall, *Early World Series,* 39; Lansche, *Forgotten Championships,* 19–27.

85. *St. Louis Post-Dispatch,* 23 October 1887, 6.

86. *Sporting Life,* 2 November 1887, 5.

87. *St. Louis Post-Dispatch,* 23 October 1887, 6; *Washington Post,* 18 October 1887, 3. The Washington newspaper reported that the use of three Palace Cars, a baggage car, and dining car created $3,280 in expenses, food costs for the entourage totaled $1,267, and mileage another $8,000. When these expenditures were coupled with advertising, umpires' salaries, and sundry items, the total reached about $15,000. *Sporting Life,* 2 November 1887, 5.

88. *St. Louis Post-Dispatch,* 23 October 1887, 6.

6—The New York Giants

1. Thorn and Palmer, *Total Baseball,* 721, 1427, 1502; Hetrick, *Von der Ahe,* 78–79.

2. Wolff, *Baseball Encyclopedia,* 1731. Bushong caught sixty-nine games for Brooklyn in 1889, but his batting average declined to .209, and as his skills waned he was relegated to the status of a reserve player before he was finally released in 1890. Foutz's odyssey in the major leagues was also in eclipse. He remained with the Brooklyn team for two years and then moved to the Brooklyn NL team in 1890, but his achievements were undistinguished. He won only thirty-three games in his last seven years in the major leagues.

3. Robert L. Tiemann, "Curt Welch," in *Nineteenth Century Stars,* 132; Thorn and Palmer, *Total Baseball,* 1319. Clubs' trading for players in the 1880s was less

frequent than in modern times. It was more common for clubs to buy players from other clubs. Two classic examples of this practice in the 1880s were when Spalding sold Kelly to Boston and when Stearns purchased the Buffalo club to acquire the Big Four. In a few cases players changed clubs when they were left off a reserve list. John Montgomery Ward, for example, moved to the New York Giants in 1883 when the Providence Grays, thinking his career as a pitcher was ending, left him off the club's reserve list. John B. Day signed Buck Ewing, Roger Connor, Mickey Welch, and Tim Keefe to contracts when the Troy, New York, club died after the 1882 season. He assigned Ewing, Connor, and Welch to his New York Giants (NL) and sent Keefe to his New York Metropolitans (AA). When Keefe blossomed as a pitcher Day transferred him to the Giants in 1885. The fairly familiar modern spectacle of clubs trading several players in a single transaction was virtually unknown in the 1880s. Players were bought, sold, or occasionally traded for the usual reasons: Clubs sought to strengthen their rosters or to eliminate players who had become personae non grata.

4. Robert L. Tiemann, "William G. Gleason," in *Nineteenth Century Stars,* 52; Thorn and Palmer, *Total Baseball,* 870.

5. During his four years in St. Louis, McCarthy collected 697 hits in 2,241 times at bat for a .311 batting average. It must be recalled, however, that his average was somewhat inflated by the rule allowing bases on balls to be counted as hits in 1887. McCarthy's lifetime batting average for ten full years in the major leagues was a respectable .292. James D. Smith and Robert L. Tiemann, "Thomas Francis Michael McCarthy," in *Baseball's First Stars,* 102. Some baseball historians suggest that McCarthy is the poorest player honored with membership in baseball's Hall of Fame.

6. Thorn and Palmer, *Total Baseball,* 1023.

7. Ibid., 1326; Wright, *Nineteenth Century Baseball,* 175. The year 1888 was White's final year in the major leagues.

8. *Sporting News,* 8 September 1888, 1.

9. Joseph M. Overfield, "Elton P. Chamberlain (Icebox)," in *Nineteenth Century Stars,* 27.

10. The fact that the Browns managed to do so well in 1888 with only two pitchers caused some comment. In its section called "Local Hits," *Sporting News* observed, "Think of It! Only Two Pitchers. They Are Winning the Championship for the Browns." 1 September 1888, 2. The news that Von der Ahe had purchased Chamberlain reached St. Louis later that day.

11. *Sporting News,* 30 June 1888, 2. Brooklyn's record was thirty-eight wins and seventeen losses compared to the Browns' thirty-four wins and fifteen losses, but St. Louis's winning percentage of .693 gave them a slim lead over the Trolley Dodgers.

12. *Sporting News,* 26 July, 30 August, 27 September 1888, 2, 2, 2.

13. Wright, *Nineteenth Century Baseball,* 175.

14. Thorn and Palmer, *Total Baseball,* 1907. Cincinnati's club stole 469 bases, one better than the Browns.

15. *Sporting News,* 28 July 1888, 1; *New York Daily Tribune,* 5 October 1888, 4; *New York Times,* 5 October 1888, 2.

16. David Pietrusza, "John B. Day," in *Baseball's First Stars,* 49.

17. John J. O'Malley, "James J. Mutrie," in *Nineteenth Century Stars,* 98; Hardy, *New York Giants Base Ball Club,* 32.

18. O'Malley, "James J. Mutrie," 98.

19. Irv Bergman, "William Ewing" and "Michael Francis Welch"; Bernard Crowley, "Roger Connor"; and John J. O'Malley, "Timothy John Keefe," in *Baseball's First Stars,* 60–61, 170–71, 38–39, 83–84.

20. Mark Alvarez, "John Montgomery Ward," *Baseball's First Stars,* 167–68; Di Salvatore, *A Clever Base-Ballist,* 136; Stevens, *Baseball's Radical,* 25.

21. According to David Stevens, the club's name—the Giants—originated in a statement made by Jim Mutrie in 1885 who then managed the New Yorks. Mutrie boasted of "My Giants" when he referred to his club, and Stevens observed that the "team wasn't particularly tall, but Mutrie's nickname of Truthful James was half in jest anyway. The team's improvement sparked writers and fans to pick up the new name. It stuck, and the New York Giants were born." Stevens, *Baseball's Radical,* 33. Another account of the origins of the name recounts, "A few days before the opening of the 1885 season, during an exhibition game, Mutrie exhorted his team with the words 'come on you giants,' creating a name in sports that has endured for a century." O'Malley, "James J. Mutrie."

22. O'Malley, "Timothy John Keefe."

23. Burrows and Wallace, *Gotham,* 1222; Di Salvatore, *A Clever Base-Ballist,* 138.

24. Thorn and Palmer, *Total Baseball,* 1174; Hardy, *New York Giants Base Ball Club,* 60; Joe Klein, "Daniel Richardson," in *Baseball's First Stars,* 138. Klein was correct when he said Richardson's "steady play at second base for the New York Giants was an important factor in their winning the World's Championships in 1888 and 1889."

25. Bernard J. Crowley, "James Henry O'Rourke," in *Baseball's First Stars,* 125.

26. Thorn and Palmer, *Total Baseball,* 1283; Randy Linthurst, "Michael Joseph Tiernan," in *Nineteenth Century Stars,* 126. Silent Mike earned his nickname by his obvious dislike of publicity and by his calm style on the field.

27. *St. Louis Post-Dispatch,* 10 October 1888, 8.

28. *New York Times,* 5 October 1888, 2; *New York Daily Tribune,* 5 October 1888, 4.

29. *Sporting Life,* 10 October 1888, 1. By 1888 many journalists simply referred to the annual games as the "World's Series" and dropped the more cumbersome "World's Championship."

30. Ibid., 17 October 1888, 1; *St. Louis Post-Dispatch,* 10 October 1888, 8.

31. *Sporting Life,* 10 October 1888, 1.

32. *Sporting Life,* 17 October 1888, 1.

33. *St. Louis Post-Dispatch,* 10 October 1888, 8; Hardy, *New York Giants Base Ball Club,* 83.

34. *St. Louis Post-Dispatch,* 10 October 1888, 8; *Sporting Life,* 24 October 1888, 5.

35. Hetrick, *Von der Ahe,* 88–89; *New York Times,* 16 October 1888, 2.

36. *New York Daily Tribune,* 15 October 1888, 7; *Sporting Life,* 24 October 1888, 6.

37. Jim Moore and Natalie Vermilyea, *Ernest Thayer's "Casey at the Bat": Background and Characters of Baseball's Most Famous Poem* (Jefferson, N.C.: McFarland, 1994), 260–61; *New York Times,* 15 August 1888, 4; *New York Daily Tribune,* 15 August 1888, 8.

38. De Wolf Hopper, *Once a Clown, Always a Clown: Reminiscences of De Wolf Hopper* (Boston: Little, Brown, 1927), 80–81.

39. Moore and Vermilyea, *"Casey at the Bat"*, 260–61.

40. *New York Times*, 25 September 1935, 23; Hardy, *New York Giants Base Ball Club*, 77. An interesting sidelight to Hopper's career onstage is the fact that one of his wives, Elda Furry, whom he married in 1913, later became famous as the Hollywood columnist Hedda Hopper. Their son William became well known as Perry Mason's investigator in the television series. Ephraim Katz, *The Film Encyclopedia* (New York: G. P. Putnam's Sons, 1979), 576.

41. Spalding, *America's National Game*, 450.

42. Wright, *Nineteenth Century Baseball*, 175; Thorn and Palmer, *Total Baseball*, 1567.

43. *St. Louis Post-Dispatch*, 1 October 1888, 8. Perhaps, some speculated, Hudson felt that after Icebox Chamberlain joined the Browns Comiskey favored Chamberlain and King when handing out starting pitching assignments. According to one writer, Hudson "felt sore over Comiskey's preference for King and Chamberlain and probably he never thought his club would need his services." Ibid., 23 October 1888, 8.

44. *New York Times*, 1 November 1888, 1; Hetrick, *Von der Ahe*, 91.

45. *Sporting Life*, 24 October 188, 1; *New York Daily Tribune*, 17 October 1888, 12.

46. The Giants' mascot was not identified by the press reports, but Cliff Latham, Arlie's young son, served as the Browns' mascot during the series. *Sporting Life*, 17 October 1888, 1. During much of the regular season a man named Fred Blundt, a Chicago bootblack, served as the Giants' mascot. He did not get along well with manager Mutrie and was replaced by a young man whose mother operated a Harlem boarding house. *Sporting News*, 8 September 1888, 2.

47. Kelly had recently been arrested for assault and battery of a prostitute, when he and two friends visited Kit Howard's brothel in Detroit while Kelly was in town umpiring NL games. Their stay ended when Honest John assaulted one of the prostitutes, one Emma Gordon, and knocked out two of her teeth. The group moved on to Kit Flemming's bordello and still drunk and disorderly broke up some furniture, whereupon they proceeded to a third house of ill repute. Kelly finally returned to his room in the Cadillac Hotel where he was arrested on a complaint filed by Ms. Gordon. His friends contacted her, gave her twenty-five dollars, and Gordon withdrew the complaint. *Sporting News*, 29 September 1888, 5; Hardy, *New York Giants Base Ball Club*, 8.

48. *New York Times*, 17 October 1888, 3; *St. Louis Post-Dispatch*, 16 October 1888, 2; *New York Clipper*, 27 October 1888, 529.

49. *New York Daily Tribune*, 17 October 1888, 12.

50. *Sporting Life*, 24 October 1888, 3; *St. Louis Post-Dispatch*, 17 October 1888, 1.

51. Hetrick, *Von der Ahe*, 89.

52. *New York Daily Tribune*, 19 October 1888, 3.

53. *New York Times*, 19 October 1888, 3.

54. Ibid., 20 October 1888, 4; *Sporting Life*, 24 October 1888, 3.

55. *St. Louis Post-Dispatch*, 19 October 1888, 1; *New York Daily Tribune*, 20 October 1888, 4; *New York Times*, 20 October 1888, 3.

56. *New York Daily Tribune*, 21 October 1888, 4.

57. Tattersall, *Early World Series*, 48–49; *St. Louis Post-Dispatch*, 20 October 1888, 1; *New York Times*, 21 October 1888, 6; *New York Daily Tribune*, 21 October 1888, 4; *Sporting Life*, 31 October 1888, 3.

58. New York City began an aggressive program of streetlighting in 1881 that first centered on lower Fifth Avenue and the crosstown streets of 14th and 34th. Soon electric illumination appeared on selected streets such as Fourth and Seventh Avenues and 59th Street and up the thoroughfares flanking Central Park. By 1888, although the vicinity of the Polo Grounds was not extensively illuminated, the sportswriters could see the streetlights from their vantage point in the press box. Burrows and Wallace, *Gotham*, 1063–69.

59. *Sporting News*, 31 October 1888, 3.

60. *St. Louis Post-Dispatch*, 21 October 1888, 10 (quotation); Thorn and Palmer, *Total Baseball*, 1023.

61. *Sporting Life*, 31 October 1886, 6.

62. Ibid., 5. Henry Chadwick, the author of "Chadwick's Chat" for *Sporting Life*, described the scene at the park and reported sharing a box with De Wolf Hopper and Digby Bell, their spouses, and Helen Dauvray. Lowry, *Green Cathedrals*, 205–6.

63. *New York Daily Tribune*, 23 October 1888, 10; *Sporting Life*, 31 October 1888, 5. Another writer observed that O'Rourke "used so many big words that we spent a week scouring the dictionary, but could not find any of them." *National Police Gazette*, 10 November 1888, 3.

64. *Sporting Life*, 31 October 1888, 3; Lansche, *Forgotten Championships*, 30.

65. *New York Times*, 23 October 1888, 3.

66. *Sporting Life*, 31 October 1888, 3. Some newspapers, critical of Von der Ahe's careless remarks, informed their readers that Chris also went so far as to state he believed Kelly bet money on the Giants. Ibid.; *New York Times*, 25 October 1888, 2.

67. *St. Louis Post-Dispatch*, 23 October 1888, 3.

68. Ibid., 24 October 1888, 1.

69. *Sporting Life*, 31 October 1888, 3.

70. *New York Daily Tribune*, 25 October 1888, 3; *New York Times*, 25 October 1888, 2; *Sporting Life*, 31 October 1888, 3; *St. Louis Post-Dispatch*, 24 October 1888, 1.

71. *Sporting Life*, 31 October 1888, 3; Stevens, *Baseball's Radical*, 74.

72. *New York Daily Tribune*, 25 October 1888, 3.

73. *St. Louis Post-Dispatch*, 25 October 1888, 7.

74. *New York Daily Tribune*, 26 October 1888, 7.

75. *Sporting Life*, 31 October 1888, 3.

76. Lansche, *Forgotten Championships*, 33; Tattersall, *Early World Series*, 52–53.

77. *Sporting Life*, 7 November 1888, 3.

78. Ibid.; *New York Daily Tribune*, 26 October 1887, 7; *New York Clipper*, 3 November 1888, 545. Thomas H. Hall, the manufacturer of "Between the Acts" cigarettes, donated the Hall Cup to honor the 1888 championship games. Tiffany's in New York fashioned the cup, which contained one hundred and six ounces of silver. *Sporting News*, 15 September 1888, 1.

79. Mutrie had a purpose in mind when he announced the team was disbanded. He knew that some of his players had agreed to an exhibition game with the Browns the next afternoon, which happened to be Sunday. So long as the team

remained under his jurisdiction, it was an NL team and could not play on the sabbath. Now, after he made his statement, the Giants were free agents to play the game and to put a little cash in their pockets. *St. Louis Post-Dispatch,* 28 October 1888, 18.

80. *Sporting News,* 7 November 1888, 3.

81. *Sporting Life,* 7 November 1888, 3.

82. Ibid.

7—New York and Brooklyn

1. *Sporting Life,* 17 October 1888, 4. For a concise account of Spalding's tour, see Levine, *Spalding,* 99–109. At the time the tour left Chicago, John Montgomery Ward and Ed Cannonball Crane were with the New York Giants finishing the World's Championship playoff in St. Louis. They joined the team in Oxford, Nebraska, as the tour prepared to play three exhibition games in Denver and Colorado Springs. *Sporting Life,* 31 October 1888, 7. For eyewitness (sometimes rambling) accounts, consult Anson, *A Ball Player's Career,* 141–282; Spalding, *America's National Game,* 251–65; and Palmer, *Athletic Sports,* 151–400.

2. Larry G. Bowman, "'The Players Redeemed Themselves': Major League Baseball Visits Colorado, 1888," *Colorado Heritage* (spring 1999), 31. Spalding, always the shrewd businessman with a nearly unerring sense for ticket sales, garnered about eleven thousand dollars from the games played in Denver and Colorado Springs. Once the tourists' food and lodging costs, the games' advertising, and other expenses were deducted from the gate receipts, Spalding's visit to Colorado provided enough profit to fund approximately one-third of the entire trip.

3. According to Peter Levine, Spalding revealed his secondary motive when he declared to a reporter that he went to Australia for the purpose of "extending [his] sporting goods business to that quarter of the globe and to create a market for goods there." Levine, *Spalding,* 100.

4. *New York Times,* 7 April 1889, 11; *New York Daily Tribune,* 9 April 1889, 1.

5. *Sporting News,* 20 April 1889, 1.

6. *Sporting Life,* 28 November 1888, 1; *Sporting News,* 24 November 1888, 2.

7. Rich Eldred, "John Tomlinson Brush," in *Baseball's First Stars,* 14.

8. *Sporting Life,* 29 August 1888, 3. The players threw and batted balls (an old one and a new one) into the air and claimed they had little difficulty catching them. A small crowd of local baseball fans attended the experiment, and they apparently were both awed and enthusiastic by the prospect of major leaguers playing ball in artificial light.

9. Ibid., 12 September 1888, 2. See also Pietrusza, *Lights On!,* 13–15.

10. *Sporting Life,* 5 December 1888, 1; Di Salvatore, *A Clever Base-Ballist,* 244–46. The Brush plan was adopted while the Brotherhood of Professional Base Ball Players' leader, John Montgomery Ward, was occupied playing in Spalding's world tour. Ward apparently believed he was recruited in order to get him out of the country while the Brush plan was formalized, and that he had been betrayed by Spalding who always played a major role in any important decision rendered by the NL owners.

11. *Sporting News,* 24 November 1888, 2; Burk, *Never Just a Game,* 101–3. Ac-

cording to Daniel Pearson, at least thirty-three major league players in 1889 earned salaries in excess of the $2,500 cap imposed by the Brush plan. Daniel M. Pearson, *Baseball in 1889: Players versus Owners* (Bowling Green, Ohio: Bowling Green State University Popular Press, 1993), 223–24.

12. *Sporting Life,* 12 December 1888, 1.

13. Titcomb managed to win only one game for the Giants in 1889. After that he played only one more season, in the minor leagues, before exiting professional baseball. Wright, *Nineteenth Century Baseball,* 168, 182; Thorn and Palmer, *Total Baseball,* 1804.

14. Norman L. Macht, "Henry Francis O'Day," in *Baseball's First Stars,* 123.

15. Pearson, *Baseball in 1889,* 32; Lowry, *Green Cathedrals,* 224–25. Erastus Wiman owned the New York Metropolitans in 1886 and 1887, and his Mets made the St. George their home park until the franchise collapsed at the conclusion of the 1887 season.

16. Hardy, *New York Giants Base Ball Club,* 87. Henry Chadwick, a columnist for *Sporting Life,* visited the construction site about a week before it was scheduled to open on July 8 and reported that the work was nearly completed. The new Polo Grounds, he judged, appeared adequate to major league standards. *Sporting Life,* 10 July 1889, 5.

17. Lowry, *Green Cathedrals,* 190. When the third Polo Grounds opened on July 8, 1889, it drew a throng of fans. De Wolf Hopper was among those who attended the opening, and as one reporter observed, "As soon as De Wolf Hopper, the comedian, got inside the grounds he uttered the most blood-curdling war whoop ever heard. Then he jumped in the air, kicking his heels three times, and went and sat down, the happiest man in the world." *New York Daily Tribune,* 9 July 1889, 2. The event carried the air of a holiday weekend series or playoff game. A group of Wall Street brokers who fashioned themselves the "cranks on 'Change'" attended the game and presented Buck Ewing with a gold watch and chain reportedly worth $250. *New York Daily Tribune,* 9 July 1889, 2. To put the value of Ewing's gift in perspective, the average working man's annual salary was about $500 a year in the 1880s. Many fans could not get into the sold-out Polo Grounds, and an estimated five thousand of the disappointed fans simply gathered on the high ground overlooking the ballpark, then called Dead-Head Hill, to watch the game. *New York Times,* 9 July 1889, 3.

18. *Sporting Life,* 24 August 1889, 1; Di Salvatore, *A Clever Base-Ballist,* 256.

19. Hardy, *New York Giants Base Ball Club,* 85; O'Malley, "Timothy John Keefe."

20. See John Montgomery Ward, "Is the Base-Ball Player a Chattel?" *Lippincott's Monthly Magazine* 40 (1887): 310–19; "Our National Game," *Cosmopolitan* 5 (October 1888): 442–55.

21. Di Salvatore, *A Clever Base-Ballist,* 191; *Sporting Life,* 20 July 1887, 2.

22. *Sporting Life,* 28 November 1888, 2; Pearson, *Baseball in 1889,* 85; Hardy, *New York Giants Base Ball Club,* 84–85. Ward's reluctance to join Washington's Statesmen was certainly understandable; the team was inept, and he must have viewed such a move as exile. New York City was an ideal place from which to lead the Brotherhood; and at that time his ill-fated marriage to Helen Dauvray had entered a difficult phase, and he wanted to be closer to her as he sought to effect a

reconciliation. Stevens, *Baseball's Radical*, 78–81; Bowman, "Baseball's Intriguing Couple."

23. Di Salvatore, *A Clever Base-Ballist*, 255.

24. Andy McCue, "Charles H. Byrne," in *Baseball's First Stars*, 19.

25. *New York Clipper*, 14 April 1883, 53. Although his team did not join the AA in 1883, Byrne was in full agreement with the AA's marketing strategies, including selling alcohol at his park. He also endorsed the AA's concept of ladies' days, and he converted a nearby building on the grounds into a ladies' room to attract women to the ballpark. Washington Park was destroyed by fire on May 19, 1889, and was replaced by Washington Park II, which served as Brooklyn's home field throughout the 1890 season. Lowry, *Green Cathedrals*, 115.

26. *New York Clipper*, 23 June, 28 July 1883, 218, 302.

27. Ibid., 13 October 1883, 491; Pearson, *Baseball in 1889*, 19.

28. *New York Clipper*, 19 May 1883, 133. The attendance figure was all the more impressive because the weather was cloudy and rainy that afternoon, and the last-minute decision to play the game came as a surprise to both players and spectators alike. The Mets won the six-inning game by a score of 8–1.

29. Terry played fourteen years in the major leagues with four teams and recorded a lifetime record of 197 wins and 196 losses. John Corcoran, a pitcher, and infielders Charlie Householder, William Henry Harrison Geer, and William F. Greenwood also were promoted from Byrne's minor league team to his major league franchise, but they all had brief and undistinguished careers. Thorn and Palmer, *Total Baseball*, 764, 861, 882, 935, 1799–800.

30. Ibid., 1898, 1901, 1903, 1905.

31. Wright, *Nineteenth Century Baseball*, 174–75.

32. Richard Puff, "Thomas Joseph Lovett," in *Baseball's First Stars*, 97.

33. Caruthers won forty games, Terry won twenty-two, and Lovett registered seventeen wins in 1889. Lovett's arrival was critical to Brooklyn's success that season. Mickey Hughes had been one of the team's pitching mainstays, but he faltered in 1889, winning nine and losing eight. In 1890 Hughes spent part of the season with Brooklyn before he was released to Philadelphia in the AA. He compiled a composite five and seven record and was finished as a major league player. Thorn and Palmer, *Total Baseball*, 1568.

34. *Sporting Life*, 17 April 1889, 8; Pearson, *Baseball in 1889*, 29–30.

35. *Sporting Life*, 10 April 1889, 1.

36. *New York Times*, 7 April 1889, 11; *New York Daily Tribune*, 9 April 1889, 1.

37. *Sporting Life*, 17 April 1889, 8.

38. Ibid., 8 May 1889, 8.

39. *New York Daily Tribune*, 20 May 1889, 3; Lowry, *Green Cathedrals*, 115.

40. *Sporting News*, 25 May 1889, 1.

41. *New York Daily Tribune*, 31 May 1889, 2.

42. *Sporting Life*, 5 June 1889, 3; Pearson, *Baseball in 1889*, 45–46; Hetrick, *Von der Ahe*, 97–98. The Browns' games in Brooklyn proved a bonanza for Byrne in 1889. According to Byrne's count, a record-setting 353,690 fans attended the Bridegrooms sixty-nine home games for an average of 5,125 per contest. But when Von der Ahe's "poys" were in Brooklyn, they drew 95,395 fans for eight games, an average of 11,924. Drawing better than ten thousand spectators to a game in the 1880s

was well above average for a major league game. *Sporting Life,* 23 October 1889, 3.

43. *St. Louis Post-Dispatch,* 5 July 1889, 3; *Sporting Life,* 10 July 1889, 3.

44. *Sporting Life,* 8 May 1889, 1.

45. *Sporting News,* 19 October 1889, 3.

46. Pearson, *Baseball in 1889,* 168–69; Hetrick, *Von der Ahe,* 101–2.

47. *Sporting Life,* 18 September 1889, 3.

48. Ibid., 16 October 1889, 3. For an excellent account of Brooklyn's championship season, see Nemec, *Beer and Whiskey League,* 165–201.

49. Thorn and Palmer, *Total Baseball,* 1908; Wright, *Nineteenth Century Baseball,* 182.

50. Wright, *Nineteenth Century Baseball,* 182.

51. Hoss Radbourn won 309 games in his long and illustrious career in the major leagues. He joined the Players' League in 1890 and won twenty-seven games. After the demise of the Players' League, he signed a contract with the NL's Cincinnati club, played a final season, and won eleven while losing seventeen. Radbourn pitched a total of 4,335 innings in eleven seasons. Nolan Ryan, for example, pitched 3,869 innings in his twenty-six-year career. The fact that Radbourn lasted as long as he did is a tribute to his skill and stamina. He was gone from the major leagues after the 1891 season. Thorn and Palmer, *Total Baseball,* 1723, 1747.

52. Ibid., 25 September 1889, 2.

53. *Sporting Life,* 16 October 1889, 1.

54. The slogan "We Are the People" was one that Giants' manager Jim Mutrie popularized. Prior to games, he frequently strode up and down in front of the stands shouting, "Who are the People? We are the People!" His antics became popular with New York fans, and his chant became the club's battle cry. *New York Daily Tribune,* 3 November 1889, 2; Hardy, *New York Giants Base Ball Club,* 47.

55. *New York Daily Tribune,* 7 October 1889, 2.

56. *New York Times,* 21 October 1889, 5. Sunday evening was chosen for the gala event at the Broadway Theatre since World's Championship games rested on the sabbath to honor the NL's ban on Sunday games. At that point the Giants and the Bridegrooms were tied at one victory apiece in the series. Accounts of the evening's entertainment do not indicate that Hopper revisited mighty Casey's fateful turn at bat for the audience. *Sporting News,* 2 November 1889, 4.

57. *Sporting Life,* 23 October 1889, 2.

58. Henry Chadwick, the premiere baseball columnist of his day, wrote, "I am glad to see that both Messrs. Day and Byrne are of one accord in their views of ending the series the moment the championship has been decided. Experience has shown that the after games are useless and unprofitable." Ibid., 3.

59. *New York Clipper,* 26 October 1889, 555.

60. *Sporting Life,* 23 October 1889, 3; *Sporting News,* 19 October 1889, 1. After the series concluded, Brooklyn paid Lynch's salary and the Giants paid Gaffney's. *Sporting Life,* 6 November 1889, 2. When the Brooklyn club chose Lynch to umpire in the series, "Honest John" Kelly was bypassed. Kelly had officiated in every World's Championship since 1885, and he was dismayed when Byrne elected to summon Tom Lynch to serve as the AA's umpire. Byrne and Day agreed to select umpires from among those currently employed by their respective leagues, and in 1889 Honest John did not umpire in the major leagues. Nevertheless, he seemed to think

his bad relationship with Byrne disqualified him. Kahn, *Umpire Story,* 239. See also *Sporting News,* 3 November 1889, 2.

61. *Sporting Life,* 23 October 1889, 3; Pearson, *Baseball in 1889,* 158.

62. Kahn, *Umpire Story,* 237; *Sporting Life,* 23 October 1889, 3; Tattersall, *Early World Series,* 58. Ferguson had a long history in major league baseball. He played on several major league teams, often serving as captain-manager, and later umpired in the NL in 1885, in the AA from 1887 through 1889, and in the Players' League in 1890. Frank V. Phelps, "Robert V. Ferguson," in *Nineteenth Century Stars,* 43.

63. Tattersall, *Early World Series,* 58–59; Lansche, *Forgotten Championships,* 34–35; *Sporting Life,* 23 October 1889, 3.

64. *New York Times,* 19 October 1889, 3.

65. Lynch originally demanded eight hundred dollars but finally compromised at six. Gaffney profited from Lynch's holdout and received an equal sum. *Sporting Life,* 23 October 1889, 3; *New York Times,* 20 October 1889, 12. Considering the fact that none of the Giants or the Bridegrooms received more than four hundred dollars for their play in the series, the umpires, unlike modern times, did comparatively well financially.

66. *Sporting Life,* 30 October 1889, 3; Lansche, *Forgotten Championships,* 35; Jerry Lansche, *Glory Fades Away: The Nineteenth-Century World Series Rediscovered* (Dallas: Taylor Publishing, 1991), 175–78.

67. *New York Times,* 20 October 1889, 12.

68. *Sporting Life,* 30 October 1889, 3; *New York Times,* 20 October 1889, 12; *New York Daily Tribune,* 20 October 1889, 4.

69. Unable to resist the temptation to pocket additional profits, Byrne chose to pit his club against their rivals from Baltimore rather than give his men a day of rest. *Sporting Life,* 30 October 1889, 6; Lansche, *Glory Fades Away,* 164; *New York Times,* 21 October 1889, 2.

70. Lansche, *Glory Fades Away,* 165–66; Tattersall, *Early World Series,* 61–62; *New York Daily Tribune,* 23 October 1889, 10.

71. *New York Times,* 24 October 1889, 3.

72. *Sporting Life,* 30 October 1889, 3.

73. Ibid.; Lansche, *Glory Fades Away,* 168–69. No one bothered to explain the fifteen-minute differential between games in the city and in Brooklyn.

74. Errors were common in the series games. Wet grounds, damp baseballs, and poor playing surfaces often contributed to frequent errors. In the first four games of the series, the Bridegrooms and the Giants committed a total of thirty-four errors, or an average of about eight per contest. Lansche, *Forgotten Championships,* 35–37; *Sporting Life,* 30 October 1889, 3; *New York Times,* 25 October 1889, 9. Concerning the umpiring, one reporter observed, "The umpiring gave more satisfaction than at any of the previous games." *New York Daily Tribune,* 26 October 1889, 4.

75. Clark's injury was so severe he did not return to the Bridegrooms' lineup for the remainder of the series. His loss proved disastrous to Brooklyn's efforts in the playoffs. Clark was hitting .417 at the time he sustained his injury, but (perhaps even more important) he curtailed the Giants' running game on the bases. While he was playing in the first four games, New York stole twelve bases; they stole twenty-one in the last five games after he no longer was available to catch. Joe Vis-

ner and Doc Bushong shared the catching duties after Clark was injured, and *Sporting Life* observed, "The miserable throwing of Visner and Bushong was a big factor in New York's success." *Sporting Life*, 6 November 1889, 2.

76. *New York Daily Tribune*, 26 October 1889, 10; Lansche, *Glory Fades Away*, 172; *New York Times*, 26 October 1889, 2.

77. *Sporting Life*, 6 November 1889, 2; *New York Times*, 27 October 1889, 3; *New York Clipper*, 2 November 1889, 571–72.

78. *New York Daily Tribune*, 29 October 1889, 2; *New York Times*, 29 October 1889, 3.

79. *New York Daily Tribune*, 30 October 1889, 3.

80. Lansche, *Glory Fades Away*, 175. O'Day's accomplishments in the series were impressive. He pitched a total of twenty-three innings, won two games and lost none, and recorded an earned run average of only 1.17. Cannonball Crane won four games and posted a 3.72 earned run average, and Brooklyn's Adonis Terry, who won two games for the Bridegrooms and lost three, had an earned run average of 5.97. Crane clearly was the series' star, but O'Day provided steady pitching at critical junctures in the series. Tattersall, *Early World Series*, 72–74; Pearson, *Baseball in 1889*, 182.

81. Tattersall, *Early World Series*, 75; *Sporting News*, 2 November 1889, 4.

82. *New York Times*, 31 October 1889, 3; *Sporting Life*, 20 November 1889, 4.

83. *Sporting Life*, 20 November 1889, 4; Pearson, *Baseball in 1889*, 182–83.

84. *Sporting Life*, 6 November 1889, 2. The first two games of the championship series attracted 25,670 paid admissions, or 53 percent of the total. Inclement weather clearly had its effect on the series' attendance and profits.

85. Ibid.; *New York Daily Tribune*, 31 October 1889, 3.

8—Brooklyn and Louisville

1. *Sporting News*, 9 November 1889, 3.

2. *Sporting Life*, 13 November 1889, 1.

3. Ibid. For handy access to the text of the players' manifesto, see Sullivan, *Early Innings*, 188–89.

4. *Sporting Life*, 25 December 1889, 1; Levine, *Spalding*, 60; Thorn and Palmer, *Total Baseball*, 2258–59. Brunell began his journalistic career with the *Cleveland Herald* in 1883 and was appointed the official scorekeeper for the Cleveland Blues' home games. Brunell took a strong stand against the UA in 1884, but by 1889 he apparently believed that the players had suffered enough abuse, and he openly allied with their cause. Spink, *The National Game*, 358. Another early ally came in the person of Albert L. Johnson of Cleveland, a wealthy streetcar magnate. Johnson realized that new ballparks meant new business opportunities for streetcar companies where he could merge "outrage at player mistreatment and the reserve clause with lucrative possibilities of the enterprise for his transit business." Burk, *Never Just a Game*, 104. See also Rader, *Baseball*, 58–59, and Sullivan, *Early Innings*, 185–87.

5. Burk, *Never Just a Game*, 105–9; *Sporting Life*, 25 December 1889, 1. In spite of all the forward-thinking elements of the PL's constitution, the Brotherhood proved unable to avoid certain arbitrary decisions. As Charles Alexander points out, "Yet for all its past complaints about players having no voice in when and where

they were sent, the Brotherhood made compulsory player assignments to constitute the eight club rosters." *Our Game,* 55.

6. *New York Clipper,* 9, 19 November 1889, 588, 603; *Sporting News,* 28 September 1889, 2; Burk, *Never Just a Game,* 106.

7. *Sporting Life,* 19 March 1890, 1.

8. As the Brotherhood settled one issue after another, the *New York Daily Tribune* alerted its readers that Keefe sought the contract to supply equipment to PL teams, and observed: "furnishing balls, bats, uniforms and other paraphernalia of the game would prove a neat item for any sporting-goods house. Keefe is a member of such a firm [Keefe and Becannon, at 157 Broadway, New York City], and if he does not get that contract there will be some excitement." 7 November 1890, 3. Keefe got the contract, and in the 25 December 1890 issue of *Sporting Life,* Keefe and Becannon announced that the PL had officially adopted their baseball; they offered the baseball to the general public at fifteen dollars a dozen. *Sporting Life,* 25 December 1889, 8. Keefe and Becannon continued the advertisements through August 1890. *Sporting Life,* 23 August 1890, 15. Keefe and Becannon also placed identical advertisements in *Sporting News.* The advertisements began on 18 January 1890 and appeared in the journal throughout the baseball season. See *Sporting News,* 18 January 1890, 3.

9. *New York Clipper,* 16, 23 November 1889, 604, 651. Day's appointment to the committee was especially significant. He was popular with the players and several of his Giants tried to persuade him to take his club into the PL. Had he chosen to do so, the impact on the NL would have been devastating. Instead, he elected to remain loyal to his fellow owners in the NL and suffered severe financial reverses in 1890. Hardy, *New York Giants Base Ball Club,* 102–3. Spalding was the backbone of the NL's war effort. His cunning, fortitude, and acumen served the NL owners well as they dealt with the multitude of problems plaguing his colleagues during the tense and costly players' revolt. Arthur Bartlett, *Baseball and Mr. Spalding: The History and Romance of Baseball* (New York: Farrar, Strauss and Young, 1951), 209–22; Hetrick, *Von der Ahe,* 116–17.

10. *Sporting Life,* 20 November 1889, 1; Thorn and Palmer, *Total Baseball,* 1908, 1910.

11. Spalding, *America's National Game,* 273–75; Sullivan, *Early Innings,* 189–95. The NL attacked the emerging PL in other ways as well. In December 1889, the New York club sought relief in the courts by seeking a temporary injunction against Ward in an effort prevent him from playing for another club. Early in 1890 the Giants also filed for an injunction against Buck Ewing. While the courts' rulings in each case were somewhat ambiguous, Ward and Ewing were in no way restrained from playing for any team other than the Giants. Had the decisions gone against Ward and Ewing, the PL could have suffered a death blow long before the season commenced. Di Salvatore, *A Clever Base-Ballist,* 295–97. See also *Sporting Life,* 22 January 1890, 2.

12. *Sporting Life,* 13 November 1889, 1. Also see Nemec, *Beer and Whiskey League,* 189.

13. *Sporting Life,* 11 December 1889, 2. Von der Ahe did not attend the meeting. Instead, he authorized Ralph Lazarus—who was speaking for his own club, the Columbus Buckeyes—to attend to the Browns' interests as well.

14. Wright, *Nineteenth Century Baseball,* 197; Hardy, *New York Giants Base Ball Club,* 102–6.

15. Di Salvatore, *A Clever Base-Ballist,* 300–305.

16. Levine, *Spalding,* 60; Wright, *Nineteenth Century Baseball,* 183, 189, 197.

17. For Cap's views on the Brotherhood and the players' revolt, see Anson, *A Ball Player's Career,* 286–94. Cap's memoirs were published a decade after the PL blossomed and withered. Cap contented himself with reviewing the trend of events and focused principally upon his problems of training and leading a relatively poor club during 1890. Cap did not excoriate his erstwhile foes. In an effort to keep one of the league's brightest stars from joining the PL, Spalding tried to tempt King Kelly to stay in the NL by offering him a ten-thousand-dollar bonus and a generous three-year contract, but the King declared, he "could not go back on the boys." Appel, *Slide, Kelly, Slide,* 150–52.

18. O. P. Caylor, "Opening Day of the Baseball Season of 1890," *Harper's Weekly* 34 (May 1890): 353–56.

19. Thorn and Palmer, *Total Baseball,* 1894, 1896, 1898, 1901, 1903, 1905, 1907, 1909.

20. Sydney Cowell was born in England in 1846 into a famous family of performers. She emigrated to the United States in 1871, pursued a career on the New York stage until 1903 when poor health forced her to retire, and died in 1925. *New York Times,* 22 April 1903, 6; Raymond D. McGill, ed., *Notable Names in the American Theatre* (Clifton, N.J.: James T. White, 1976), 373; Larry Bowman, "A Celebrity Allegory: Fame, Indeed, for John Montgomery Ward," *National Pastime* 20 (2000): 90–92.

21. Sydney Cowell, "The Enchanted Baseball: A Fairy Story of Modern Times," *The Cosmopolitan: A Monthly Illustrated Magazine* 8 (November 1889–April 1890): 659.

22. Ibid., 560.

23. Wright, *Nineteenth Century Baseball,* 182–93.

24. Ibid., 189–215.

25. Thorn and Palmer, *Total Baseball,* 712, 911, 1217, 1299, 1488.

26. L. Robert Davids and Richard A. Puff, "William Van Winkle Wolf," in *Nineteenth Century Stars,* 140.

27. Thorn and Palmer, *Total Baseball,* 711–12; Philip Von Borries, "Louis Rogers Browning," in *Nineteenth Century Stars,* 19, 143. During Browning's years with the Colonels, Chicken amassed a composite batting average of .285. Browning clearly was the superior hitter. Nevertheless, the ungainly Wolf won the fans' affections. Part of his attractiveness to the Louisville fans was because he, as Browning, was born in Louisville, and when Chicken chose to remain with the Colonels, the esteem in which he was held among the Colonels' fans became limitless.

28. Wright, *Nineteenth Century Baseball,* 193.

29. *Sporting News,* 18 October 1890, 2. Hamburg was a familiar face to the Louisville fans. Before playing in minor league baseball he had been a member of the Eclipse Juniors, the best amateur team in Louisville. He signed with Columbus, Georgia, in the Southern League in 1884 and after two seasons there moved to Bridgeport for two seasons, then to Buffalo in the International League. He became a major leaguer in 1890.

30. Thorn and Palmer, *Total Baseball,* 896, 1197, 1164, 1223, 1273, 1317, 1340, 1482, 1654; Wright, *Nineteenth Century Baseball,* 210.

31. Joseph M. Overfield, "John Curtis Chapman," in *Nineteenth Century Stars,* 28. During his career Chapman managed teams in Louisville, Detroit, Milwaukee, and Buffalo in addition to his minor league managing stints at Buffalo, Holyoke and Springfield, Massachusetts, Syracuse and Rochester, New York, and Toronto. Tall and courtly in appearance, "Jack Chapman knew and practiced the virtue of silence." Ibid.

32. Nemec, *Beer and Whiskey League,* 184.

33. The New York City newspapers, for example, provided readers extensive accounts of the Louisville disaster. Losses in lives and property were ghastly. Readers soon learned that Louisville was not the only victim of the series of tornadoes that swept through the upper Ohio River Valley and adjacent areas. Such towns as Princeton, Indiana, Bowling Green, Kentucky, and several others also were in the path of the atmospheric conditions that spawned several tornadoes. The use of the term *cyclone* reflected contemporary theory regarding catastrophic winds. A tornado was defined as a local event that affected only a small area. A cyclone was viewed as a large, elliptical weather disturbance that punished extensive geographical areas. Modern meteorologists rarely use the term *cyclone,* and then usually only to describe severe weather conditions in Asia. Louisville and neighboring areas were probably in the path of an advancing cold front that collided with warm moist air, and the volatile ingredients spawned a rash of tornadoes over a large area much like the series of storms that swept through Alabama, Georgia, Tennessee, Kentucky, and Ohio on the night of May 26–27, 1973, and killed over three hundred people. For a discussion of late-nineteenth-century Americans' differentiation between a cyclone and a tornado, see *New York Times,* 29 March 1890, 2.

34. *Sporting Life,* 26 April 1890, 8.

35. Ibid., 13; *Sporting News,* 26 April 1890, 3.

36. *Sporting Life,* 31 May 1890, 13.

37. Ibid., 19 July 1890, 13; *Sporting News,* 19 July 1890, 5. In a report by a special correspondent, *Sporting News* informed its readers that "they [the Cyclones] are winning games right along, and are to the Association what Comiskey's team [the Browns], in the days of old, were." *Sporting News,* 2 August 1890, 1.

38. Wolf's .300 batting average in 1884 came during a year in which the AA expanded from eight to thirteen teams to counter the AA's challenge to establish itself as a third major league. Good pitching was a scarce commodity in 1884, and Wolf, in his third year in the AA, enjoyed the second-best batting average of his career.

39. Thorn and Palmer, *Total Baseball,* 1340.

40. Wright, *Nineteenth Century Baseball,* 210. Taylor's career in the major leagues was brief, and his .306 average in 1890 was his career average as well; Charlie Hamburg spent only one year in the major leagues. Phil Tomney and Farmer Weaver each recorded batting averages slightly above their earlier performances. The Louisville club batting average of .279 led the AA in 1890. Thorn and Palmer, *Total Baseball,* 1911.

41. Thorn and Palmer, *Total Baseball,* 1482, 1788.

42. Ibid.

43. *Sporting Life,* 7 July 1890, 12.

44. *Louisville Courier-Journal,* 15 October 1890, quoted in *Sporting News,* 18 October 1890, 2.

45. *Sporting News,* 26 April 1890, 5.

46. *Sporting Life,* 6 September 1890, 10; *Sporting News,* 13 September 1890, 3.

47. Thorn and Palmer, *Total Baseball,* 1910. Slugging averages are computed by dividing a club's total number of bases garnered from hits by the total number of times at bat.

48. Ibid.; Wright, *Nineteenth Century Baseball,* 203. Only one other National League club, the Chicago White Stockings, committed fewer than 350 errors in 1890.

49. Thorn and Palmer, *Total Baseball,* 1910.

50. *Sporting News,* 4 October 1890, 1.

51. *Sporting Life,* 11 October 1890, 8.

52. *Sporting News,* 18 October 1890, 2.

53. *New York Daily Tribune,* 13 October 1890, 2; *Sporting Life,* 18 October 1890, 9. No one bothered to explain the reason why the Cyclones insisted on an extra ten cents per seat. Parsons and Byrne wished to maximize receipts, and perhaps they reasoned that Louisville fans would gladly pay the extra ten cents to attend the city's first World's Championship.

54. *Sporting Life,* 18 October 1890, 9. Division of receipts proved a moot point. Attendance for the series was among the worst of the seven World's Championships, and Byrne and Parsons barely recovered expenses.

55. Ibid. Richter was not alone in his tepid endorsement of the playoffs. "It is to be regretted," Spink observed, "that the Boston Players' team, winners of the Brotherhood pennant[,] are barred from taking part in the series in question. It has been claimed by many that the Boston is a better team than either the Brooklyn or Louisville and that the battle between the two latter will by no means decide which is the best in the country." *Sporting News,* 25 October 1890, 2.

56. *New York Clipper,* 25 October, 1890, 521; *New York Daily Tribune,* 18 October 1890, 3; *Sporting News,* 25 October 1890, 2; *Sporting Life,* 25 October 1890, 6.

57. *Sporting News,* 25 October 1890, 2.

58. Ibid.; *Sporting Life,* 30 August 1890, 1. Ever the astute strategist, Chapman lured Daily back to the AA late in the summer of 1890. The New York Giants were in dreadful condition that summer, and Daily's case was unique. When Chapman sought to enlist Daily to his roster, none of the AA clubs protested since Daily's dilemma was not of his own making.

59. Wright, *Nineteenth Century Baseball,* 210; Thorn and Palmer, *Total Baseball,* 1456.

60. Tattersall, *Early World Series,* 79; *Sporting News,* 25 October 1890, 2.

61. *New York Clipper,* 11 November 1890, 537; Lansche, *Glory Fades Away,* 196.

62. Lansche, *Glory Fades Away,* 196.

63. Tattersall, *Early World Series,* 80.

64. *Sporting News,* 1 November 1890, 5; Lansche, *Forgotten Championships,* 43; *New York Times,* 26 October 1890, 8.

65. *New York Daily Tribune,* 28 October 1890, 4.

66. Tattersall, *Early World Series,* 80.

67. *Sporting Life,* 1 November 1890, 5. Throughout the series, *Sporting Life* persisted in its mild scorn of the World's Championship and continued to term it "Inter-League Play." In its final coverage of the Louisville-Brooklyn match, *Sporting Life* declared, "neither team has shown any marked superiority over the other, and the result of the series will strengthen the belief of many [that] the Boston Players' team would have no trouble winning a series from either or both of the teams which contested for what was called by courtesy the 'world's championship.'" Ibid.

68. *New York Daily Tribune,* 29 October 1890, 3.

69. *Sporting News,* 1 November 1890, 5.

Conclusion

1. *Sporting Life,* 1 November 1890, 2.

2. Rader, *Baseball,* 61.

3. Bob Bailey, "The Forgotten War: The American Association–National League War of 1891," *National Pastime* 19 (1999): 81–84.

4. Nemec, *Beer and Whiskey League,* 232; *Sporting News,* 25 December 1891, 1.

5. *Sporting News,* 14 November 1891.

6. Nemec, *Beer and Whiskey League,* 234–35.

7. Lansche, *Forgotten Championships,* 45.

8. Ibid., 49–61; Lansche, *Glory Fades Away,* 229–306; Rader, *Baseball,* 71; Burk, *Never Just a Game,* 127; McGraw, *My Thirty Years in Baseball,* 107, 115–16.

9. *Sporting Life,* 17 January 1903, 4.

10. Ibid., 17 February 1905, 7.

Bibliography

Newspapers and Magazines

Boston Daily Globe

Chicago Daily News

Chicago Tribune

Current Biography

Detroit Evening News

Detroit Free Press

Detroit Sunday News

Kansas City Star

Lippincott's Monthly Magazine

Louisville Courier-Journal

The National Pastime:
A Review of Baseball History

National Police Gazette

New York Clipper

New York Daily Tribune

New York Herald

New York Times

New York World

Nine: A Journal of Baseball History and
Social Policy Perspectives

Providence Daily Journal

Rocky Mountain News

Sporting Life

Sporting News

St. Louis Post-Dispatch

Washington Post

Encyclopedias and Directories

Grobani, Anton. *Guide to Baseball Literature*. Detroit: Gale Research Company, 1975.

Hartroll, Phyllis, ed. *The Oxford Companion to the Theatre*. New York: Oxford University Press, 1983.

Hatch, Tom. *Custer and Battle of the Little Big Horn: An Encyclopedia of the People, Places, Events, Indian Cultures and Customs, Information Sources, Art, and Films*. Jefferson, N.C.: McFarland, 1997.

Holli, Melvin, and Peter d'A. Jones. *Biographical Dictionary of American Mayors*. Westport, Conn.: Greenwood Press, 1981.

Ivor-Campbell, Frederick, Robert L. Tiemann, and Mark Rucker, eds. *Baseball's First Stars*. Cleveland, Ohio: Society for American Baseball Research, 1996.

Jackson, Kenneth T., ed. *The Encyclopedia of New York City*. New Haven: Yale University Press, 1995.

Jobes, Gertrude, ed. *Dictionary of Mythology, Folklore, and Symbols*. 3 vols. New York: Scarecrow Press, 1961–1962.

Jones, Donald D. *Former Major League Teams: An Encyclopedia*. Jefferson, N.C.: McFarland, 1995.

Jones, Michael, and Frances Cattermoll-Tally, eds. *Guide to the Gods*. Santa Barbara, Calif.: ABC-CLIO, 1992.

Katz, Ephraim. *The Film Encyclopedia*. New York: G. P. Putnam's Sons, 1979.

Leach, Maria L. *Dictionary of Folklore, Mythology and Legend*. 2 vols. New York: Funk and Wagnalls, 1949.

McGill, Raymond, ed. *Notable Names in the American Theatre*. Clifton, N.J.: James T. White, 1976.

Nemec, David. *The Great Encyclopedia of Nineteenth Century Major League Baseball*. New York: Donald Fine Books, 1997.

Porter, David L., ed. *Biographical Directory of American Sports: Baseball*. Westport, Conn.: Greenwood Press, 1987.

Smith, Myron L., Jr. *Baseball: A Comprehensive Bibliography*. Jefferson, N.C.: McFarland, 1986.

———. *Baseball: A Comprehensive Bibliography, Supplement I*. Jefferson, N.C.: McFarland, 1993.

Thorn, John, and Peter Palmer, eds. *Total Baseball: The Ultimate Encyclopedia of Baseball*. New York: HarperCollins, 1993.

Tiemann, Robert L., and Mark Rucker, eds. *Nineteenth Century Stars*. Manhattan, Ks.: Ag Press, 1989.

Turkin, Hy, and S. C. Thompson. *The Official Encyclopedia of Baseball*. New York: A. S. Barnes, 1951.

Wilson, James Grant, and John Fiske, eds. *Appleton's Cyclopedia*. New York: D. Appleton, 1900.

Wolff, Rick, editorial director. *The Baseball Encyclopedia*. 8th ed. New York: Macmillan, 1990.

Government Documents

Department of Commerce, Bureau of the Census. *Historical Statistics of the United States, Colonial Times to 1970*. Washington, D.C.: U.S. GPO, 1975.

Department of the Interior, Census Office. Report on the Population of the United States at the Eleventh Census, 1890. Washington, D.C.: U.S. GPO, 1895.

———. Report on Transportation Business in the United States at the Eleventh Census, 1890, part 1—Transportation by Land. Washington, D.C.: GPO, 1895.

———. Statistics of the Population of the United States at the Tenth Census. Washington, D.C.: U.S. GPO, 1883.

House of Representatives. Exec. doc. no. 406, 51st Cong., 2d sess., Statistical Abstract of the United States, 1890. Washington, D.C.: U.S. GPO, 1891.

Books, Articles, and Unpublished Material

Addams, Jane. *The Spirit of Youth and the City Streets*. Urbana: University of Illinois Press, 1972.

———. *Twenty Years at Hull House*. New York: Macmillan, 1911.

Adelman, Melvin L. *A Sporting Time: New York City and the Rise of Modern Athletics, 1820–1870*. Urbana: University of Illinois Press, 1986.

Alexander, Charles C. *John McGraw*. New York: Viking Penguin, 1988.

———. *Our Game: An American Baseball History*. New York: Henry Holt, 1991.

Anson, Adrian C. *A Ball Player's Career*. Chicago: Era Publishing, 1900.

Appel, Marty. *Slide, Kelly, Slide: The Wild Life and Times of Mike "King" Kelly, Baseball's First Superstar*. Lanham, Md.: Scarecrow Press, 1996.

Asbury, Herbert. *Gem of the Prairie: An Informal History of the Chicago Underworld*. New York: A. A. Knopf, 1940.

Axelson, G. W. *Commy: The Life Story of Charles A. Comiskey*. Chicago: Reilly and Lee, 1919.

Bailey, Bob. "The Forgotten War: The American Association–National League War of 1891." *National Pastime* 19 (1999): 81–84.

Baker, William J. *Sports in the Western World*. Towata, N.J.: Rowman and Littlefield, 1982.

Bald, F. Clever. *Michigan in Four Centuries*. New York: Harper Brothers, 1954.

Barney, Robert Knight, and Frank Dallier. "I'd Rather Be a Lamppost in Chicago, than a Millionaire in Any Other City: William A. Hulbert, Civic Pride, and the Birth of the National League." *Nine: A Journal of Baseball History and Social Policy Perspectives* 2 (fall 1993): 40–59.

Barth, Gunther. *City People: The Rise of Modern City Culture in Nineteenth Century America*. New York: Oxford University Press, 1980.

Bartlett, Arthur. *Baseball and Mr. Spalding: The History and Romance of Baseball*. New York: Farrar, Strauss and Young, 1951.

Bass, Cynthia. "The Making of a Baseball Radical." *National Pastime* (fall 1982): 63–65.

Battiste, William Powell. "History of the St. Louis Brown Stockings, 1875–1877: The First Professional Baseball Club in St. Louis." Master of Arts thesis, Washington University, 1962.

Berlage, Gai Ingham. "Transition of Women's Baseball: An Overview." *Nine: A Journal of Baseball History and Culture* 9 (spring 2001): 73–83.

Betts, John Rickards. "Sporting Journalism in Nineteenth-Century America." *American Quarterly* 5 (spring 1953): 39–56.

———. "The Technological Revolution and the Rise of Sport, 1850–1900." *Mississippi Valley Historical Review* 40 (September 1953): 231–56.

"Big League Superstitions." *Literary Digest* 48 (May 1914): 1151–54.

Bode, E. A. *A Dose of Frontier Soldiering: The Memoirs of Corporal E. A. Bode, Frontier Regular Infantry, 1877–1882*. Edited by Thomas T. Smith. Lincoln: University of Nebraska Press, 1994.

Bowman, Larry G. "Baseball's Intriguing Couple: Helen Dauvray and John Montgomery Ward." *National Pastime* 18 (1998): 69–72.

———. "A Celebrity Allegory: Fame, Indeed, for John Montgomery Ward." *National Pastime* 20 (2000): 90–92.

———. "Christian Von der Ahe, the St. Louis Browns, and the World's Championship Playoffs, 1885–1888." *Missouri Historical Review* 91 (July 1997): 385–405.

———. "Detroit's First World Champions." *Michigan History* 81 (September/October 1997): 40–45.

———. "The First World's Championship of Professional Baseball: The New York Metropolitans and the Providence Grays, 1884." *Nine: A Journal of Baseball History and Social Policy Perspectives* 6 (spring 1998): 2–14.

———. "The Helen Dauvray Cup." *National Pastime* 17 (1997): 73–76.

———. "'I Think It Is Pretty Ritzy, Myself': Kansas Minor League Teams and Night Baseball." *Kansas History* 18 (winter 1995–1996): 248–58.

———. "Moses Fleetwood Walker." In *Baseball History: An Annual of Original Baseball Research,* ed., Peter Levine. Westport, Conn.: Meckler Books, 1989.

———. "Night Baseball Comes to the Texas League." *Nine: A Journal of Baseball History and Social Policy Perspectives* 5 (spring 1997): 207–27.

———. "'The Players Redeemed Themselves': Major League Baseball Visits Colorado: 1888." *Colorado Heritage* (spring 1999): 20–31.

———. "Soldiers at Play: Baseball on the American Frontier." *Nine: A Journal of Baseball History and Culture* 9 (spring 2001): 35–50.

Boyer, Paul. *Urban Masses and Moral Order in America, 1820–1920.* Cambridge, Mass.: Harvard University Press, 1978.

Brewer, William A. "Barehanded Catcher." *Negro Digest* 60 (1951): 85–87.

Burk, Robert F. *Never Just a Game: Players, Owners, and American Baseball to 1920.* Chapel Hill: University of North Carolina Press, 1994.

Burrows, Edwin G., and Mike Wallace. *Gotham: A History of New York City to 1898.* New York: Oxford University Press, 1999.

Carroll, John M., ed. *Private Theodore Ewert's Diary of the Black Hills Expedition, 1874.* Piscataway, N.J.: CRI Books, 1975.

Catton, Bruce. "The Great American Game." *American Heritage* 10 (April 1959): 16–26.

Caylor, O. P. "Opening Day of the Baseball Season of 1890." *Harper's Weekly* 34 (May 1890): 353–56.

Chalk, Ocania. *Pioneers of Black Sport.* New York: Dodd, Mead, 1975.

Chudacoff, Howard P., and Judith E. Smith. *The Evolution of American Urban Society.* Englewood Cliffs, N.J.: Prentice-Hall, 1994.

Constitution and Playing Rules of the National League of Professional Base Ball Clubs, 1876. Philadelphia: Reach and Johnston, 1876.

Cook, Adrian. *The Armies of the Streets: The New York City Draft Riots of 1863.* Lexington: University Press of Kentucky, 1974.

Cook, Ann, Marilyn Gittell, and Herb Mack. *City Life, 1865–1900: Views of Urban America.* New York: Praeger, 1973.

Cowell, Sydney. "The Enchanted Baseball: A Fairy Story of Modern Times." *The Cosmopolitan: A Monthly Illustrated Magazine* 8 (November 1889–April 1890): 659–68.

Dickens, Charles. *American Notes for General Circulation.* London: Penguin Books, 1985.

Di Salvatore, Bryan. *A Clever Base-Ballist: The Life and Times of John Montgomery Ward.* New York: Pantheon Books, 1999.

Dixon, David. *Hero of Beecher's Island: The Life and Military Career of George A. Forsyth.* Lincoln: University of Nebraska Press, 1994.

Dixon, Phil, and Patrick J. Hannigan. *The Negro Baseball Leagues: A Photographic History.* Mattituck, N.Y.: Ameron, 1992.

Eckley, Grace. *Finley Peter Dunne.* Boston: Twayne, 1981.

Eddleton, Oscar. "Under the Lights." *Baseball Research Journal* (1980): 37–42.

Eigenriether, Richard. "Chris Von der Ahe: Baseball's Pioneering Huckster." *Baseball Research Journal* 18 (1989): 27–31.

————. "Chris Von der Ahe: Baseball's Pioneering Huckster." *Nine: A Journal of Baseball History and Social Policy Perspectives* 7 (spring 1999): 14–39.

Evers, John L. "Timothy John Keefe." In *Biographical Directory of American Sports: Baseball,* ed. David L. Porter. Westport, Conn.: Greenwood Press, 1987.

Fanning, Charles. *Finley Peter Dunne & Mr. Dooley: The Chicago Years.* Lexington: University of Kentucky Press, 1978.

Folsom, Lowell Edwin. "America's 'Hurrah Game': Baseball and Walt Whitman." *Iowa Review* 2 (1980): 68–80.

Forbes-Robertson, Diana. *My Aunt Maxine.* New York: Viking, 1964.

Foster, Mark S. "Playing by the Rules: The Evolution of Baseball in the Nineteenth Century." *Colorado Heritage* (spring 1995): 44–52.

Gerlach, Larry. "On Umpires: Historical Perspective, Contemporary Observations." *Nine: A Journal of Baseball History and Social Policy Perspectives* 7 (fall 1998): 16–45.

Goldstein, Warren. *Playing for Keeps.* Ithaca, N.Y.: Cornell University Press, 1989.

Grella, George. "Baseball and the American Dream." *Massachusetts Review* 16 (summer 1975): 550–67.

Guttmann, Allen. *Sports Spectators.* New York: Columbia University Press, 1986.

————. *A Whole New Ball Game: An Interpretation of American Sports.* Chapel Hill: University of North Carolina Press, 1988.

Hardy, James D., Jr. *The New York Giants Base Ball Club: The Growth of a Team and a Sport, 1870 to 1900.* Jefferson, N.C.: McFarland, 1996.

Harshman, Jack E. "The Radbourn and Sweeney Saga." *Baseball Research Journal* 19 (1990): 7–10.

Henderson, Robert W. *Ball, Bat and Bishop: The Origin of Ball Games.* New York: Rockport Press, 1947.

Hetrick, J. Thomas. *Chris Von der Ahe and the St. Louis Browns.* Lanham, Md.: Scarecrow Press, 1999.

Holst, David L. "Charles G. Radbourne: The Greatest Pitcher of the Nineteenth Century." *Illinois Historical Journal* 81 (winter 1988): 255–68.

Hopper, De Wolf. *Once a Clown, Always a Clown: Reminiscences of De Wolf Hopper.* Boston: Little, Brown, 1927.

Horton, Ralph. "The Big Four Come to Detroit." *National Pastime* 19 (1998): 34–37.

Husman, John Richard. "Walter Arlington Latham." In *Nineteenth Century Stars,* ed. Tiemann and Rucker.

Jahoda, Gustav. *The Psychology of Superstition.* London: Penguin, 1969.

James, Bill. *The Bill James Historical Baseball Abstract.* New York: Villard Books, 1988.

Jayne, Walter Addison. *The Healing Gods of Ancient Civilizations.* New York: University Books, 1962.

Kahn, James M. *The Umpire Story.* New York: G. P. Putnam's Sons, 1953.

Kirsch, George B. "Baseball in the Civil War." *Civil War Times* 14 (May 1998): 30–39.

————. *The Creation of Team Sports: Baseball & Cricket, 1838–1872.* Urbana: University of Illinois Press, 1989.

"Know Baseball, Know America." *American Magazine* 76 (September 1913): 94.

Krause, Herbert, and Gary B. Olson, eds. *Prelude to Glory.* Sioux Falls, S.D.: Brevet Press, 1974.

Kuklick, Bruce. *To Every Thing a Season: Shibe Park and Urban Philadelphia, 1909–1976*. Princeton: Princeton University Press, 1991.

Kull, Andrew. "Baseball's Greatest Pitcher." *American Heritage* (April–May 1985): 103–8.

Lansche, Jerry. *The Forgotten Championships: Postseason Baseball, 1882–1981*. Jefferson, N.C.: McFarland, 1989.

———. *Glory Fades Away: The Nineteenth-Century World Series Rediscovered*. Dallas: Taylor Publishing, 1991.

Lawson, Thomas W. *The Krank: His Language and What It Means*. Boston: Rand Avery, 1884.

Levine, Peter. *A. G. Spalding and the Rise of Baseball: The Promise of American Sport*. New York: Oxford University Press, 1985.

———. *Ellis Island to Ebbetts Field: Sport and the American Jewish Experience*. New York: Oxford University Press, 1992.

Lowenfish, Lee, and Tony Lupien. *The Imperfect Diamond: The Story of the Reserve System and the Men Who Fought to Change It*. New York: Da Capo Press, 1991.

Lowry, Philip J. *Green Cathedrals: The Ultimate Celebration of All 271 Major League and Negro League Ballparks Past and Present*. New York: Addison-Wesley, 1992.

McGimpsey, David. *Imagining Baseball: America's Pastime and Popular Culture*. Bloomington: University of Indiana Press, 2000.

McGraw, John J. *My Thirty Years in Baseball*. Lincoln: University of Nebraska Press, 1995.

McMahon, William E. "Albert Goodwill Spalding." In *Baseball's First Stars*, ed. Ivor-Campbell et al.

Miller, Donald L. *City of the Century: The Epic of Chicago and the Making of America*. New York: Simon and Schuster, 1996.

Moore, Jim, and Natalie Vermilyea. *Ernest Thayer's "Casey at the Bat": Background and Characters of Baseball's Most Famous Poem*. Jefferson, N.C.: McFarland, 1994.

Mote, James. *Everything Baseball*. New York: Prentice-Hall, 1989.

Mrozek, Donald J. *Sport and American Mentality, 1880–1910*. Knoxville: University of Tennessee Press, 1983.

Murrin, John M., and James M. Rosenheim. "America at Play: The National Pastime versus College Football, 1860–1914." *Princeton Alumni Weekly*, 6 October 1975, 13–17, 19.

Nemec, David. *The Beer and Whiskey League: The Illustrated History of the American Association—Baseball's Renegade Major League*. New York: Lyons and Burford, 1994.

———. *The Rules of Baseball*. New York: Lyons and Burford, 1994.

Noble, Richard E. "Saving Face: The Genesis of the Catcher's Mask." *Baseball History* (fall 1987): 46–49.

Nugent, William Henry. "The Sports Section." *American Mercury* 16 (March 1929): 329–38.

Nye, W. S. *Carbine and Lance: The Story of Old Fort Sill*. Norman: University of Oklahoma Press, 1943.

Oliva, Leo E. *Fort Hays: Keeping the Peace on the Plains*. Topeka: Kansas State Historical Society, 1996.

———. *Fort Larned: Guardian of the Santa Fe Trail*. Topeka: Kansas State Historical Society, 1997.

O'Malley, John J. "James J. Mutrie." In *Nineteenth Century Stars*, ed. Tiemann and Rucker.

———. "Timothy John Keefe." In *Baseball's First Stars*, ed. Ivor-Campbell et al.

Ornstein, Jerry B. "The Union Association of 1884: A Glorious Failure." *Baseball Research Journal* 19 (1990): 3–6.

Overfield, Joseph M. "Dennis Joseph Brouthers." In *Baseball's First Stars*, ed. Ivor-Campbell et al.

Palmer, Harry Clay. *Athletic Sports in America, England, and Australia*. Philadelphia: Hubbard Brothers, 1889.

Pearson, Daniel M. *Baseball in 1889: Players versus Owners*. Bowling Green, Ohio: Bowling Green State University Popular Press, 1993.

Pietrusza, David. *Lights On! The Wild Century-Long Saga of Night Baseball*. Lanham, Md.: Scarecrow Press, 1997.

Primm, James Neal. *Lion of the Valley: St. Louis, Missouri*. Boulder, Colo.: Pruett, 1981.

Rader, Benjamin G. *American Sports: From the Age of Folk Games to the Age of the Spectator*. Englewood Cliffs, N.J.: Prentice-Hall, 1983.

———. *Baseball: A History of America's Game*. Urbana: University of Illinois Press, 1992.

Rammelkamp, Julian S. *Pulitzer's Post-Dispatch, 1878–1883*. Princeton: Princeton University Press, 1967.

Ribowsky, Mark. *A Complete History of the Negro Leagues, 1884 to 1955*. New York: Birch Lane Press, 1995.

Rickey, Don, Jr. *Forty Miles a Day on Beans and Hay*. Norman: University of Oklahoma Press, 1963.

Riess, Steven A. *City Games: The Evolution of American Urban Society and the Rise of Sports*. Urbana: University of Illinois Press, 1989.

———. *Sport in Industrial America, 1850–1920*. Wheeling, Ill.: Harlan Davidson, 1995.

Ritter, Lawrence. *The Glory of Their Times: The Story of the Early Days of Baseball Told by the Men Who Played It*. New York: William Morrow, 1984.

Ryczek, William J. *When Johnny Came Sliding Home: The Post–Civil War Baseball Boom, 1865–1870*. Jefferson, N.C.: McFarland, 1998.

Schaaf, Barbara C. *Mr. Dooley's Chicago*. Garden City, N.Y.: Anchor Press/Doubleday, 1977.

Schroeder, Sheila E. "When Technology and Culture Collide: The Advent of Night Baseball." *Nine: A Journal of Baseball History and Social Policy Perspectives* 3 (fall 1994): 85–106.

Seymour, Harold. *Baseball: The Early Years*. New York: Oxford University Press, 1960.

Slowkowski, C. S. "Cultural Performance and Sports Mascots." *Journal of Sport and Social Issues* 17 (April 1993): 23–31.

Smith, Leverett T. *The American Dream and the National Game*. Bowling Green, Ky.: Bowling Green University Popular Press, 1975.

Somers, Dale A. "The Leisure Revolution: Recreation in the American City, 1820–1920." *Journal of Popular Culture* 5 (summer 1971): 125–47.

Spalding, Albert G. *America's National Game*. Lincoln: University of Nebraska Press, 1992.

―――. "Base-Ball." *The Cosmopolitan: A Monthly Illustrated Magazine* 7 (October 1889): 603–12.

Spink, Alfred H. *The National Game*. St. Louis: National Game Publishing, 1910.

Spinney, Robert G. *City of Big Shoulders: A History of Chicago*. DeKalb: Northern Illinois University Press, 2000.

Spinoza, Benedict. *A Theological-Political Treatise and a Political Treatise*. Translated by R. H. M. Elwes. New York: Dover, 1951.

Spotts, David L. *Campaigning with Custer and the Nineteenth Kansas Volunteer Cavalry on the Washita Campaign, 1868–69*. Edited by E. A. Brininstool. New York: Argonaut Press, 1965.

Stevens, David. *Baseball's Radical for All Seasons: A Biography of John Montgomery Ward*. Lanham, Md.: Scarecrow Press, 1998.

Sullivan, Dean A., ed. *Early Innings: A Documentary History of Baseball, 1825–1908*. Lincoln: University of Nebraska Press, 1995.

Tattersall, John C. *The Early World Series, 1884–1890*. Havertown, Pa.: Privately printed, 1976.

Thompson, C. J. S. *The Hand of Destiny: The Folk-Lore and Superstitions of Everyday Life*. Detroit: Singing Tree, 1970.

Utley, Robert M. *Life in Custer's Cavalry: Diaries and Letters of Albert and Jennie Barnitz, 1867–1868*. New Haven: Yale University Press, 1977.

Voigt, David Quentin. *American Baseball: From Gentlemen's Sport to the Commissioner System*. 3 vols. University Park: Pennsylvania State University Press, 1983.

―――. *America Through Baseball*. Chicago: Nelson Hall, 1976.

―――. "Cash and Glory: The Commercialization of Major League Baseball as a Sports Spectacular, 1862–1892." Ph.D. thesis, Syracuse University, 1963.

Wallop, Douglas. *Baseball: An Informal History*. New York: W. W. Norton, 1969.

Ward, John Montgomery. "Is the Base-Ball Player a Chattel?" *Lippincott's Monthly Magazine* 40 (1887): 310–19.

―――. "Notes of a Base-Ballist." *Lippincott's Monthly Magazine* 38 (1886): 212–20.

―――. "Our National Game." *The Cosmopolitan: A Monthly Illustrated Magazine* 5 (1889): 443–55.

Wheatley, Richard. "The Thieves of New York." *The Cosmopolitan: A Monthly Illustrated Magazine* 9 (1890): 22–31.

Wright, Marshall D. *Nineteenth Century Baseball: Year-by-Year Statistics for the Major League Teams, 1871 through 1900*. Jefferson, N.C.: McFarland, 1996.

Zang, David. *Fleet Walker's Divided Heart: The Life of Baseball's First Black Major Leaguer*. Lincoln: University of Nebraska Press, 1995.

Index